THE MACARTHUR NEW TESTAMENT COMMENTARY

1-3 JOHN

John MacArthur

MOODY PUBLISHERS/CHICAGO

All Scripture quotations, unless otherwise indicated, are taken from the *New
American Standard Bible®*, Copyright © The Lockman Foundation 1960, 1962, 1963, 1968,
1971, 1972, 1973, 1975, 1977, 1995. Used by permission. www.Lockman.org

Scripture quotations marked NIV are taken from the *Holy Bible, New International
Version®*. NIV®. Copyright © 1973, 1978, 1984 by International Bible Society. Used by permission of Zondervan. All rights reserved.

Scripture quotations marked NKJV are taken from the *New King James Version.*
Copyright © 1982 by Thomas Nelson, Inc. Used by permission. All rights reserved.

Scripture quotations marked KJV are taken from the King James Version.

Cover Design: Smartt Guys design

Library of Congress Cataloging-in-Publication Data

MacArthur, John, 1939-
   1-3 John / by John MacArthur
     p. cm. — (The MacArthur New Testament commentary series)
   Includes bibliographical references and index.
   ISBN: 978-0-8024-0772-6
   1. Bible. N.T. Epistles of John—Commentaries. I. Title. II. Title: one-three John.

BS2805.53.M33 2007
227'.9407—dc22

2006036453

We hope you enjoy this book from Moody Publishers. Our goal is to provide high-quality,
thought-provoking books and products that connect truth to your real needs and challenges. For more information on other books and products written and produced from a
biblical perspective, go to www.moodypublishers.com or write to:

Moody Publishers
820 N. LaSalle Boulevard
Chicago, IL 60610

9 10 8

Printed in the United States of America

For Bill Shannon:
with gratitude for your years of faithful shepherding of God's flock

Contents

Preface

It continues to be a rewarding, divine communion for me to preach expositionally through the New Testament. My goal is always to have deep fellowship with the Lord in the understanding of His Word and out of that experience to explain to His people what a passage means. In the words of Nehemiah 8:8, I strive "to give the sense" of it so they may truly hear God speak and, in so doing, may respond to Him.

Obviously, God's people need to understand Him, which demands knowing His Word of Truth (2 Tim. 2:15) and allowing that Word to dwell in them richly (Col. 3:16). The dominant thrust of my ministry, therefore, is to help make God's living Word alive to His people. It is a refreshing adventure.

This New Testament commentary series reflects this objective of explaining and applying Scripture. Some commentaries are primarily linguistic, others are mostly theological, and some are mainly homiletical. This one is basically explanatory, or expository. It is not linguistically technical but deals with linguistics when that seems helpful to proper interpretation. It is not theologically expansive but focuses on the major doctrines in each text and how they relate to the whole of Scripture. It is not primarily homiletical, although each unit of thought is generally treated as one chapter, with a clear outline and logical flow of thought.

Most truths are illustrated and applied with other Scripture. After establishing the context of a passage, I have tried to follow closely the writer's development and reasoning.

My prayer is that each reader will fully understand what the Holy Spirit is saying through this part of His Word, so that His revelation may lodge in the mind of believers and bring greater obedience and faithfulness—to the glory of our great God.

Introduction to
1 John

The Greco-Roman world at the close of the first century A.D. was in a state of cultural, philosophical, and religious ferment. Religious syncretism and inclusivism were the watchwords of the day, as Donald W. Burdick notes:

> Apart from the Judaeo-Christian sphere, the world was religiously inclusivistic. There was always room for a new religion, provided of course that it was not of an exclusive nature. Syncretism, however, did not merely express itself in a mood of tolerance toward other faiths. Its characteristic expression was in the combination of various ideas and beliefs from different sources to form new or aberrant religions. This was the age of the developing mystery religions, the age of the occult, the age of the proliferation of Gnostic sects. (*The Letters of John the Apostle* [Chicago: Moody, 1985], 4)

Nowhere was that more evident than in the Roman province of Asia, located in western Asia Minor, in modern Turkey. The region forms a land bridge between the continents of Europe and Asia, across which flowed the tides of invasion and migration. As a result, it was a melting pot of ideas, philosophies, and religions. The Imperial cult of emperor worship was widespread. The region was also home to the worship of a myriad of false gods, including Asclepius, Athena, Zeus, Dionysus (Bacchus), Cybele, Apollo, and Artemis, whose magnificent temple in Ephesus was one of the Seven Wonders of the Ancient World.

In the midst of the darkness of paganism and superstition, the Christian church was a beacon of hope, shining forth the light of truth (cf. Matt. 5:14; Phil. 2:15). But the church in Asia did not exist in isolation from the surrounding culture. The plethora of competing ideologies inevitably posed a threat—both externally, from false religions, and internally, from false teachers ("savage wolves"; Acts 20:29; Matt. 7:15) and their followers (cf. 2 Cor. 11:26; Gal. 2:4) infiltrating the churches. The pressure had already begun to take its toll on the churches of Asia. Some had split, with the false teachers and their followers leaving (1 John 2:19). Only two of the seven churches in the region addressed in Revelation 2–3 were commended by the Lord (Smyrna and Philadelphia); the other five were rebuked for worldliness and tolerating false doctrine (Ephesus, Pergamum, Thyatira, Sardis, and Laodicia).

It was in this strategic location, where the battle against "the world forces of this darkness . . . the spiritual forces of wickedness in the heavenly places" (Eph. 6:12) raged most fiercely, that John, the last living apostle, ministered. He had come to Asia many years earlier and settled in Ephesus, the capital city of the province (see Date and Place of Writing below). Though he was by now an old man (most likely at least in his eighties), age had not dampened John's fiery zeal for the truth. Recognizing the dangers threatening the congregations under his care, the apostle took up his pen to defend the "faith which was once for all handed down to the saints" (Jude 3).

In our inclusivistic age of secularism, postmodern relativism, New Age cults, and militant world religions, the apostle's words of warning and assurance are both timely and relevant. As always, the church ignores them at her peril.

THE AUTHOR OF 1 JOHN

First John and Hebrews are the only two New Testament epistles that do not identify their authors. But from the first century until the rise of modern destructive higher criticism at the end of the eighteenth century, the church consistently identified the apostle John as the author of 1 John. There are possible or definite allusions to 1 John in such late first- and early second-century works as Clement of Rome's *First* and *Second Epistles to the Corinthians*, the *Didache*, the *Epistle of Barnabas*, the *Shepherd of Hermas*, the *Epistle to Diognetus*, Justin Martyr's *Apologies* and

Dialogue with Trypho, Polycarp's *Epistle to the Philippians*, and the writings of Polycarp's contemporary, Papias. But the first writer to quote directly from 1 John and name the apostle John as its author was Irenaeus, in the closing decades of the second century. His testimony is especially significant, since he was a disciple of Polycarp, who in turn was a disciple of the apostle himself. Irenaeus's contemporaries Clement of Alexandria and Tertullian also attributed 1 John to the apostle John, as did the second-century list of canonical books known as the Muratorian Canon. In the third century, Origen, Dionysius of Alexandria, and Cyprian of Carthage also named the apostle John as the epistle's author. Summarizing the evidence from the early church, the fourth-century church historian Eusebius wrote, "But of the writings of John, not only his gospel, but also the former of his epistles [1 John], has been accepted without dispute both now and in ancient times" (*Ecclesiastical History*, 3.24).

Although John does not name himself in 1 John (as he also did not do in the gospel of John), the internal evidence strongly supports the testimony of the early church that he wrote this epistle.

First, the epistle displays remarkable similarities to the gospel of John. Both works present a series of stark contrasts, with no third alternative (e.g., light and darkness; life and death; love and hate; truth and lies; love of the Father and love of the world; children of God and children of the Devil; being in the world but not of the world; to know God or not to know God; to have eternal life or not to have eternal life).

Their grammatical styles are also very similar, leading Nigel Turner to write, "The stylistic considerations in favour of unity [of authorship] are indeed overwhelming" (J. H. Moulton, *A Grammar of New Testament Greek*; vol. IV: *Style*, by Nigel Turner [Edinburgh: T. & T. Clark, 1976], 133).

The two books also have many words and phrases—some of which are found nowhere else in the New Testament—in common (for detailed lists of such similarities, see Robert Law, *The Tests of Life* [Edinburgh: T. & T. Clark, 1914], 341–45; and A. E. Brooke, *A Critical and Exegetical Commentary on the Johannine Epistles*, The International Critical Commentary [Edinburgh: T. & T. Clark, 1912], ii–ix). Some critics point to differences between 1 John and the gospel of John as evidence of two different authors. But those differences are debatable, inconsequential, or explainable by the different circumstances that prompted the two writings. Despite the differences, the vocabularies of 1 John and the gospel of John are more similar than those of Luke and Acts, Ephesians and Colossians, or 1 Timothy and Titus, which are known to have come from the same writer (D. A. Carson, Douglas J. Moo, and Leon Morris, *An Introduction to the New Testament* [Grand Rapids: Zondervan, 1992], 448–49).

Finally, the same theological themes pervade both works, including the incarnation (1 John 4:2; John 1:14) of the eternal (1 John 1:1; John 1:1), unique ("only begotten"; 1 John 4:9; John 3:16) Son of God (1 John 5:5; John 20:31); the truth that Jesus Christ is the source of eternal life (1 John 5:11; John 6:35) and is eternal life (1 John 5:20; John 11:25); that believers were once children of the Devil (1 John 3:8; John 8:44), part of his evil world system (1 John 4:5; John 15:19), walking in darkness (1 John 1:6; John 12:35), spiritually blind (1 John 2:11; John 9:39–41) and dead (1 John 3:14; John 5:25); that because of His love for lost sinners God sent His Son to lay down His life for believers (1 John 3:16; John 10:11) to take away their sin (1 John 3:5; John 1:29), so that they might be born again (1 John 5:1; John 3:5–7) and receive eternal life (1 John 5:11; John 3:15–16) through believing in Jesus (1 John 5:13; John 3:16); and that as a result, they know God (1 John 5:20; John 17:3), know the truth (1 John 2:21; John 8:32), are of the truth (1 John 3:19; John 18:37), obey the truth (1 John 2:5; John 8:51), and are God's children (1 John 3:1–2; John 1:12).

The author of 1 John also claims to have been an eyewitness to the events of Christ's life (see the exposition of 1:1–4 in chapter 1 of this volume), in contrast to the second-generation Christians he addressed. That considerably narrows the field of possible authors. It means that the writer had to have been one of the few who had been intimately acquainted with Jesus during His earthly life (cf. 1:1) and were still alive many decades later when 1 John was written.

Some critics attempt to evade the force of this argument by claiming that the writer's use of "we" in the opening verses refers to the church as a whole. But appealing to the common experience of all believers would hardly be used to authenticate the writer's message. Further, if the "we" in verses 1–4 is the church as a whole, who are the "you"? This view results in the absurdity of the Christian community addressing itself. It is nothing more than an unsuccessful attempt to avoid the obvious truth that the writer was an eyewitness. Such an eyewitness was the apostle John.

The author also writes with an air of authority:

> There is nothing tentative or apologetic about what he writes. He does not hesitate to call certain classes of people liars, deceivers or antichrists. He supplies tests by which everybody can be sorted into one or other of two categories. According to their relation to his tests they either have God or have not, know God or do not, have been born of God or have not, have life or abide in death, walk in the darkness or in the light, are children of God or children of the devil. This dogmatic authority of the writer is seen particularly in his statements and in his commands. (John R. W. Stott, *The Epistles of John*, The Tyndale New Testament Commentaries [Grand Rapids: Eerdmans, 1964], 34)

He clearly expected his readers to obey his commands unquestioningly. Only an apostle, known and respected by those whom he addressed, could have written such an authoritative letter and not given his name.

Since it is clear that the same author wrote both the gospel of John and 1 John, evidence that the apostle John wrote the gospel is also evidence that he wrote the epistle. That evidence may be briefly summarized in five points that narrow the focus unmistakably to the apostle:

First, the author of the gospel was a Jew, as his familiarity with Jewish customs and beliefs indicates.

Second, he had lived in Palestine, as evidenced by his detailed knowledge of that region.

Third, the author had to have been an eyewitness to many of the events he recorded, since he gave numerous details only an eyewitness would have known.

Fourth, the author was an apostle. He was intimately acquainted with what the Twelve were thinking and feeling.

Finally, the author was the apostle John, since his name does not appear in the fourth gospel. No other writer could possibly have failed to mention such a prominent apostle. (For a more complete discussion of the evidence that the apostle John wrote the gospel of John, see *John 1–11*, The MacArthur New Testament Commentary [Chicago: Moody, 2006], 3–7.)

Despite the unanimous testimony of the early church and the strong internal evidence that the apostle John penned this epistle, some critics perversely insist on attributing it to someone else. The usual candidate is the so-called John the Elder. The existence of that shadowy figure rests entirely on a much-disputed statement attributed by Eusebius to Papias who, like Polycarp, was a disciple of the apostle John. Eusebius quotes Papias as saying, "If, then, anyone who had attended on the elders came, I asked minutely after their sayings,—what Andrew or Peter said, or what was said by Philip, or by Thomas, or by James, or by John, or by Matthew, or by any other of the Lord's disciples: which things Aristion and the presbyter [elder] John, the disciples of the Lord, say" (*Exposition of the Oracles of the Lord*, 1).

It is doubtful, however, that Papias had two different Johns in mind. He mentions John again with Aristion because they were still alive (as the present-tense verb "say" indicates). He repeats the word "presbyter" before naming John again to show that he is referring to the John he had previously described as one of the elders (presbyters). R. C. H. Lenski notes,

> At the second mention of John, Papias carefully repeats the term, "*the presbyter* John," to show beyond question that he has in mind the John listed among the seven whom he has just called "the presbyters"; for if

in this second instance he had written only "John," the reader might take this to be a different John from the one mentioned in the list of seven termed "the presbyters." Papias makes certain that we think of the same man when "the presbyter John" is mentioned, one of the seven presbyters he has just named. (*The Interpretation of St. John's Revelation* [Minneapolis: Augsburg, 1943], 9)

It is unlikely that two such prominent men named John lived at Ephesus at the same time. But even if it could be shown that "John the Elder" actually existed, there is not one iota of evidence that he wrote the Johannine epistles (or anything else). That he exercised authority over several churches (cf. 2 and 3 John) also suggests that the writer was an apostle, since the authority of elders was limited to their own congregations. The view that "John the Elder" wrote 1 John also fails to explain why Irenaeus, a disciple of one of the apostle John's disciples, attributed it to the apostle.

John was the younger of the two sons of Zebedee (since James is almost always listed first when the two are mentioned together), a prosperous fisherman on the Sea of Galilee who owned his own boat and had hired servants (Mark 1:20). John's mother was Salome (cf. Mark 15:40 with Matt. 27:56), who contributed financially to Jesus' ministry (Matt. 27:55–56), and who may have been the sister of Mary, the mother of Jesus (John 19:25). If so, John and Jesus would have been cousins.

John was a disciple of John the Baptist (cf. John 1:35–40; though characteristically, John did not name himself). When the Baptist pointed out Jesus as the Messiah, John immediately left him and followed Jesus (John 1:37). After staying with Him for a while, John returned to his father's fishing business. Later, he became a permanent disciple of Jesus (Matt. 4:18–22) and was named an apostle (Matt. 10:2).

Along with James and Peter, John was part of the inner circle of the Twelve (cf. Matt. 17:1; Mark 5:37; 13:3; 14:33). After the Ascension, he became one of the leaders of the Jerusalem church (Acts 1:13; 3:1–11; 4:13–21; 8:14; Gal. 2:9). According to tradition, John spent the last decades of his life at Ephesus, overseeing the churches in the surrounding region (Clement of Alexandria, *Who Is the Rich Man that Shall Be Saved?*, 42) and writing his gospel (c. A.D. 80–90) and three epistles (c. A.D. 90–95). Toward the end of his life (according to Irenaeus [*Against Heresies*, 3.3.4], John lived until the time of the emperor Trajan [A.D. 98–117]) and was banished to the island of Patmos. It was there that he received and wrote the visions described in the book of Revelation (c. A.D. 94–96).

Despite his reputation as "the apostle of love," John had a fiery temperament. Jesus named John and James "Sons of Thunder" (Mark 3:17), and the two brothers lived up to that name. Indignant when a

Samaritan village refused to receive Jesus and the disciples, and overestimating their apostolic power, they eagerly asked the Lord, "Do You want us to command fire to come down from heaven and consume them?" (Luke 9:54). In the only recorded incident in the Synoptic Gospels in which John acted and spoke alone, he reveals the same attitude, saying to Jesus, "Master, we saw someone casting out demons in Your name; and we tried to prevent him because he does not follow along with us" (Luke 9:49).

Though he mellowed toward people over time (I trace the development of his spiritual character in my book *Twelve Ordinary Men* [Nashville: W Publishing Group, 2002]), John never lost his passion for the truth. Two vignettes from his years at Ephesus reveal that. According to Polycarp, "John, the disciple of the Lord, going to bathe at Ephesus, and perceiving [the heretic] Cerinthus within, rushed out of the bath-house without bathing, exclaiming, 'Let us fly, lest even the bath-house fall down, because Cerinthus, the enemy of the truth, is within'" (Irenaeus, *Against Heresies*, 3.3.4). Clement of Alexandria relates how John fearlessly entered the camp of a band of robbers and led its captain, who had once professed faith in Christ, to true repentance (see *Who Is the Rich Man that Shall Be Saved?*, 42).

DATE AND PLACE OF WRITING

Although it contains no clear historical indications of when or where it was written, John most likely composed this letter in the latter part of the first century at Ephesus. As noted above, the testimony of the early church places John in that city during that period. The apostle's repeated references to his readers as "little children" (2:1, 12, 28; 3:7, 18; 4:4; 5:21) implies that he was much older than them and that he wrote 1 John toward the end of his life. The heresy John confronted (see the discussion under Occasion and Purpose below) appears to have been an incipient form of Gnosticism, which was beginning to develop toward the end of the first century. Further, the lack of any reference to the persecution under Emperor Domitian (c. A.D. 95) suggests that John wrote before it began. Finally, 1 John was probably written after the gospel of John (cf. Burdick, *The Letters of John*, 38–40, who estimates that at least 80 percent of the verses in 1 John reflect concepts found in the gospel of John [p. 40]). Since John wrote his Gospel about A.D. 80–90 (*John 1–11*, The MacArthur New Testament Commentary, 9), a date of A.D. 90–95 for 1 John is reasonable.

OCCASION AND PURPOSE

As previously noted, the church fathers (e.g., Justin Martyr, Irenaeus, Clement of Alexandria, Eusebius) place John at Ephesus during the time this letter was written, where the aged apostle had the oversight of many churches in the surrounding region. As Paul had earlier predicted (Acts 20:29–30), false teachers, influenced by the current religious and philosophical trends, had arisen. Those heretics were infecting the churches with false doctrine. Their heretical teaching represented the beginning stages of the virulent heresy later known as Gnosticism, which developed in the second century and posed a grave threat to the truth.

Gnosticism (from the Greek word *gnōsis* ["knowledge"]) was an amalgam of various pagan, Jewish, and quasi-Christian systems of thought. Influenced by Greek philosophy (especially that of Plato), Gnosticism taught that matter was inherently evil and spirit was good. That philosophical dualism led the false teachers whom John confronted to accept some form of Christ's deity, but to deny His humanity. He could not, according to them, have taken on a physical body, since matter was evil. The denial of the Incarnation in Gnosticism took two basic forms. Some, known as Docetists (from the Greek verb *dokeō* ["to seem," or "to appear"]), taught that Jesus' body was not a real, physical body, but only appeared to be so. In sharp contrast, John forcefully asserted that he had "heard," "seen," and "touched" Jesus Christ (1:1), who had truly "come in the flesh" (4:2; cf. John 1:14).

Others (such as the heretic Cerinthus, whose presence caused John to flee the bathhouse) taught that the Christ spirit descended on the man Jesus at His baptism, but left Him before the crucifixion. John refuted that specious argument by asserting that the Jesus who was baptized was the same person who was crucified (see the exposition of 5:6 in chapter 17 of this volume).

Either of those heretical views undermines not only the biblical teaching of Jesus' true humanity, but also of the atonement. If Jesus were not truly man—as well as truly God—when He suffered and died, He could not have been an acceptable substitutionary sacrifice for sin.

The Gnostics' philosophical dualism also caused them to be indifferent to moral values and ethical behavior. To them, the body was merely the prison in which the spirit was incarcerated. Therefore, sin committed in the body had no connection to or effect on the spirit. But as John emphatically declared, "If we say that we have no sin, we are deceiving ourselves and the truth is not in us. . . . If we say that we have not sinned, we make Him a liar and His word is not in us" (1:8, 10; cf. 2:4; 3:3–10; 5:18; 3 John 11).

Since they viewed themselves as the spiritual elite, who alone had true spiritual knowledge, Gnostics scorned the unenlightened ones bereft of such knowledge. They were arrogant, unholy, and loveless. But such behavior does not mark those with a higher knowledge of God, but rather those who do not know Him at all—a truth that John stated plainly and repeatedly:

> The one who says he is in the Light and yet hates his brother is in the darkness until now. (2:9)

> By this the children of God and the children of the devil are obvious: anyone who does not practice righteousness is not of God, nor the one who does not love his brother. (3:10)

> We know that we have passed out of death into life, because we love the brethren. He who does not love abides in death. Everyone who hates his brother is a murderer; and you know that no murderer has eternal life abiding in him. (3:14–15)

> The one who does not love does not know God, for God is love. (4:8)

> If someone says, "I love God," and hates his brother, he is a liar; for the one who does not love his brother whom he has seen, cannot love God whom he has not seen. And this commandment we have from Him, that the one who loves God should love his brother also. (4:20–21)

Like any pastor, John could not stand idly by when his people were being assaulted by the satanic lies of false teachers. Responding to the serious crisis threatening the churches under his care, the apostle sent them this letter to help check the deadly plague. But John's purpose was not merely polemical, but also pastoral, expressing his deep concern for his people. He wanted not only to refute the false teachers, but also to reassure the genuine believers. Thus, while the gospel of John was "written so that [people] may believe that Jesus is the Christ, the Son of God; and that believing [they might] have life in His name" (John 20:31), 1 John was written to those "who believe in the name of the Son of God, so that [they might] know that [they] have eternal life" (1 John 5:13). By repeatedly cycling through the essential truths of Christianity, John, with increasingly deeper and broader disclosure, fortified his people against the assaults of the false teachers and reassured them that they possessed eternal life. First John thus spirals through the biblical balance of truth, obedience, and love.

DESTINATION AND READERS

Some have questioned whether 1 John is actually a letter, since it lacks some of the general characteristics of letters from that era. But its intimate tone and content indicate that it was not a general treatise, but a personal, pastoral letter. The churches it was addressed to were most likely located in Asia Minor, near John's home church at Ephesus (see under The Author of 1 John above for evidence that John lived in Ephesus).

Little is known for certain about the recipients of 1 John. Most likely, they were primarily Gentiles, as the absence of Old Testament quotes and references (apart from 3:12) and the concluding warning against idolatry (5:21) suggest.

OUTLINE

  I. The Fundamental Tests of Genuine Fellowship—SPIRAL I (1:1–2:17)
    A. The Fundamental Tests of Doctrine (1:1–2:2)
       1. A biblical view of Christ (1:1–4)
       2. A biblical view of sin (1:5–2:2)
    B. The Fundamental Tests of Morals (2:3–17)
       1. A biblical view of obedience (2:3–6)
       2. A biblical view of love (2:7–17)
         a. The love that God requires (2:7–11)
         b. The love that God hates (2:12–17)
 II. The Fundamental Tests of Genuine Fellowship—SPIRAL II (2:18–3:24)
    A. Part 2 of the Doctrinal Test (2:18–27)
       1. Antichrists depart from Christian fellowship (2:18–21)
       2. Antichrists deny the Christian faith (2:22–25)
       3. Antichrists deceive the Christian faithful (2:26, 27)
    B. Part 2 of the Moral Test (2:28–3:24)
       1. The purifying hope of the Lord's return (2:28–3:3)
       2. The Christian's incompatibility with sin (3:4–24)
         a. The requirement of righteousness (3:4–10)
         b. The requirement of love (3:11–24)
III. The Fundamental Tests of Genuine Fellowship—SPIRAL III (4:1–21)
    A. Part 3 of the Doctrinal Test (4:1–6)
       1. The demonic source of false doctrine (4:1–3)
       2. The need for sound doctrine (4:4–6)
    B. Part 3 of the Moral Test (4:7–21)
       1. God's character of love (4:7–10)
       2. God's requirement of love (4:11–21)

IV. The Fundamental Tests of Genuine Fellowship—SPIRAL IV (5:1–21)
A. The Victorious Life in Christ (5:1–5)
B. The Witness of God for Christ (5:6–12)
C. Christian Certainties Because of Christ (5:13–21)
1. The certainty of eternal life (5:13)
2. The certainty of answered prayer (5:14–17)
3. The certainty of victory over sin and Satan (5:18–21)

Certainties of the Word of Life (1 John 1:1–4)

1

What was from the beginning, what we have heard, what we have seen with our eyes, what we have looked at and touched with our hands, concerning the Word of Life—and the life was manifested, and we have seen and testify and proclaim to you the eternal life, which was with the Father and was manifested to us—what we have seen and heard we proclaim to you also, so that you too may have fellowship with us; and indeed our fellowship is with the Father, and with His Son Jesus Christ. These things we write, so that our joy may be made complete. (1:1–4)

We live in an era that looks with suspicion on any type of certainty or conviction about the truth. Our society has abandoned the idea of absolutes, choosing instead to arbitrarily grant equal validity to every opinion and philosophical musing. Sadly, today's church, influenced by the surrounding culture, has fallen prey to an inclusivism that tolerates seemingly any and every viewpoint, except dogmatism. In the realm of biblical interpretation, for instance, a significant new movement is gaining ground that says that no one can know for sure what the Bible means. According to this emerging viewpoint, the Bible is so obscure that anyone who exegetes Scripture should offer nothing more than a cautious, "humble," open-minded opinion regarding the text's meaning. But such radical, unwarranted skepticism blatantly ignores the Bible's own teaching that Christians not only can, but must, know the truth (John 8:32; cf. Pss. 19:8; 119:105; Prov. 22:21; Isa. 29:24; Luke 1:4; 1 Tim. 4:3; 2 Peter 1:12, 19; 1 John 2:21; 4:6; 2 John 1). Thus, to claim that the meaning of Scripture is unknowable is to directly attack the divinely designed clarity of the Bible; it is, in essence, to accuse God of being unable to clearly reveal Himself and His truth to humanity. The inevitable result of such arrogance—for those who embrace it—is the loss of certainty and confidence about the rich and essential doctrinal truths of the Christian faith.

The writers of Scripture, on the other hand, were absolutely certain of what they believed and, under the Holy Spirit's inspiration, wrote with a clarity and boldness that makes the message of salvation in its fullness understandable to the regenerated and illuminated mind. Still, the proper sense of dogmatism is utterly contrary to today's relativistic attitudes, and those who hold it are consistently condemned as insensitive, unloving, and anti-intellectual. The reality is that those who deny Scripture's clarity are likely motivated by rebellion against its clear message of sin and righteousness (cf. John 3:20). Denying that the Bible can be understood gives false comfort to those who do not like the truth it reveals. In contrast, those who love the truth are quick to seek it out and apply it to their lives (John 3:21). Such God-honoring adherence to divine, absolute truth is precisely what the apostle John exalts in his first epistle as the evidence of genuine salvation.

The teaching of this epistle may be divided into three categories: theological certainty regarding the gospel and the person of Jesus Christ (2:1–2, 22; 5:1, 20), moral certainty regarding the commandments of God (2:4, 7, 29; 3:9, 22), and relational certainty regarding love (2:10; 4:7, 21; 5:2–3). (For a complete overview of John's themes in his first letter, see the Introduction to 1 John at the beginning of this volume.)

Consistent with his firm commitment to the certainty of divine truth, John dispensed with all introductory amenities—he did not even name himself as the author, nor did he identify his audience. Rather, he immediately launched into writing the Spirit-inspired truth. He began by presenting five certainties about the person and work of Christ: The Word of Life is unchangeable, historical, communicable, relational, and joyful.

THE WORD OF LIFE IS UNCHANGEABLE

What was from the beginning, (1:1*a*)

The message of redemption is unchanging. **From the beginning** of the proclamation of the gospel it has been the same. Those who preach the true gospel have always commanded faith and repentance (Matt. 4:17; John 3:16–18; Acts 2:38; 17:30), declared that the kingdom of God is at hand (Matt. 3:2; Acts 19:8), announced the merciful and gracious availability of divine forgiveness (Acts 10:43; Eph. 1:7), and urged sinners to be reconciled to God through Jesus Christ (2 Cor. 5:18–21). When the apostle John wrote this epistle, an incipient Gnosticism was already threatening the churches of Asia Minor. Its proponents denied the full deity and humanity of Jesus Christ and, therefore, His true nature essential to the gospel. They further claimed to have attained, apart from the gospel, a transcendent knowledge of the divine, available only to the "spiritual" elite and otherwise beyond the reach of the common believer.

Such false teachers threatened the church in John's day, just as they still do today; and they will continue to do so until the end of the age. Jesus warned, "For false Christs and false prophets will arise and will show great signs and wonders, so as to mislead, if possible, even the elect" (Matt. 24:24). They threaten to undermine the church (Acts 20:29–30; 2 Tim. 3:1–9), seeking to lure it away from the apostolic body of faith (cf. Acts 2:42; 13:8; 14:22; 16:5; 1 Cor. 16:13; 2 Cor. 13:5; Eph. 4:4–6; Col. 1:23; 1 Tim. 4:1, 6; 6:10, 21; 2 Tim. 3:8; 4:7; Titus 1:13; 3:15; 2 Peter 1:20–21; Jude 3, 4, 20) —the inspired truth that nothing can ever supersede (cf. Heb. 13:8–9).

Any alteration of this heavenly revelation, whether by adding to it or taking from it, constitutes an attack on the truth and its sovereign Author. All preachers, teachers, and witnesses for the gospel—in any generation or location, for any reason, including making the message more acceptable or marketable—should know they cannot freely change with impunity any element of God's revelation.

The apostle Paul also earlier warned in unambiguous words of those who propagate an altered or false gospel:

> I am amazed that you are so quickly deserting Him who called you by the grace of Christ, for a different gospel; which is really not another; only there are some who are disturbing you and want to distort the gospel of Christ. But even if we, or an angel from heaven, should preach to you a gospel contrary to what we have preached to you, he is to be accursed! As we have said before, so I say again now, if any man is preaching to you a gospel contrary to what you received, he is to be accursed! (Gal. 1:6–9)

With a simple opening statement John establishes that the gospel message concerning the Word of Life is permanent and unalterable (cf. Rev. 22:18–19).

THE WORD OF LIFE IS HISTORICAL

what we have heard, what we have seen with our eyes, what we have looked at and touched with our hands, concerning the Word of Life—and the life was manifested, (1:1b–2a)

Contrary to what the false teachers taught, experiencing Christ and His gospel is not some mystical, spiritually transcendent, secret insight reserved only for those elite who ascend to some higher understanding. John told his readers—even those who were young in their faith (cf. 2:12)—that they could apprehend the actual, historical truth about **the Word of Life** (the person and work of Jesus Christ as proclaimed in the gospel). In his record of the life and ministry of Christ, John wrote that "the Word became flesh, and dwelt among us, and we saw His glory, glory as of the only begotten from the Father, full of grace and truth" (John 1:14; cf. Rom. 1:3; Gal. 4:4; Heb. 1:1–3; 1 Tim. 3:16; Rev. 19:13). Jesus Christ was the God-man (John 10:30), fully divine (Phil. 2:6; Col. 2:9); and fully human (Luke 1:31; Phil. 2:7–8; Heb. 2:14; 4:15). John had experienced that reality through his natural senses and was a true witness to the incarnation in its completeness.

John listed four ways he had actually perceived the Word of Life with his senses. First he had **heard** the Lord speak. John heard the parables (e.g., Matt. 13:3–33; Mark 4:26–29; Luke 15:11–32), sermons (Matt. 4:23; 5–7), and private words of instruction and counsel from Jesus (Matt. 10:5–42; John 13:12–17; 14–16). **Have heard** translates a perfect tense form of the verb *akouō*, indicating a completed occurrence in the past with an impact in the present. John did not merely hear something from Jesus on a single occasion. He was present throughout Jesus' earthly ministry (cf. John 20:30–31; 21:24–25). Though John wrote this letter some sixty years later, what he had heard firsthand was still a vivid truth in his heart.

Not only had John heard the Lord; he had also seen Him. The verb translated **have seen** is also in the perfect tense, again suggesting a past, completed action with a present, ongoing impact. John added **with our eyes** to make it clear that he was referring to the physical experience of seeing; he was not referring to some kind of spiritual vision that was only in his mind. Christ was not a mystical, phantom image, as some have alleged, but a real man whom John had observed daily for three years by means of normal eyesight.

Third, reinforcing the truth that he had actually seen Jesus, John added the term **looked at.** That word involves more than a mere glance or quick look; instead, it denotes a long, searching gaze (cf. 4:14; Matt. 11:7; Luke 23:55). It is the same verb (*theaomai*) that the *New King James*

Version translates "beheld" in John 1:14. Beyond the works that Jesus performed, John and the other apostles watched Him intently for several years and saw the stunning and unmistakable realities of who He is (cf. Matt. 13:16–17)—the Lord and God, Messiah and Savior (Luke 2:25–32; John 1:29, 41), with supernatural power over demons, disease, nature, and death (Matt. 4:23–24; 8:28–32; Mark 1:23–27; Luke 5:4–6; 7:12–15; John 2:6–10; 4:46–53; 5:5–9; 9:1–7; 11:38–45), and the authority to forgive sins (Mark 2:5, 9; Luke 7:48) and grant eternal life (Luke 19:10; John 11:24–27). As intimate and constant eyewitnesses to His earthly ministry, they had ample proof that Jesus Christ was God in human flesh (John 14:8–11).

Finally, John told his readers that he had **touched with** his **hands** the Word of Life. The word rendered **touched** (*psēlaphaō*) means "to feel after," or "grope" (like a blind man). Jesus used the same word in Luke 24:39, "Touch Me and see, for a spirit does not have flesh and bones as you see that I have." The apostles would have touched Jesus all the time in the daily course of their companionship with Him. John even described himself as one who leaned on Jesus' chest (John 13:23, 25; 21:20). The Lord encouraged Thomas to touch Him on that postresurrection occasion, "Reach here with your finger, and see My hands; and reach here your hand and put it into My side; and do not be unbelieving, but believing" (John 20:27).

With the incarnation of Jesus Christ **the life was manifested.** The verb translated **was manifested** (*phaneroō*) means "to reveal," or "to make visible what was hidden." God did not reveal Himself in human flesh until Christ's earthly ministry when the divine or eternal **life** became visible to mankind. As Jesus said, "For just as the Father has life in Himself, even so He gave to the Son also to have life in Himself" (John 5:26; cf. 1:1–4; 5:39–40; 11:25–26; 1 John 5:12). The Father and the Son have the same divine life, and both can grant eternal life (John 6:37–40).

THE WORD OF LIFE IS COMMUNICABLE

and we have seen and testify and proclaim to you the eternal life, which was with the Father and was manifested to us—what we have seen and heard we proclaim to you also, (1:2b–3a)

For John, that which **was manifested to** him—the Word of Life—became the basis for his proclamation of truth. His privileged life in the presence of the Lord Christ was not a private experience to elevate him above others who were not so blessed, as if he were somehow one of God's "favorite sons." Rather, his privilege became the platform for his responsibility and mandate, as an apostle and eyewitness, to bear witness (**testify**) of the truth (John 20:30–31; 21:24; cf. 1:41–42; 2 Cor. 5:14–15) and **proclaim** the gift of **eternal life** in Him (cf. Ps. 145:11–12; 1 Cor. 2:2; 9:16) to those, including his readers, who had never seen Jesus. Because of his widespread reputation as one who had been with Jesus as an apostle (cf. John 1:14, 16–18, 37–51), John was a true and credible witness (John 19:35–37). Other New Testament books written by apostles or their associates also present eyewitness accounts of Jesus and the truth of the gospel. The other Gospels do that (cf. Luke 1:1–4), as does the book of Acts (cf. 1:1–3) and the epistles (e.g., 2 Peter 1:16–21).

The apostle John knew that the matter of communicating the Word of Life was not an option but a command. The content of the message was not to be hoarded but its unchanging truth declared far and wide. Commenting on this passage, John R. W. Stott provided this key perspective:

> The historical manifestation of the Eternal Life was proclaimed, not monopolized. The revelation was given to the few for the many. They were to dispense it to the world. . . . He [Christ] not only manifested Himself to the disciples to qualify them as *eyewitnesses*, but gave them an authoritative commission as *apostles* to preach the gospel. The author [John] insists that he possess these necessary credentials. Possessing them, he is very bold. Having heard, seen and touched the Lord Jesus, he bears witness to Him. Having received a commission, he proclaims the gospel with authority, for the Christian message is neither a philosophical speculation, nor a tentative suggestion, nor a modest contribution to religious thought, but a dogmatic affirmation by those whose experience and commission qualified them to make it. (*The Epistles of John*, Tyndale New Testament Commentaries [Grand Rapids: Eerdmans, 1964], 61, 62–63, emphases in original)

THE WORD OF LIFE IS RELATIONAL

so that you too may have fellowship with us; and indeed our fellowship is with the Father, and with His Son Jesus Christ. (1:3*b*)

John proclaimed the Word of Life **so that** (*hina*, "in order that") all believers would realize they have **fellowship** (an authentic partnership) **with** Jesus Christ and fellow believers (cf. Acts 1:14; 2:42, 44–47; 1 Cor. 12:26–27; Eph. 4:1–3; Heb. 10:25; 12:22–24). The word rendered **fellowship**, the familiar Greek term *koinonia*, signifies a mutual participation in a common cause or shared life (cf. Gal. 2:9; 6:6; 1 Tim. 6:18; Titus 1:4; Philem. 6; 1 Peter 4:13; Jude 3). It is far more than a mere partnership of those who have the same beliefs and are thus drawn together. Rather, it is the mutual life and love of those who are one in spirit (1 Cor. 6:17; cf. Eph. 5:30–32).

The aim of gospel preaching is to produce faith that rests in Christ (John 6:29; Acts 20:21). Those who believe savingly in Jesus enter into a genuine union with **the Father, His Son Jesus Christ,** and the Holy Spirit. The apostle Paul wrote,

> God is faithful, through whom you were called into fellowship with His Son, Jesus Christ our Lord. (1 Cor. 1:9; cf. Gal. 2:20)

> The grace of the Lord Jesus Christ, and the love of God, and the fellowship of the Holy Spirit, be with you all. (2 Cor. 13:14; cf. John 17:21)

Even sinning Christians who lose the joy of their fellowship with God never lose the reality of that eternal life from Him (1 Cor. 1:9; 2 Cor. 13:14; Phil. 2:1; Heb. 12:10), given them through their union with Christ (Rom. 6:3–5; Eph. 2:5; Col. 3:3). Jesus said, "Truly, truly, I say to you, he who hears My word, and believes Him who sent Me, has eternal life, and does not come into judgment, but has passed out of death into life" (John 5:24; cf. Eph. 5:26; Titus 3:5). The new birth produces new life, so that believers are regenerated into everlasting fellowship with the triune God (cf. John 3:5–8).

THE WORD OF LIFE IS JOYFUL

These things we write, so that our joy may be made complete. (1:4)

Because it is transforming truth, John's message is one that brings consummate **joy,** produces full satisfaction and **complete** fulfillment that can never be lost (John 10:28–29; Rom. 8:35–39; Phil. 1:6; 2 Peter 1:10–11). Jesus told the apostles in the upper room, "These things I have spoken to you so that My joy may be in you, and that your joy may be made full" (John 15:11; cf. 16:22, 33; Luke 2:10). As the apostle Paul explained, "For the kingdom of God is not eating and drinking, but righteousness and peace and joy in the Holy Spirit" (Rom. 14:17; cf. Phil. 4:4; 1 Thess. 5:16).

The secular, dictionary definition of **joy**—"the emotion evoked by well-being, success, or good fortune or by the prospect of possessing what one desires"—is thoroughly inadequate when applied to the Christian life. Martyn Lloyd-Jones correctly observed,

Another thing we must bear in mind, in any definition we may give of New Testament joy, is that we do not go to a dictionary; we go to the New Testament instead. This is something quite peculiar which cannot be explained; it is a quality which belongs to the Christian life in its essence, so that in our definition of joy we must be very careful that it conforms to what we see in our Lord. The world has never seen anyone who knew joy as our Lord knew it, and yet He was "a man of sorrows and acquainted with grief." So our definition of joy must somehow correspond to that. (*Life in Christ: Studies in 1 John* [Wheaton, Ill.: Crossway, 2002], 28)

Lloyd-Jones went on to appropriately summarize the sort of joy of which the apostle John was speaking:

Joy is something very deep and profound, something that affects the whole and entire personality. In other words it comes to this; there is only one thing that can give true joy and that is contemplation of the Lord Jesus Christ. He satisfies my mind; He satisfies my emotions; He satisfies my every desire. He and His great salvation include the whole personality and nothing less, and in Him I am complete. Joy, in other words, is the response and the reaction of the soul to a knowledge of the Lord Jesus Christ. (*Life in Christ*, 30)

John wanted his readers to experience the **joy** that comes from understanding the reality of Christ, the saving truth of the gospel, and the fellowship that each Christian has with God and fellow believers. It is then that all true followers of Jesus will have His "joy made full in themselves" (John 17:13; cf. 15:11; 16:24; Ps. 16:11).

Tests of Salvation—Part 1: Belief in God and the Certainty of Sin (1 John 1:5–6, 8, 10)

2

This is the message we have heard from Him and announce to you, that God is Light, and in Him there is no darkness at all. If we say that we have fellowship with Him and yet walk in the darkness, we lie and do not practice the truth; . . . If we say that we have no sin, we are deceiving ourselves and the truth is not in us. . . . If we say that we have not sinned, we make Him a liar and His word is not in us. (1:5–6,8,10)

In addition to leading and feeding their sheep, godly pastors, as spiritual shepherds, must warn their flocks about false teachers and the doctrinal errors they spread. As the apostle Paul charged the Ephesian elders,

> Be on guard for yourselves and for all the flock, among which the Holy Spirit has made you overseers, to shepherd the church of God which He purchased with His own blood. I know that after my departure savage wolves will come in among you, not sparing the flock; and from among your own selves men will arise, speaking perverse things, to draw away the disciples after them. Therefore be on the alert, remembering that night and day for a period of three years I did not cease to admonish each one with tears. (Acts 20:28–31; cf. 1 Tim. 6:20; 2 Tim. 1:13–14)

Similarly, John wrote this letter to protect his flock of faithful believers in Asia Minor by reiterating God's truth to them. John's zealous concern for the certainties of divine teaching also motivated him to write his second and third letters. Thus, the apostle addressed his second epistle "to the chosen lady and her children, whom I love in truth; and not only I, but also all who know the truth, for the sake of the truth which abides in us and will be with us forever" (vv. 1–2). Three times in that opening salutation John refers to "the truth," underscoring its significance for him. Then in verse 4 he adds, "I was very glad to find some of your children walking in truth, just as we have received commandment to do from the Father" (cf. 3 John 3–4).

To the degree that John was passionate in his love for the truth, he was equally passionate in his opposition to error. In 2 John 7, he warned his readers that "many deceivers have gone out into the world, those who do not acknowledge Jesus Christ as coming in the flesh. This is the deceiver and the antichrist." Then he admonished them to separate themselves from all such heretics:

> Anyone who goes too far and does not abide in the teaching of Christ, does not have God; the one who abides in the teaching, he has both the Father and the Son. If anyone comes to you and does not bring this teaching, do not receive him into your house, and do not give him a greeting; for the one who gives him a greeting participates in his evil deeds. (vv. 9–11; cf. 3 John 9–10)

To guard one's flock from those who would destroy it, a faithful pastor must know and teach sound doctrine (cf. Titus 1:9). He must also give his people tests by which they can distinguish true believers from counterfeit professors. Making that fundamental distinction is essential to the church's protection and spiritual growth. The wheat must be differentiated from the tares (cf. Matt. 13:24–30), the sheep distinguished from the goats, or the godly shepherd will never be able to clarify to his people their true condition or protect them from the deadly deceptions of false teachers.

In these verses, John presents two crucial doctrinal tests to determine who is genuine: an accurate belief in the nature of God, and a genuine belief in the certainty of sin.

The Nature of God

This is the message we have heard from Him and announce to you, that God is Light, and in Him there is no darkness at all. (1:5)

The message, preached by John and the other apostles, was one they **heard from Him** [Jesus] and **announce**[d] **to** their audience. As God in human flesh (John 1:1–4, 18; Titus 2:13; Heb. 1:8; 1 John 5:20; cf. John 4:26; 8:24, 28, 58; 18:5), Jesus Christ is the perfect source of revelation regarding the nature and character of God. The apostle earlier recorded Jesus' statement, "God is spirit" (John 4:24); here in his first letter he declared, **God is Light** and later would affirm, "God is love" (4:8).

The description of **God** as **Light** captures the essence of His nature and is foundational to the rest of the epistle. However, unlike the straightforward expressions "God is spirit" (meaning that God is immaterial in form; compare John 4:24 with Luke 24:39) and "God is love" (meaning that the persons of the Trinity love one another and mankind; cf. 3:17; 4:7, 16; Mic. 7:18; Zeph. 3:17; John 5:42; 15:10; Rom. 5:5, 8; 8:39; Eph. 2:4; Titus 3:4), the idea that **God is Light** (cf. Ps. 78:14; Isa. 60:19–20; John 1:9; 3:19; 8:12; 9:5; 12:46; Acts 9:3; Rev. 21:23) is more complex.

Throughout the Scriptures, God and His glory are often described in terms of light. For example, during the exodus God appeared to the Israelites in the form of light:

> The Lord was going before them in a pillar of cloud by day to lead them on the way, and in a pillar of fire by night to give them light, that they might travel by day and by night. He did not take away the pillar of cloud by day, nor the pillar of fire by night, from before the people. (Ex. 13:21–22; cf. 40:34–38; 1 Kings 8:11)

When Moses came down from Mount Sinai after meeting with the Lord, his face glowed with a reflection of God's light (Ex. 34:29–35; cf. 2 Cor. 3:7–8). In Psalm 104:1–2, the psalmist says, "Bless the Lord, O my soul! O Lord my God, You are very great; You are clothed with splendor and majesty, covering Yourself with light as with a cloak, stretching out heaven like a tent curtain" (cf. 1 Tim. 6:14–16). Not only is God light in His essence, but He also is the source of the believer's light (Ps. 27:1; John 1:9; 12:36).

At the transfiguration, when Jesus gave the three apostles a glimpse of His full glory, He manifested Himself as light: "He was transfigured before them; and His face shone like the sun, and His garments became as white as light" (Matt. 17:2). Second Corinthians 4:4–6 summarizes well the importance of God as light and its role in a Christian's life:

> The god of this world has blinded the minds of the unbelieving so that they might not see the light of the gospel of the glory of Christ, who is the image of God. For we do not preach ourselves but Christ Jesus as Lord, and ourselves as your bond-servants for Jesus' sake. For God, who said, "Light shall shine out of darkness," is the One who has shone in our

hearts to give the Light of the knowledge of the glory of God in the face of Christ. (cf. Matt. 5:14–16; Eph. 5:8–10; Phil. 2:15; Col. 1:12–13; 1 Peter 2:9)

Although the foregoing passages describe the significance of divine light, they do not define it. However, Psalm 36:9 does: "For with You is the fountain of life; in Your light we see light" (cf. 1 Peter 2:9). Here the psalmist employed a Hebrew parallelism, using two statements to say the same thing. He equates light and life—God is light in the sense that He is life, and He is the source and sustainer of both physical and spiritual life.

John expressed that truth in the prologue to his gospel:

> In the beginning was the Word, and the Word was with God, and the Word was God. He was in the beginning with God. All things came into being through Him, and apart from Him nothing came into being that has come into being. In Him was life, and the life was the Light of men. The Light shines in the darkness, and the darkness did not comprehend it. There came a man sent from God, whose name was John. He came as a witness, to testify about the Light, so that all might believe through him. He was not the Light, but he came to testify about the Light. There was the true Light which, coming into the world, enlightens every man. He was in the world, and the world was made through Him, and the world did not know Him. He came to His own, and those who were His own did not receive Him. But as many as received Him, to them He gave the right to become children of God, even to those who believe in His name, who were born, not of blood nor of the will of the flesh nor of the will of man, but of God. (John 1:1–13; cf. 2:23–3:21; Col. 1:15–17)

"I am the Light of the world," Jesus declared; "he who follows Me will not walk in darkness, but will have the Light of life" (John 8:12; cf. 12:45–46). God, the source of true light, bestows it on believers in the form of eternal life through His Son, who was the light incarnate.

Scripture reveals two fundamental principles that flow from the foundational truth that God is light. First, light represents the truth of God, as embodied in His Word. The psalmist wrote these familiar words: "Your word is a lamp to my feet and a light to my path. . . . The unfolding of Your words gives light; it gives understanding to the simple" (Ps. 119:105, 130; cf. Prov. 6:23; 2 Peter 1:19). The light and life of God are inherently connected to and characterized by truth.

Second, Scripture also links light with virtue and moral conduct. The apostle Paul instructed the Ephesians, "You were formerly darkness, but now you are Light in the Lord; walk as children of Light (for the fruit of the Light consists in all goodness and righteousness and truth)" (Eph. 5:8–9; cf. Isa. 5:20; Rom. 13:12; 1 Thess. 5:5–6).

Those two essential properties of divine light and life are crucial in distinguishing genuine faith from a counterfeit claim. If one professes to possess the Light and to dwell in it—to have received eternal life—he will show evidence of spiritual life by his devotion both to truth and to righteousness, as John writes later in this letter:

> The one who says he is in the Light and yet hates his brother is in the darkness until now. The one who loves his brother abides in the Light and there is no cause for stumbling in him. But the one who hates his brother is in the darkness and walks in the darkness, and does not know where he is going because the darkness has blinded his eyes. (2:9–11; cf. Matt. 5:16; 25:34–40; Luke 1:6; 11:28; Rom. 6:17; 16:19; Phil. 1:11; Titus 2:7; James 2:14–20)

If truth and righteousness are absent from one's life, that person, no matter what he or she says, does not possess eternal life (Matt. 7:17–18, 21–23; 25:41–46). They cannot belong to God, because **in Him there is no darkness at all.** God is absolutely perfect in truth and holiness (Ex. 15:11; 1 Sam. 2:2; Pss. 22:3; 48:10; 71:19; 98:2; Isa. 6:3; Rev. 4:8; 15:4). Obviously, believers fall far short of that perfection, but they manifest a godlike desire for and continual striving toward heavenly truth and righteousness (cf. Phil. 3:7–16).

THE CERTAINTY OF SIN

If we say that we have fellowship with Him and yet walk in the darkness, we lie and do not practice the truth; . . . If we say that we have no sin, we are deceiving ourselves and the truth is not in us. . . . If we say that we have not sinned, we make Him a liar and His word is not in us. (1:6, 8, 10)

Ever since the fall, mankind has tried to deny the reality of sin, even though every human being is innately aware of its presence.

> For when Gentiles who do not have the Law do instinctively the things of the Law, these, not having the Law, are a law to themselves, in that they show the work of the Law written in their hearts, their conscience bearing witness and their thoughts alternately accusing or else defending them, on the day when, according to my [Paul's] gospel, God will judge the secrets of men through Christ Jesus. (Rom. 2:14–16; cf. Eccles. 7:20; Rom. 5:12; Gal. 3:22)

People today minimize and redefine sin, often alleging that the "failures" of their lives and certain "disorders" exist because of how others have treated them. The victim mentality reigns supreme as popular culture comforts itself in affirming that people are basically good and whatever may be wrong is not really wrong, but merely a preference of personal freedom. Instead of accepting responsibility for their behavior, people demand to be accepted as they are. They reclassify serious and heart issues "illnesses" and "addictions" and try to "cure" them with prescription drugs and psychotherapy. But because that fails to deal with sin, the actual root cause of the problem, society goes from bad to worse. In contrast to all that delusion, Jesus taught that every person is sinful at the very core of his or her being:

> That which proceeds out of the man, that is what defiles the man. For from within, out of the heart of men, proceed the evil thoughts, fornications, thefts, murders, adulteries, deeds of coveting and wickedness, as well as deceit, sensuality, envy, slander, pride and foolishness. All these evil things proceed from within and defile the man. (Mark 7:20–23; cf. Gen. 6:5; Jer. 17:9; James 1:15; 4:1)

Yet, many in the church today seem to be reluctant to make the diagnosis Jesus did, for fear they might offend someone or be deemed "unloving." Thus, sin is explained away in culturally acceptable terms.

The people of Judah in Malachi's day were equally adept at denying their sin. God had given them very clear and detailed instructions concerning what offerings were acceptable to Him (Lev. 1:1–7:38). Yet they continued to present defiled food and defective animals to the Lord. Then they acted surprised (as though they had done nothing wrong) when the Lord, through the prophet Malachi, confronted them about their clear disobedience:

> " 'A son honors his father, and a servant his master. Then if I am a father, where is My honor? And if I am a master, where is My respect?' says the Lord of hosts to you, O priests who despise My name. But you say, 'How have we despised Your name?' You are presenting defiled food upon My altar. But you say, 'How have we defiled You?' In that you say, 'The table of the Lord is to be despised.' But when you present the blind for sacrifice, is it not evil? And when you present the lame and sick, is it not evil? Why not offer it to your governor? Would he be pleased with you? Or would he receive you kindly?" says the Lord of hosts. (Mal. 1:6–8)

God then moved from an expression of displeasure to a warning of severe judgment on the religious leaders, the priests:

> And now this commandment is for you, O priests. "If you do not listen, and if you do not take it to heart to give honor to My name," says the Lord of hosts, "then I will send the curse upon you and I will curse your blessings; and indeed, I have cursed them already, because you are not taking it to heart. Behold, I am going to rebuke your offspring, and I will spread refuse on your faces, the refuse of your feasts; and you will be taken away with it. Then you will know that I have sent this command-ment to you, that My covenant may continue with Levi," says the Lord of hosts. (2:1–4)

The Lord's rebuke was necessarily harsh because the people had dis-obeyed Him so grievously (2:11–16) and yet were acting as though they had done nothing wrong. They had arbitrarily (and wrongly) excused their wicked behavior, to the point that they audaciously accused God of being unjust and unfair to them (v. 17). In a similar sense, there are many today who think God would be brutally unjust for sending any human being to hell. It is not until people accept both the absolute holiness of God and full responsibility for their sin that they admit God has the right to judge and punish them (cf. Ezra 9:13; Neh. 9:33; Luke 15:21; 23:41).

The apostle John faced a similar situation in the churches to whom he wrote his letter. Flooding into Ephesus and the other cities and churches of Asia Minor were deceitful, sin-denying false teachers (cf. 2:18; 4:1–3; 2 Peter 2:1–2; Jude 4). In addition to the heresies of Docetism (that said Christ's body only appeared to be physical) and Cerinthianism (that claimed that Christ's "divine spirit" descended upon the human Jesus at His baptism but departed just prior to His crucifixion), John had to contend with Greek philosophical dualism (the basis of Gnosti-cism)—a view that denied the reality of sin and evil. Those who held to this mystical, elitist philosophy argued the spiritual was always good and the physical was always bad; they therefore created an artificial dichoto-my between the spiritual realm and the physical world—contending that spiritual realities were all that mattered, and that what was done in the flesh (including sin) was a nonissue. As John encountered this heresy, he had to unmask those who denied sin's existence and thereby sidestepped their own responsibility for it and its consequences.

John divided those who claimed to be in the fellowship but rejected the truth into three similar but distinct categories: those in dark-ness, those in deception, and those who defame God. All three groups of people either willfully rejected or completely ignored the reality that true believers and sin are incompatible. "How shall we who died to sin still live in it?" Paul exclaimed in Romans 6:2. Later in that chapter he added, "But thanks be to God that though you were slaves of sin, you became obedi-ent from the heart to that form of teaching to which you were committed, and having been freed from sin, you became slaves of righteousness"

(vv. 17–18; cf. Eph. 2:1–5). By refusing to repent, these sin-denying false professors revealed that they were outside of God's plan of salvation, which begins with election (Rom. 8:29; Eph. 1:4, 11); includes redemption (1 Cor. 1:30; Gal. 3:13; Heb. 9:12), sanctification (1 Cor. 6:11; Eph. 5:26–27; Phil. 2:12–13), and spiritual growth (John 16:13; 17:17; cf. 2 Thess. 2:13; 1 Tim. 3:15); and culminates with glorification (2 Cor. 3:18; 2 Thess. 2:14; 2 Tim. 2:10).

If we say that we have fellowship with Him and yet walk in the darkness, we lie and do not practice the truth; (1:6)

The first category of false professors consists of those who ignored their sin as if it were not a reality to them. They claimed to **have fellowship with** God, to share common aspects of life with **Him,** that is, eternal life (cf. John 17:3). However, that claim is meaningless if one continues to **walk in the darkness. Walk** refers to manner of life or conduct (Rom. 8:4; cf. 13:13; Eph. 4:1; Col. 1:10; see also Deut. 10:12–13; Ps. 119:1; Mic. 6:8), and it is there that genuine salvation is manifest, not in a mere profession that one possesses eternal life. To profess one thing and live in contradiction to it is to **lie** and **not practice the truth.** Jesus indicted the Jews' superficial earthly religion by declaring to them, "The eye is the lamp of the body; so then if your eye is clear, your whole body will be full of light. But if your eye is bad, your whole body will be full of darkness. If then the light that is in you is darkness, how great is the darkness!" (Matt. 6:22–23). In this analogy, the Lord argued from the lesser to the greater. If it is a negative thing to be in the dark physically (blind), it is much worse to be in the dark spiritually. John in his gospel taught that Jesus was the true light for a sin-darkened world (John 1:4–5; cf. 8:12). But since sinful humanity prefers darkness over light (John 3:19–20), no one who claims to be a Christian and yet lives in darkness (meaning that they continually practice evil deeds) is actually saved (1 John 3:4, 9; cf. Matt. 7:17–18; 13:38; John 8:42–44).

Those who really embrace the truth heed James's admonition:

> But prove yourselves doers of the word, and not merely hearers who delude themselves. For if anyone is a hearer of the word and not a doer, he is like a man who looks at his natural face in a mirror; for once he has looked at himself and gone away, he has immediately forgotten what kind of person he was. But one who looks intently at the perfect law, the law of liberty, and abides by it, not having become a forgetful

hearer but an effectual doer, this man will be blessed in what he does. (James 1:22–25)

Believers possess God's life, are new creations in Christ made for good works (1 John 5:20; Rom. 6:11–17; 8:1–2; 12:5; 1 Cor. 1:2; 2 Cor. 1:21; 5:17; Gal. 3:28; Eph. 2:10; Phil. 1:1; Col. 1:27–28), and have the indwelling Holy Spirit (Rom. 8:11; 1 Cor. 3:16; 2 Tim. 1:14). Thus they cannot ignore the existence of personal iniquity and walk in darkness (cf. Col. 1:12–14). No matter what anyone claims for himself, the genuineness of faith can always be seen in one's life by the love of righteousness (Matt. 7:15–20).

THOSE IN DECEPTION

If we say that we have no sin, we are deceiving ourselves and the truth is not in us. (1:8)

A second group of false professors claimed to **have no sin.** This position was prouder than the stance of those in the first category who ignored their sin (cf. Jer. 17:9). Any so-called Christians who claim to have reached a higher spiritual plane, where sin no longer exists in their lives, completely misunderstand their condition and the Spirit's work of progressive sanctification.

Again, any who ignore the existence of sin give clear evidence that **the truth is not in** them. The Bible plainly teaches the principle of human depravity. In Romans 3:10–23 Paul wrote:

"There is none righteous, not even one; there is none who understands, there is none who seeks for God; all have turned aside, together they have become useless; there is none who does good, there is not even one. Their throat is an open grave, with their tongues they keep deceiving, the poison of asps is under their lips; whose mouth is full of cursing and bitterness; their feet are swift to shed blood, destruction and misery are in their paths, and the path of peace they have not known. There is no fear of God before their eyes." Now we know that whatever the Law says, it speaks to those who are under the Law, so that every mouth may be closed and all the world may become accountable to God; because by the works of the Law no flesh will be justified in His sight; for through the Law comes the knowledge of sin. But now apart from the Law the righteousness of God has been manifested, being witnessed by the Law and the Prophets, even the righteousness of God through faith in Jesus Christ for all those who believe; for there is no distinction; for all have sinned and fall short of the glory of God. (cf. Gen. 8:21; 2 Chron. 6:36; Ps. 51:5; Jer. 13:23; Rom. 8:7–8; 1 Cor. 2:14; Titus 3:3)

Jesus Christ was the only human being who could ever claim to be without sin (Heb. 4:15). All who make such an outlandish claim are only fooling themselves. It is not until believers are glorified in heaven that their sanctification process will be complete (Rom. 8:19, 23), and then they will be without sin.

THOSE WHO DEFAME GOD

If we say that we have not sinned, we make Him a liar and His word is not in us. (1:10)

The list of those who deny the certainty of sin culminates with a third group, those who not only claim not to sin now, but who **say that** they **have** never **sinned.** By making that ridiculous assertion they blasphemously **make** God a **liar** (cf. Titus 1:2; 1 John 5:10–11) in two ways. First, they explicitly deny His teaching that all have sinned (see above), and second, they implicitly deny the need for a Savior (cf. Isa. 53:10–11; Zech. 9:9; Matt. 1:21; Luke 2:11; 19:10; Acts 5:31; 13:38–39; Rom. 6:23; 1 Tim. 1:15; Heb. 5:9). After all, why would they need a Substitute to take their punishment for something they claim to have never committed?

All three categories of false claimants to fellowship with God fail John's second doctrinal test by denying sin's certainty. Thus they prove that **His word** [truth] **is not in** them. Anyone, even a professed believer seeking to cover up his or her sin, is in the depths of spiritual darkness and deception, and blasphemes God. Conversely, when those truly in the fellowship fall into sin, they do not deny sin's presence or their propensity toward it (Rom. 7:14–25; 1 Tim. 1:12–15; cf. Pss. 32:5; 51:1, 3; Prov. 28:13). Instead, they openly and honestly confess their sins before the Lord and repent of them.

Scripture corroborates the validity and necessity of John's first two doctrinal tests of salvation—belief in God and belief in the certainty of sin. Concerning essential faith, the author of Hebrews declares,

> Now faith is the assurance of things hoped for, the conviction of things not seen. . . . And without faith it is impossible to please Him, for he who comes to God must believe that He is and that He is a rewarder of those who seek Him. (11:1, 6; cf. John 6:47; 20:31; Rom. 1:17; 3:21–22, 28; 1 John 5:1)

Jesus' parable of the Pharisee and the publican (tax collector) makes clear that one cannot be justified apart from an honest confession of his or her sinfulness:

But the tax collector [in contrast to the self-righteous Pharisee], standing some distance away, was even unwilling to lift up his eyes to heaven, but was beating his breast, saying, "God, be merciful to me, the sinner!" I tell you, this man went to his house justified rather than the other; for everyone who exalts himself will be humbled, but he who humbles himself will be exalted. (Luke 18:13–14; cf. Prov. 26:12; 1 Cor. 6:9–10; Gal. 5:19–21; Eph. 5:5)

Tests of Salvation— Part 2: Belief in the Forgiveness of Sins and Confession (1 John 1:7, 9; 2:1*a*)

3

But if we walk in the Light as He Himself is in the Light, we have fellowship with one another, and the blood of Jesus His Son cleanses us from all sin. . . . If we confess our sins, He is faithful and righteous to forgive us our sins and to cleanse us from all unrighteousness. . . . My little children, I am writing these things to you so that you may not sin. (1:7, 9; 2:1*a*)

The glorious promise of the gospel is the free and gracious forgiveness of sin given to everyone who truly repents and believes in the person and work of the Son of God. That divine pardon is so comprehensive that God removes all believing sinners' defilement, guilt, and punishment and replaces those things with righteousness, sanctification, and heavenly reward. Moreover, God's forgiveness is eternal and unchangeable (cf. John 5:24; Heb. 10:17–18). The apostle Paul summarized that all-surpassing blessing in his epistle to the Romans:

Therefore there is no condemnation for those who are in Christ Jesus. . . . And we know that God causes all things to work together for good to those who love God, to those who are called according to His purpose. For those whom He foreknew, He also predestined to become conformed to the image of His Son, so that He would be the firstborn among many brethren; and these whom He predestined, He also called; and these whom He called, He also justified; and these whom He justified, He also glorified. What then shall we say to these things? If God is for us, who is against us? He who did not spare His own Son, but delivered Him over for us all, how will He not also with Him freely give us all things? Who will bring a charge against God's elect? God is the one who justifies; who is the one who condemns? Christ Jesus is He who died, yes, rather who was raised, who is at the right hand of God, who also intercedes for us. Who will separate us from the love of Christ? Will tribulation, or distress, or persecution, or famine, or nakedness, or peril, or sword? . . . But in all these things we overwhelmingly conquer through Him who loved us. For I am convinced that neither death, nor life, nor angels, nor principalities, nor things present, nor things to come, nor powers, nor height, nor depth, nor any other created thing, will be able to separate us from the love of God, which is in Christ Jesus our Lord. (Rom. 8:1, 28–35, 37–39; cf. Ps. 103:12; Rom. 5:20–21; Gal. 3:13–14; Eph. 1:7; see also Ps. 32:1–2; Rom. 4:6–8)

The fact that forgiveness is complete and irrevocable, however, has led some to wrongly conclude that those who have received salvation need never again confess their sins before God and request forgiveness. The proponents of this view contend that, in order for Christians to accept genuinely their full pardon and fully enjoy their liberty in Christ, they must ignore sin and focus solely on God's grace. But historically, such teaching has consistently led to the error of antinomianism—a practical disregard for the law of God and a callous lack of concern for violating it. If such people are truly saved, they are indifferent toward the disciplines that produce holiness in their lives. The effects of such faulty thinking are disastrous. (For further discussion of this issue, see John MacArthur, *The Freedom and Power of Forgiveness* [Wheaton, Ill.: Crossway, 1998], chapter 3.)

In order to justify their indifference toward God's moral law, many who hold such a position relegate Christ's teaching on forgiveness to another dispensation (contending that Jesus' instruction applies to Old Testament Israel only, and not to the New Testament church). Thus, they argue, when Jesus commanded the apostles to pray for the Father's forgiveness (cf. Luke 11:4), His words reflected the era of law, not grace. They further suggest that the reason Christ gave such stipulations to His disciples was because He understood salvation in the Old Testament to be conditional—based on confessing sin, offering sacrifices, and keeping the law. But their claims are ultimately unfounded, for salvation never functioned that way during any part of the Old Testament era (and, obviously, that was not how Jesus understood it). God saved people then on the same basis that He saves them now—by the substitutionary, atoning death of Jesus Christ, which the sacrificial system pictured. Sinners then as now were saved by faith only, demonstrated when, overwhelmed by their sin and inability to keep God's holy law, they cried out to God for mercy and received His pardon (cf. Ps. 32:1–2*a*; Isa. 55:6–7; Mic. 7:18–19; Luke 18:13–14). Those whom He saved before the cross, God in eternity past chose, and looking ahead to the death of "the Lamb slain from the foundation of the world" (Rev. 13:8, NKJV) applied Christ's coming death to their account, even as He now looks back to Calvary and extends the same electing grace to all who have believed the gospel. The just have always lived by faith (Hab. 2:4; Rom. 1:17), so no sacrifice, confession, or law keeping in any era could earn a right standing before God or satisfy His just judgment against sinners (cf. Rom. 4:1–24; Heb. 9:11–15). Only the perfect, substitutionary death of the Lamb of God could satisfy justice and save believing sinners from God's wrath. And only the righteous life of Christ credited to their accounts could make them acceptable to God (John 1:29; 2 Cor. 5:21; 1 Peter 1:18–19).

So how can one reconcile the comprehensiveness and permanence of God's forgiveness and the imputing of perfect righteousness to believers at salvation with the continual need for Christian penitence (e.g., Pss. 6; 32; 38; 51; 102; 130; 143; Matt. 6:14–15)? It is necessary to recognize that divine forgiveness consists of two interrelated aspects: the judicial (or legally forensic) and the sanctifying (or personal, paternal). The Lord illustrated those two aspects of forgiveness when He washed the apostles' feet in the upper room:

> Jesus, knowing that the Father had given all things into His hands, and that He had come forth from God and was going back to God, got up from supper, and laid aside His garments; and taking a towel, He girded Himself. Then He poured water into the basin, and began to wash the disciples' feet and to wipe them with the towel with which He was girded. So He came to Simon Peter. He said to Him, "Lord, do You wash my feet?" Jesus answered and said to him, "What I do you do not realize now, but you will understand hereafter." Peter said to Him, "Never shall You wash my feet!" Jesus answered him, "If I do not wash you, you have no part with Me." Simon Peter said to Him, "Lord, then wash not only my feet, but also my hands and my head." Jesus said to him, "He who has bathed needs only to wash his feet, but is completely clean; and you are clean, but not all of you." (John 13:3–10)

Modeling humility and servanthood, the Lord performed one of the most frequent menial acts of courtesy found in the ancient Middle East—a task normally done by the lowest-level slave. Instead of asking one of His disciples to do the dirty work, Jesus Himself removed the sandals of His followers and washed their grimy feet in preparation for the Passover meal.

When Jesus told Peter, "He who has bathed needs only to wash his feet, but is completely clean" (John 13:10), the Lord made a distinction between the two aspects of forgiveness. The all-cleansing bath represents God's forensic application of Christ's death to repentant sinners, completely and forever justifying them (Acts 13:39; Rom. 3:22, 24; 4:6–8; 5:1; Gal. 2:16), and freeing them forever from eternal hell. Washing feet, on the other hand, represents the paternal forgiveness of sanctification. Although repentant sinners have already been justified once-for-all, they have not yet been delivered from the presence and power of sin in their daily lives (Rom. 7:15–20; Gal. 5:17). Therefore believers need to confess and forsake sin regularly, thereby washing the metaphorical dirt of sin off their feet (cf. Pss. 38:18; 97:10; 139:23–24; Prov. 28:13; Rom. 8:13; 12:9; Col. 3:5; Heb. 12:1). But in so doing, since they have already been fully cleansed, they come to confess, not to a condemning Judge (cf. Matt. 25:41; Rev. 20:11–15), but rather to their loving Father (1 John 2:5; 4:16; cf. Ps. 36:7; Rom. 5:5; 8:39; Eph. 2:4), endeavoring to avoid His displeasure and discipline (cf. Heb. 13:17). It is this kind of forgiveness that confessing Christians seek, and why they forgive others so that God does not withhold the relational forgiveness that blesses (Matt. 6:14–15).

Repentance is not only God's work in the heart leading to salvation (Acts 2:38; 3:19; 11:18; 2 Cor. 7:10; 2 Tim. 2:25), but also an essential element of every believer's sanctification (cf. 2 Cor. 7:1). John concludes the opening section by applying two tests of genuine salvation that are related to repentance: a belief in God's forgiveness of sin and a regular practice of confessing sins. This instruction suggests three terms that describe true believers in contrast to those who falsely profess to be in the fellowship of faith (cf. 1:6, 8, 10). True believers are cleansed from sin; yet, confessing sin; and even conquering sin.

CLEANSED

but if we walk in the Light as He Himself is in the Light, we have fellowship with one another, and the blood of Jesus His Son cleanses us from all sin. (1:7)

Walk is used throughout the New Testament, especially in Paul's letters, to describe the effect, not of justification, but of sanctification. Salvation is not only a change in one's legal status as divine righteousness is credited to one's account, but a change in behavior as actual righteousness is given to believers by the very indwelling presence of God's Spirit. Daily living of the Christian life is a Spirit-enabled walk (John 8:12; 12:35; Rom. 6:4; 8:4; 1 Cor. 7:17; 2 Cor. 5:7; Gal. 5:16, 25; Eph. 2:10; 4:1; 5:8; Col. 1:10;

1 Thess. 4:1). The verb is a present subjunctive, expressing continuous action that is nevertheless hypothetical because it applies only to some people.

Those who **walk** in the **Light** do so because the power of God has regenerated them. As "new creature[s]" for whom "new things have come" (2 Cor. 5:17), they will behave in a way that reflects the power of God's righteous life in them, just **as** God **Himself is in the Light** (see the discussion of 1:5 in the previous chapter of this volume). The general pattern of their day-to-day actions and attitudes will be godlike. Such walkers will experience **fellowship with one another** (1:3, 7; Acts 2:42; cf. Col. 1:12; Phil. 2:17–18), which derives from their union with the triune God (1:6; 1 Cor. 1:9; 6:17; 12:6, 13). All true Christians live and walk in the Light (i.e., the life of God) and the communion of the saints.

To all who **walk in the Light,** God grants His grace so that throughout their lives **the blood of Jesus Christ His Son cleanses** them **from all sin.** This is not to say that Christians no longer struggle with sin, for no one will ever be totally free in this life from the unredeemed humanness of their flesh (Matt. 26:41; Rom. 7:18–24; Gal. 5:17; cf. Rom. 13:14). However, because **the blood of Jesus Christ** continually **cleanses** away every impurity, sin can never change a believer's standing before God (cf. Rom. 8:33–39). The term **blood** is often used in the New Testament as a dramatic and graphic way to represent Christ's sacrificial death on the cross (cf. Acts 20:28; Rom. 3:25; 5:9; Eph. 1:7; Heb. 9:12; 10:19), by which He "released us from our sins by His blood" (Rev. 1:5; cf. Col. 1:20–22; 1 Tim. 2:6; Heb. 2:17; Rev. 5:9).

The salvation cleansing John described encompasses all the sinner's transgressions, past and future, and depends on no condition but God's sovereign grace in response to saving faith. John is unmistakably in agreement with the Spirit-inspired teaching of Paul that the redeemed enjoy complete, unalterable, and unrepeatable forgiveness (cf. 1 Cor. 6:11; 2 Cor. 5:18–19; Eph. 1:7; Col. 1:14; Heb. 10:10).

CONFESSING

If we confess our sins, He is faithful and righteous to forgive us our sins and to cleanse us from all unrighteousness. (1:9)

Confession of sin is absolutely crucial to entering the Light (justification) (cf. Mark 1:15; Luke 18:13–14) and walking in it (sanctification). Though this is obvious in Scripture, there are many who even claim that one needs only to accept the facts about Jesus for salvation, arguing that the confession and repentance of sin are unnecessary—or optional at best—for justification. Out of the soil of that errant soteriology comes the antinomian indifference toward a Christian life of repentance and confession for the sake of holiness. (For an in-depth discussion of this erroneous viewpoint and an exposition of the biblical doctrine of salvation, see John MacArthur, *The Gospel According to Jesus* [Grand Rapids: Zondervan, 1988, 1994], and *The Gospel According to the Apostles* [Nashville: Thomas Nelson, 1993, 2000].)

Such views exist in spite of biblical calls to repentance and examples of people who openly acknowledged their sins to God. "So Judah said, 'What can we say to my lord? What can we speak? And how can we justify ourselves? God has found out the iniquity of your servants'" (Gen. 44:16*a*; cf. 41:9; Jon. 3:5–10). Overwhelmed by a vision of God's majestic holiness, the prophet Isaiah cried out, "Woe is me, for I am ruined! Because I am a man of unclean lips, and I live among a people of unclean lips; for my eyes have seen the King, the Lord of hosts" (Isa. 6:5; cf. 1 Chron. 21:17; Dan. 9:20). The Psalms are filled with confessions, most notably David's in Psalm 51:

> Be gracious to me, O God, according to Your lovingkindness; according to the greatness of Your compassion blot out my transgressions. Wash me thoroughly from my iniquity and cleanse me from my sin. For I know my transgressions, and my sin is ever before me. Against You, You only, I have sinned and done what is evil in Your sight, so that You are justified when You speak and blameless when You judge. Behold, I was brought forth in iniquity, and in sin my mother conceived me. Behold, You desire truth in the innermost being, and in the hidden part You will make me know wisdom. Purify me with hyssop, and I shall be clean; wash me, and I shall be whiter than snow. Make me to hear joy and gladness, let the bones which You have broken rejoice. Hide Your face from my sins and blot out all my iniquities. (vv. 1–9; cf. 32:5; 38:1–8, 17–18; 41:4)

The New Testament includes similar expressions. No less than John the Baptist preached repentance with manifest evidence as necessary for entering into God's salvation kingdom (Matt. 3:2–12; Luke 3:4–14). Jesus demanded recognition of sin and a response of repentance for all who desired salvation (Matt. 4:17), even saying that sinners had to repent or perish (Luke 13:3, 5). The repentance and confession of sin He demanded was so strong it required total self-denial (Luke 9:23–26) and hatred of self (Luke 14:25–27), which made coming to salvation too demanding for some (Luke 13:23–24). Peter and Paul each confessed their sinfulness (Luke 5:8; 1 Tim. 1:12–16), and two of Jesus' parables concerned men who recognized their own sinful conditions (Luke 15:18; 18:13). Moreover, as the apostles proclaimed the gospel, they made it clear that God calls upon sinners everywhere to admit their sin and repent (Acts 17:30; cf. Isa. 45:22; Acts 2:38).

First John 1:9 fits this pattern with perfect consistency, when rightly interpreted. Because John is writing to believers ("my little children," 2:1), to those who are antinomian it appears to make forgiveness conditional (i.e., if believers confess, God will forgive; if they do not confess, He will not forgive). This confusion is easily cleared away, first of all by noting that the verse is actually a reiteration of God's faithfulness to His New Covenant promise of salvation in the Old Covenant: "I will forgive their iniquity, and their sin I will remember no more" (Jer. 31:34; cf. Luke 1:77–78; Heb. 9:13–14). The reminder that **He is faithful and righteous to forgive us our sins and to cleanse us from all unrighteousness** reemphasizes the truth John had just stated in verse 7, that God will, because of His character, secure their eternal glory by continuing to cleanse believers from all future sin. He is faithful to His promise and always does what is righteous. (The aorist tense of the verb *aphiēmi* [**forgive**] carries a past connotation and further demonstrates that God's forgiveness derives from a historical event, the atonement, which has lasting benefits for all who believe.) In chapter 2 John writes, "your sins have been forgiven you for His name's sake" (v. 12). Forgiveness is consistent with who Jesus Christ is and with what the Father promised, according to His perfectly faithful (Isa. 49:7; 1 Cor. 1:9; Heb. 2:17; Rev. 19:11), righteous (Ps. 7:11; Isa. 53:11), just (Gen. 18:25; Col. 3:25), holy (Ex. 15:11; Rev. 4:8), and loving (Jer. 31:3; 1 John 4:8) nature. Forgiveness is not incomplete or dependent in the saving sense on believers' confessing.

With that established, it is possible to understand the place of ongoing confession. The word translated **confess** (*homologeō*) means "to say the same thing." Thus believers are those who **confess** their **sins,** agreeing with God about their sin—they acknowledge its reality and affirm that it is a transgression of His law and a violation of His will, the presence of which the truly penitent seek to eliminate from their lives (3:4; James 2:10–11; 4:17; cf. Rom. 7:24). What John is actually saying here about confession is that since believers are forgiven, they will regularly confess their sins. Stated another way, their forgiveness is not because of their ongoing confession, but their ongoing pattern of penitence and confession is because of their forgiveness and transformation. As the Holy Spirit sanctifies believers, He continually produces within them a hatred for sin (Ps. 97:10; Prov. 8:13; Rom. 7:15–25; Phil. 3:8–9; cf. Ps. 1:1–2), which results in penitent hearts and a sincere acknowledgment of their sins. The more believers grow in Christ, the greater their hatred of sin becomes and the deeper is their penitence. Paul, the most devout and dedicated Christian, at the end of his earthly sanctification, saw himself as the foremost of sinners (1 Tim. 1:15).

If confession is genuine, it will always stem from proper sorrow over sin and a real longing to turn from sin. In 2 Corinthians 7:9–11 Paul wrote:

> I now rejoice, not that you were made sorrowful, but that you were made sorrowful to the point of repentance; for you were made sorrowful according to the will of God, so that you might not suffer loss in anything through us. For the sorrow that is according to the will of God produces a repentance without regret, leading to salvation, but the sorrow of the world produces death. For behold what earnestness this very thing, this godly sorrow, has produced in you: what vindication of yourselves, what indignation, what fear, what longing, what zeal, what avenging of wrong! In everything you demonstrated yourselves to be innocent in the matter. (cf. 2 Sam. 12:13)

The apostle was not referring to feeling bad about the consequences of one's sinful conduct, which is the worldly sorrow characterized by despair, depression, and sometimes suicide (Matt. 27:3–5). Rather, he was describing the kind of godly sorrow that produces real repentance that leads to salvation. Biblical repentance will result in "earnestness," "vindication," "indignation," "fear," "longing," "zeal," and "avenging." (For more on these results, see comments on 2 Corinthians 7:9–11 in John MacArthur, *2 Corinthians*, MacArthur New Testament Commentary [Chicago: Moody, 2003], 264–67.) When repentance is present, believers will have a strong desire for God to deal with sin at any cost (cf. Matt. 5:29–30), even when that cost may be high for them personally (cf. Luke 19:8–10). True believers are therefore habitual confessors who demonstrate that God has not only pardoned their sin and is faithfully cleansing them daily from it, but has truly regenerated them, making them new creatures with holy desires that dominate their will. (Later in this epistle, John shows how true believers do not go on sinning [3:4–10], but strive to obey God [3:19–24].)

In spite of this straightforward meaning, many throughout history have misinterpreted and misapplied the concept of confession. The Roman Catholic Church, for example, sees confession as the anonymous divulging of sins to a human priest in a confessional booth. Catholics believe such confession to be a meritorious act, one that earns the confessor forgiveness, if followed by the performance of some penitential ritual (such as repeating a prayer or saying the rosary a certain number of times). Under that system, one essentially receives forgiveness based on the good works of confession and penance.

Others view confession as psychologically and emotionally therapeutic—an act that helps people feel good about feeling bad, ensuring that they "feel" forgiven and experience healing. Still others teach that the confession in this verse refers only to the moment of salvation, with no regard for subsequent times of acknowledging sin. But if one truly trusts in Christ as Lord and Savior (Luke 9:23; Acts 2:38–39; 16:31; Rom. 10:9–10; cf. Mark 10:21–27; John 15:4–8), he will regularly admit his sins before God, as the present, active form of the verb *confess* indicates.

Perhaps the most popular but erroneous view of confession in this context is that believers are forgiven of only those sins they confess. If that were correct, it would mean that unconfessed sins remain with believers until the judgment seat of Christ, at which time they will have to give an account for those iniquities. But such is simply not the case. No one will enter heaven with a list of unconfessed sins still hanging over his head (cf. 1 Cor. 15:50; Gal. 5:21; Eph. 5:5; Rev. 22:15), because the finished work of Jesus Christ completely covers all of the sins of those who believe, including those that remain unconfessed (see commentary on 2:12 in chapter 7 of this volume). As the apostle Paul wrote:

> David also speaks of the blessing on the man to whom God credits righteousness apart from works: "Blessed are those whose lawless deeds have been forgiven, and whose sins have been covered. Blessed is the man whose sin the Lord will not take into account." (Rom. 4:6–8; cf. 8:33; 2 Cor. 5:21; Gal. 3:13; Col. 2:13).

CONQUERING

My little children, I am writing these things to you so that you may not sin. (2:1*a*)

The New Testament makes it clear that Christians, no longer slaves to sin, are given the spiritual means to have victory over sin. Paul's strong command to believers assumes their resources to conquer the sin that still remains in the unglorified body:

> Therefore do not let sin reign in your mortal body so that you obey its lusts, and do not go on presenting the members of your body to sin as instruments of unrighteousness; but present yourselves to God as those alive from the dead, and your members as instruments of righteousness to God. For sin shall not be master over you, for you are not under law but under grace. (Rom. 6:12–14; cf. 2 Cor. 5:15; 1 Peter 2:24)

The law made demands but provided no power or equipping to fulfill them. As a result, it only condemns and does not save.

John's strong love for his readers and his desire for them to heed his words and **not sin** comes across in his tender designation, **my little children,** an expression that occurs six other times in this letter (2:12, 28; 3:7, 18; 4:4; 5:21; cf. 2:13, 18). Being faithful, diligent confessors of sin, as an expression of their new creation, made it contrary to their own disposition to abuse God's grace by indulging in further sin (cf. Rom. 6:1–2; Gal. 5:13; 1 Peter 2:16). John was **writing these things to** encourage them in consistent holiness, because they were regenerate people indwelt by the Holy Spirit, who had been delivered from habitual sin (cf. Rom. 8:12–13; Titus 2:11–12; 1 Peter 1:13–16). Again John echoes, in a concise way, Paul's following exhortation from Romans 6,

> What then? Shall we sin because we are not under law but under grace? May it never be! Do you not know that when you present yourselves to someone as slaves for obedience, you are slaves of the one whom you obey, either of sin resulting in death, or of obedience resulting in righteousness? But thanks be to God that though you were slaves of sin, you became obedient from the heart to that form of teaching to which you were committed, and having been freed from sin, you became slaves of righteousness. (vv. 15–18)

So, at the close of 1 John 1, the aging apostle presents further tests of salvation and a clear picture of who passes those tests. Those who pass are true Christians who embrace God's forgiveness but are nonetheless constant confessors of their sin. That characteristic is a reality in their lives due to God's regenerating and sanctifying work in their hearts, by means of the Holy Spirit (John 16:13; Rom. 8:15) and the Word of truth (John 17:17). Genuine believers are thus people who have been cleansed from all sin, yet feel its presence powerfully and are eager to confess their remaining sins and, by the power of new life in the Spirit, conquer temptation.

Jesus Christ: The Divine Defense Attorney and the Perfect Propitiation (1 John 2:1*b*–2)

4

And if anyone sins, we have an Advocate with the Father, Jesus Christ the righteous; and He Himself is the propitiation for our sins; and not for ours only, but also for those of the whole world. (2:1*b*–2)

People in contemporary society are hooked on courtroom dramas. Television shows and movies dealing with crime and trials hold people spellbound. There are even cable television and satellite channels that broadcast such programming full time. Thousands avidly follow the latest high-profile trials, turning them into the judicial system's offering of entertainment, pandering to this jaded culture's appetite.

Infinitely transcending such trifles is a cosmic courtroom drama that dwarfs all human trials in scope and severity. God the Father is the Judge (Gen. 18:25; Ps. 7:11; Heb. 12:23), Satan is the accuser (Zech. 3:1; Rev. 12:10; cf. Job 1:9–11; 2:4–5), and every person who ever lived is on trial. The issue is how unjust sinners can be justified before a holy God. R. C. Sproul writes,

> The doctrine of justification involves a legal matter of the highest magnitude. It involves a matter of judgment before the supreme tribunal of

God. The most basic of all issues we face as fallen human beings is the issue of how we as unjust sinners can hope to survive a judgment before the court of an absolutely holy and absolutely just God. God is the Judge of all the earth. Herein lies our dilemma. He is just; we are unjust. If we receive from His hands what justice is due to us, we face the everlasting punishment of hell. ("The Forensic Nature of Justification," in Don Kistler, ed., *Justification by Faith Alone* [Morgan, Pa.: Soli Deo Gloria, 1995], 24)

All those standing before the bar of divine justice are guilty of violating God's holy law; they "are all under sin; as it is written, 'There is none righteous, not even one'" (Rom. 3:9–10), and "whoever keeps the whole law and yet stumbles in one point, he has become guilty of all" (James 2:10). The just sentence the divine court should hand down is eternal punishment in hell, "for the wages of sin is death" (Rom. 6:23).

But all is not hopeless for the guilty, because there is one more character to consider in this divine courtroom scene: the Lord Jesus Christ. He acts as the Advocate, or Defense Attorney, for all those who believe savingly in Him. He is a most unusual defense attorney, however, since He does not maintain His clients' innocence, but rather acknowledges their guilt. Nonetheless, He has never lost a case—and never will (John 6:39; cf. Rom. 8:29–30). Using the language of the courtroom, Paul declared, "Who will bring a charge against God's elect? God is the one who justifies; who is the one who condemns? Christ Jesus is He who died, yes, rather who was raised, who is at the right hand of God, who also intercedes for us" (Rom. 8:33–34; cf. Col. 2:13–14). That last phrase is the key to how the Lord Jesus Christ infallibly wins acquittal for those who put their faith in Him. He intercedes with the Father on the basis of His own substitution for sinners in sacrificial death, which fully paid sin's penalty for all who trust Him for salvation, thus meeting the demands of God's justice. Because "He ... did not spare His own Son, but delivered Him over for [them] all" (Rom. 8:32) and "made Him who knew no sin to be sin on [their] behalf, so that [they] might become the righteousness of God in Him" (2 Cor. 5:21), God "justified [them] freely by His grace through the redemption that is in Christ Jesus" (Rom. 3:24, NKJV). The result of the divine verdict is that believers, "having been justified [declared righteous] by faith ... have peace with God through [their] Lord Jesus Christ" (Rom. 5:1).

The Father's predetermined design and acceptance of His Son's sacrifice as payment in full for their sins answers the dilemma of how He can be both "just and the justifier of the one who has faith in Jesus" (Rom. 3:26). God's love and justice were equally satisfied when He accomplished redemption through Jesus Christ.

It is that divine courtroom drama that underlies the apostle John's thought in this section. Building on the glorious affirmation of 1:9

that God "is faithful and righteous to forgive us our sins and to cleanse us from all unrighteousness," John explains that He can do so because His Son is both the believers' Defense Attorney and the Perfect Propitiation for their sins. That twofold truth is central to the gospel.

THE DIVINE DEFENSE ATTORNEY

And if anyone sins, we have an Advocate with the Father, Jesus Christ the righteous; (2:1*b*)

This portrait of **Jesus Christ** fits perfectly with John's legal vocabulary. As noted earlier, the apostle's language pictures a courtroom setting in which accused sinners come before God's bar and Christ steps up as their legal advocate. With that portrayal in mind, John gave his readers vital instruction on how divine justice relates to salvation.

Sins translates a form of the verb *hamartanō*, the most common New Testament word for sin, which literally means "to miss the mark." God's holiness sets the standard of behavior (Ex. 15:11; Lev. 19:2; 1 Sam. 2:2; Rev. 15:4), and humanity has missed that supreme benchmark (Gen. 6:5; Eccl. 7:20; Rom. 5:12; Gal. 3:22*a*), utterly violating God's requirements of perfect obedience (Rom. 3:23; James 2:10).

The Greek grammar of the phrase **if anyone sins** is instructive. The verb is an aorist subjunctive third-class conditional that conveys the strong probability of actual occurrence. John's expression could be translated "if anyone sins, and it will happen." Immediately following his emphasis in the first part of verse 1 that believers do not have to sin, the apostle acknowledges that they definitely will (cf. 1:8, 10). (The pronoun **we** encompasses the apostle with the "little children," also referred to earlier in verse 1, showing that the apostle has to be referring to the sins of true believers.

In keeping with the imagery, God appears as the supreme Judge of the universe, seated at the heavenly bench and judging all people according to the absolute perfection of His holy law. He is the author (Lev. 26:46), interpreter (Ps. 119:34), and applier (Jer. 31:33) of the law. But believers must view the reality of divine justice with great sobriety and respect (1 Peter 1:17; cf. Acts 17:31; Col. 3:25), since God possesses the power and authority to condemn to hell every sinner who ever lived. Jesus gave this sober admonition: "Do not fear those who kill the body but are unable to kill the soul; but rather fear Him who is able to destroy both soul and body in hell" (Matt. 10:28; cf. Luke 12:5; 2 Thess. 1:5–9). The Old Testament prophets also gave clear warning about that kind of divine judgment (cf. Amos 5:18–20; Zeph. 1:14–18).

Those who are saved, however, need not fear divine justice because they have **an Advocate with the Father,** none other than **Jesus Christ the righteous.** Here **Advocate** translates *paraklētos* ("one who comes alongside") and denotes in legal settings the defender or counselor who comes to aid his client. (In his gospel, John used the same term, translated there as "Helper" or "Comforter" [14:16, 26; 16:7] to refer to the support given to each believer by the Holy Spirit.) Christ is the perfect Advocate, since the Judge is His Father and they are always in perfect harmony (cf. Matt. 26:39; John 4:34). Further, the Son completely understands the saints' human weaknesses because He came to earth as the fully human Son of Man (Heb. 4:14–15; cf. Gal. 4:4; Phil. 2:5–8). He accepts as clients only those who confess their guilt and their desperate need to receive Him as Savior and Lord (cf. Matt. 7:21–23; 25:31–46; John 6:37; 10:3, 14–15); and He becomes for them the incomparable intercessor who always gains acquittal for those who trust in Him. In Old Testament language, He is their great High Priest (Heb. 7:25–28).

THE PERFECT PROPITIATION

and He Himself is the propitiation for our sins; and not for ours only, but also for those of the whole world. (2:2)

Christ could never make His case for the saints as their divine Defense Attorney if He were not also their Propitiator who completely turned God's wrath from sinners to Himself, thus removing all their guilt and condemnation. **Propitiation** through the death of Christ is one of the critical doctrines of the Christian faith, at the very center of God's redemptive plan (Rom. 3:25; 5:1, 10–11; 1 Cor. 15:3; 2 Cor. 5:18–19; Col. 1:20–22; 1 Peter 1:18–20; cf. Lev. 10:17; 17:11; Matt. 26:28; Luke 24:47; Acts 20:28; Heb. 12:24; 13:20). An accurate understanding of this truth in all its essential aspects is vital to salvation and the pursuit of a life of holiness.

The term **propitiation,** in definition and application, is most notably a biblical and theological word. It is a translation of *hilasmos,* which means "appeasement," or "satisfaction." Christ's sacrificial death on the cross satisfied the demands of God's justice, thus appeasing His holy wrath against believers' sins.

Several related words provide additional understanding of the nature of propitiation. The verb *hilaskomai,* "to make satisfaction for," occurs in Luke 18:13 and Hebrews 2:17. *Hilastērion* refers to the sacrifice of atonement required to placate God's wrath (cf. Rom. 3:25). The translators of the Septuagint (LXX) used this term to designate the mercy seat, which establishes propitiation's link to the Old Testament sacrificial system:

They shall construct an ark of acacia wood two and a half cubits long, and one and a half cubits wide, and one and a half cubits high. You shall overlay it with pure gold, inside and out you shall overlay it, and you shall make a gold molding around it. You shall cast four gold rings for it and fasten them on its four feet, and two rings shall be on one side of it and two rings on the other side of it. You shall make poles of acacia wood and overlay them with gold. You shall put the poles into the rings on the sides of the ark, to carry the ark with them. The poles shall remain in the rings of the ark; they shall not be removed from it. You shall put into the ark the testimony which I shall give you. You shall make a *mercy seat* of pure gold, two and a half cubits long and one and a half cubits wide. You shall make two cherubim of gold, make them of hammered work at the two ends of the *mercy seat*. Make one cherub at one end and one cherub at the other end; you shall make the cherubim of one piece with the *mercy seat* at its two ends. The cherubim shall have their wings spread upward, covering the *mercy seat* with their wings and facing one another; the faces of the cherubim are to be turned toward the mercy seat. You shall put the *mercy seat* on top of the ark, and in the ark you shall put the testimony which I will give to you. There I will meet with you; and from above the *mercy seat*, from between the two cherubim which are upon the ark of the testimony, I will speak to you about all that I will give you in commandment for the sons of Israel. (Ex. 25:10–22; emphases added to indicate uses of *hilastērion* in the LXX)

The mercy seat was the lid or cover of the ark, situated between the divine Shekinah glory cloud above the ark and law tablets inside the ark. Because the priests sprinkled the seat with blood from the sacrifices, it was the place at which atonement for sin occurred. The sprinkled blood thus stood between God (the Shekinah) and His broken law (the tablets). The sacrificial blood of animals never did placate God (cf. Heb. 7:26–28; 9:6–15; 10:1–18), but it pictured the future sacrifice of Christ that would fully satisfy the Father (Heb. 9:23–28; cf. Isa. 53:6, 10; Matt. 20:28; Eph. 5:2). If the Old Testament sacrificial system had appeased God's wrath once and for all, the Jews would not have continued endlessly to bring burnt offerings (Lev. 1:3–17; 6:8–13), sin offerings (Lev. 4:1–5:13; 6:24–30), and trespass offerings (Lev. 5:14–6:7; 7:1–10) over the centuries.

Propitiation is necessary because of **sins** (cf. Ps. 7:11; Ezek. 18:4; Rom. 1:18; 3:23; 6:23; 1 Thess. 1:10). Sinners continually shatter God's perfect law (Jer. 17:9; Matt. 15:19–20*a*; John 8:34; Rom. 3:9–19; 5:12–20; James 1:14–15; 2:10–11) and He, as the righteously offended Creator, must react justly in holy anger, wrath, and judgment (Gen. 6:6–7; Deut. 25:16; Job 34:21–22, 25; Ps. 5:4–6; Prov. 6:16–19; Isa. 59:1–2; Jer. 10:10; Nah. 1:2–3; Luke 13:27; 16:15; John 3:36; Rom. 1:18; 2:5, 8; Eph. 5:6; Heb. 3:17). God's justice must be satisfied. Every sin ever committed by every person who has ever lived will be punished in one of two ways. Either God's wrath will be satisfied when all unrepentant and unbelieving sinners suffer eternally in hell (Matt. 13:42; 25:41, 46; 2 Thess. 1:9; Rev. 20:15), or for all who, by the convicting and regenerating power of the Spirit, repent and believe savingly in Jesus, God's wrath is satisfied by the punishment of Christ **Himself** on the cross (John 3:14–18). Divine punishment rendered forgiveness according to God's sovereign love and grace (cf. Rom. 3:24–26).

By God's design, pictured in the law's requirement of a lamb without blemish (Num. 6:14), the Lord Jesus Christ had to be sinless (cf. 2:1). Otherwise He would not have been acceptable to the Father (cf. Heb. 9:14) and would have been subject to the judgment of God for His own sins. But He is righteous (Isa. 53:11), holy (Rev. 3:7), innocent (John 8:46; 18:37–38), undefiled (Heb. 7:26), and separate from sinners—not merely the agent who made propitiation for sinners, He *is* the propitiation. The prophet Isaiah portrayed Him as the ideal sacrifice:

> But He was pierced through for our transgressions, He was crushed for our iniquities; the chastening for our well-being fell upon Him, and by His scourging we are healed. All of us like sheep have gone astray, each of us has turned to his own way; but the Lord has caused the iniquity of us all to fall on Him. He was oppressed and He was afflicted, yet He did not open His mouth; like a lamb that is led to slaughter, and like a sheep that is silent before its shearers, so He did not open His mouth. By oppression and judgment He was taken away; and as for His generation, who considered that He was cut off out of the land of the living for the transgression of my people, to whom the stroke was due? His grave was assigned with wicked men, yet He was with a rich man in His death, because He had done no violence, nor was there any deceit in His mouth. But the Lord was pleased to crush Him, putting Him to grief; if He would render Himself as a guilt offering, He will see His offspring, He will prolong His days, and the good pleasure of the Lord will prosper in His hand. (Isa. 53:5–10; cf. 2 Cor. 5:21; Eph. 5:2; Gal. 3:13; 1 Peter 2:24; 3:18)

The entire divine plan of redemption flows from the Father's love for unworthy and undeserving sinners (Rom. 5:8; Eph. 1:4–7). John made this truth plain when he wrote, "In this is love, not that we loved God, but that He loved us and sent His Son to be the propitiation for our sins" (4:10; cf. Titus 3:5).

The apostle's words **and not for ours only, but also for those of the whole world** have been understood by many to refer to an unlimited atonement, by which Christ provides a potential salvation for all people without exception. Logically, such an interpretation strips the work of Christ on the cross of any actual atonement for anyone specifically, and it provides only a potential satisfaction for God's wrath. (For an analysis of other aspects of the extent of the atonement, see John MacArthur, *2 Peter & Jude,* MacArthur New Testament Commentary [Chicago: Moody, 2005], 72–76.)

To be faithful to the truth revealed in Scripture, **the whole world** must be comprehended as a generic expression that refers to humanity throughout the earth, but not necessarily to every individual. **World** simply identifies the earthly realm of mankind to which God directed His reconciling love and provided propitiation (cf. John 1:29; 3:16; 6:51; 1 Tim. 2:5–6; Titus 2:11; Heb. 2:9). The language of Scripture is strong and clear, stating that Christ's death actually satisfies fully and eternally the demands of God's wrath for those who believe (John 10:11, 15; 17:9, 20; Acts 20:28; Rom. 8:32, 37; Eph. 5:25). Though the Savior's death intrinsically had infinite value, it was designed to actually (not potentially) secure the satisfaction for divine justice only on behalf of those who would believe.

Jewish believers would have understood propitiation because they were familiar with the Old Testament sacrificial system, the function of the mercy seat, and the meaning of the Day of Atonement, as recorded in Leviticus 16:15–17:

> He [the high priest] shall slaughter the goat of the sin offering which is for the people, and bring its blood inside the veil and do with its blood as he did with the blood of the bull, and sprinkle it on the mercy seat and in front of the mercy seat. He shall make atonement for the holy place, because of the impurities of the sons of Israel and because of their transgressions in regard to all their sins; and thus he shall do for the tent of meeting which abides with them in the midst of their impurities. When he goes in to make atonement in the holy place, no one shall be in the tent of meeting until he comes out, that he may make atonement for himself and for his household and for all the assembly of Israel.

However, they now understood "the assembly of Israel" as including proselytes. In Christ all national limitations were abolished (cf. Acts 11:18; Rom. 1:17; 2:28–29). Jesus' propitiatory death is for all classes of God's elect, which He is calling out for His name "from every tribe and tongue and people and nation" (Rev. 5:9; cf. John 10:16; Acts 15:14–18; 26:23; Rom. 9:25–26; Titus 2:14). Christ's work on the cross atoned for all those who would be sovereignly drawn by God to repent and believe (cf. Rom. 5:18), **not for** those believers **only** who constituted the church in John's day. However, His death did not atone for or satisfy divine justice regarding the unrepentant, unbelieving millions who will appear before the

Judge at the great white throne, from where they will be sentenced to eternal punishment in the lake of fire (Rev. 20:11–15).

Even in planning Jesus' death, the high priest Caiaphas unwittingly uttered words that providentially affirmed the true extent of Christ's propitiation. John 11:45–52 records the setting:

> Therefore many of the Jews who came to Mary, and saw what He had done, believed in Him. But some of them went to the Pharisees and told them the things which Jesus had done. Therefore the chief priests and the Pharisees convened a council, and were saying, "What are we doing? For this man is performing many signs. If we let Him go on like this, all men will believe in Him, and the Romans will come and take away both our place and our nation." But one of them, Caiaphas, who was high priest that year, said to them, "You know nothing at all, nor do you take into account that it is expedient for you that one man die for the people, and that the whole nation not perish." Now he did not say this on his own initiative, but being high priest that year, he prophesied that Jesus was going to die for the nation, and not for the nation only, but in order that He might also gather together into one the children of God who are scattered abroad.

Caiaphas meant only that Jesus should be executed to spare the nation and the leaders' positions from Roman reprisals against them because of Jesus. Caiaphas spoke *politically,* unaware of the weighty *theological* implications of his words. However, because he was the high priest the Holy Spirit directed his words (cf. 2 Sam. 15:27*a*) to prophesy that Christ would die for the nation. But obviously "nation" does not mean every individual Jew because virtually the whole nation had rejected Him (John 1:11; cf. Rom. 2:28–29; 9:6–18, 27). The designation is thus limited to those Jews who believed. As the apostle explained in John 11:52, Jesus died not only for the believing Jews but also for the children of God scattered abroad. In the original context of his gospel, John's reference to "children of God" referred primarily to believing Jews of the dispersion who would be regathered into the kingdom of God (cf. Isa. 43:5; Ezek. 34:12). But in the broader sense, that expression anticipated the outreach to the Gentiles (cf. John 12:32; Heb. 2:9). So as a result of Christ's atoning work, all throughout the world for whom Christ was the propitiation become, by faith, part of the same body, His church (Eph. 2:11–22; cf. Gal. 3:7–9, 26–29; Eph. 3:1–6).

The Certainty of Christian Assurance (1 John 2:3–6)

5

By this we know that we have come to know Him, if we keep His commandments. The one who says, "I have come to know Him," and does not keep His commandments, is a liar, and the truth is not in him; but whoever keeps His word, in him the love of God has truly been perfected. By this we know that we are in Him: the one who says he abides in Him ought himself to walk in the same manner as He walked. (2:3–6)

"Assurance," wrote the seventeenth-century English Puritan Thomas Brooks,

> is a reflex act of a gracious soul, whereby he clearly and evidently sees himself in a gracious, blessed, and happy state; it is a sensible feeling, and an experimental [experiential] discerning of a man's being in a state of grace ... assurance is a believer's ark, where he sits, Noah-like, quiet and still in the midst of all distractions and destructions, commotions and confusions. (*Heaven on Earth: A Treatise on Christian Assurance* [reprint; Edinburgh: Banner of Truth, 1982], 14, 11)

Assurance causes believers to rejoice with the hymn writer, "Blessed assurance, Jesus is mine! O what a foretaste of glory divine!" To possess assurance is, in a sense, to experience heaven on earth.

But sadly, as Brooks goes on to lament, assurance

> is a pearl that most want, a crown that few wear. . . . Little well-grounded assurance . . . is to be found among most Christians. Most Christians live between fears and hopes, and hang, as it were, between heaven and hell, sometimes they hope that their state is good, at other times they fear that their state is bad: now they hope that all is well, and that it shall go well with them forever; anon [shortly] they fear that they shall perish by the hand of such a corruption, or by the prevalency of such or such a temptation; and so they are like a ship in a storm, tossed here and there. (*Heaven on Earth,* 15, 11)

Assurance is not only a privilege; it is also a birthright that Christians possess as members of the body of Christ (Rom. 5:1; 8:16; cf. Ps. 4:3; John 10:27–29; Phil. 1:6; 1 Thess. 1:4). Not having it, on the other hand, and thereby doubting one's salvation, produces uncertainty and fear that brings misery and despair.

Though the assurance of salvation is part of redemption and vital to joy and comfort, God's Word teaches that it is possible to forfeit it, unless one pursues it. The apostle Peter wrote, "Therefore, brethren, be all the more diligent to make certain about His calling and choosing you" (2 Peter 1:10*a*; cf. Heb. 10:22). Peter revealed that this certainty comes to those who pursue all the features of holiness with increasing diligence (vv. 5–8).

Yet, in spite of such biblical mandates, many in contemporary Christianity simply ignore the biblical understanding of assurance. Teachers frequently assure them that if they have repeated a certain prayer, gone forward at an evangelistic rally, made a profession of faith, given mental assent to the gospel, or even been baptized, they are definitely saved and should never question their salvation. Such people do not want to examine themselves as the Bible teaches (2 Cor. 13:5), because to do so, they reason, might damage their fragile self-esteem or make them guilty of doubting God. As a result, the entire subject of assurance is often de-emphasized or ignored altogether.

But that has not always been the case. Throughout church history, the personal assurance of salvation has been a major issue (see John MacArthur, *The Gospel According to the Apostles* [Nashville: Thomas Nelson, 1993, 2000], chap. 10). On the one hand, Roman Catholicism has always adamantly denied the possibility of assurance. This perspective stems from the Catholic heresy that salvation is a joint effort between God and sinners. God will always do His part, but the sinner might not continue to do his or her part; thus no one can be assured of salvation in this life. In the words of the Council of Trent (1545–63), any "believer's assurance of the pardon of his sins is a vain and ungodly confidence" (cited in J.C. Ryle, *Holiness* [1877, 1879; reprint, Moscow, Idaho: Charles Nolan, 2002], 123). Cardinal Roberto Bellarmine, a Jesuit theologian of that era, once stated that assurance is "a prime error of heretics" (ibid., n. 1). In other words, according to Roman Catholicism, no one can truly know whether or not he or she has received salvation until the afterlife—and to think one can is heretical.

When the sixteenth-century Protestant Reformers recovered the true gospel from the Roman harlot and reasserted the biblical doctrine of salvation, they also accurately expounded the issue of assurance. Contrary to Roman theology, they were convinced by Scripture that believers can and should enjoy the confident hope of salvation. John Calvin correctly taught that such confidence is not some addition to but is actually the essence of faith—since those who truly trust the gospel do so because they inherently enjoy a measure of assurance in it. When people experience saving faith, they recognize both the truth of the gospel and the wickedness of their sinful condition (cf. Eph. 2:4–6), and they repent of their sins and embrace Jesus Christ as Savior and Lord (Luke 18:13; Acts 2:37–39; cf. 8:35–37; 16:27–34). When that divine work (of conversion and regeneration) takes place (Acts 11:18; 16:14; 18:27), energized by the Holy Spirit, believers sense their new-found faith and are assured of their salvation based on Scripture's promises (e.g., Luke 18:14; John 1:12–13; 3:16; 6:37; 10:9; Acts 13:38–39; Rom. 10:9–13). By setting forth the promises of God upon which salvation rests, the Word of God provides believers with an objective source of certainty and, additionally, the Holy Spirit gives subjective assurance through manifest spiritual fruit.

Nearly a century after Calvin, the writers of the Westminster Confession of Faith (1648) composed the following paragraph:

> This infallible assurance doth not so belong to the essence of faith, but that a true believer may wait long, and conflict with many difficulties before he be partaker of it: yet, being enabled by the Spirit to know the things which are freely given him of God, he may, without extraordinary revelation, in the right use of ordinary means, attain thereunto. And therefore it is the duty of everyone to give all diligence to make his calling and election sure, that thereby his heart may be enlarged in peace and joy in the Holy Ghost, in love and thankfulness to God, and in strength and cheerfulness in the duties of obedience, the proper fruits of this assurance; so far is it from inclining men to looseness. (Chapter XVIII, Article III)

Moving beyond some of the earlier Reformers (who had primarily focused on refuting Rome), the Westminster divines addressed the antinomian tendencies of their day by stressing subjective assurance in addition to John Calvin's (and Scripture's) teaching on objective assurance. They emphasized personal examination that would lead believers to recognize practical evidences in their lives of obedience to God's moral law and commands. But some in the church pressed to the extreme the Westminster idea "that a true believer may wait long, and conflict with many difficulties" before gaining full assurance. For example, the seventeenth-century English Puritans' sober, searching preaching caused many people to be generally lacking in assurance, unable to enjoy the confidence even of the evident fruit of salvation. As a result, some became frightened, insecure, and obsessed with morbid introspection, stringent self-examination, and heavy doubts as to whether or not they were elect, or even could be. Puritan pastors wrote many treatises to exhort, encourage, and comfort such troubled souls, especially expositing what the apostle Paul wrote concerning the Spirit's witness:

> For all who are being led by the Spirit of God, these are sons of God. For you have not received a spirit of slavery leading to fear again, but you have received a spirit of adoption as sons by which we cry out, "Abba! Father!" The Spirit Himself testifies with our spirit that we are children of God. (Rom. 8:14–16)

The witness of this assurance entails the Holy Spirit's working in believers' conscience and emotions so that they feel the joy of their forgiveness and long to be in God's presence, like children with a beloved father. They sense how the Spirit leads and directs them (1 Cor. 2:14–16; Gal. 5:16–18, 25; cf. Luke 24:44–45; Eph. 1:17–19; 3:16–19; Col. 1:9), not through their own wisdom and discernment, but through granting them the desire to live godly lives and obey the Scripture.

To be sure, the Bible clearly teaches that those who are truly saved can never lose their salvation (cf. John 10:28). They have been permanently sealed with the Holy Spirit (Eph. 1:13), and nothing can separate them from the love of their Savior (Rom. 8:38–39). At the same time, however, God's Word also commands every professing Christian to examine his or her life, to see if the salvation that is claimed is actually authentic (2 Cor. 13:5). If salvation is indeed genuine, there will be signs of the Spirit's working in that person's life, both in attitude and behavior. The Bible refers to these attitudes as the "fruit of the Spirit." Paul lists them in Galatians 5:22–23: "But the fruit of the Spirit is love, joy, peace, patience, kindness, goodness, faithfulness, gentleness, self-control; against such things there is no law." Assurance of salvation, in the subjective sense, comes by examining one's life to see if there is evidence of the Spirit's working in one's attitudes. Such spiritual dispositions manifest themselves in corresponding acts of "love, joy, peace," and so forth, in submission to the commands of Scripture.

John's purpose in writing this epistle is clearly stated in 5:13: "These things I have written to you who believe in the name of the Son of God, so that you may know that you have eternal life." It is to give assurance of salvation to those who might otherwise be led to doubt. So again in verses 3 to 6 of chapter 2, John addresses manifest assurance—from the perspective of obedience, which constitutes visible, objective evidence that someone is a Christian. That is a crucial element in John's moral test for believers, an aspect that he divides into three parts: the test stated, the test applied, and the test exemplified.

THE TEST STATED

By this we know that we have come to know Him, if we keep His commandments. (2:3)

By this is a transitional phrase John used to introduce a new set of tests that verify salvation and encourage assurance. John presented his readers with some additional ways they could verify that they were walking in the light and had a genuine relationship with God.

The apostle states the case with certainty; he does not say "we hope," "we think," or "we wish," but **we know. We know** translates the present tense form of the verb *ginōskō*, and means to continually perceive something by experience. Assurance comes from obeying God's **commandments** in Scripture. Those who fail to do so will and should wonder if they are converted and the Holy Spirit is truly leading them. But obedient believers can be assured that they **have come to know Him** (Christ). The perfect tense of the verb *ginōskō* (**have come to know**) looks back on a past action (savingly believing in Jesus Christ) that has continuing results in the present.

The knowledge of which John spoke is not the mystical "hidden" knowledge of Gnosticism (which promoted a secret, transcendent knowledge whose possessors were members of an elitist religious fraternity), the rationalistic knowledge of Greek philosophy (which taught that unaided human reason could unlock the mysteries of the universe, both natural and supernatural), or the experiential knowledge of hedonism (which claimed that ultimate truth was discovered through experiencing the pleasures of the physical world). Instead, it is the saving knowledge of Christ that comes from being in a right relationship with Him.

John's point, then, is that external obedience provides evidence for whether or not an internal, transforming reality—that of coming **to know** Jesus Christ in salvation—has taken place.

Writing to Titus, Paul emphasized the difference between false knowledge and true knowledge: "[Some] profess to know God, but by their deeds they deny Him, being detestable and disobedient and worthless for any good deed" (Titus 1:16; cf. 2 Tim. 3:5, 7).

But that is not true of the Christian faith that John and the other apostles taught. The people who truly know God are those who pursue holy lives, consistent with God's new covenant. The prophet Jeremiah spelled out the nature of that covenant:

> "Behold, days are coming," declares the Lord, "when I will make a new covenant with the house of Israel and with the house of Judah, not like the covenant which I made with their fathers in the day I took them by the hand to bring them out of the land of Egypt, My covenant which they broke, although I was a husband to them," declares the Lord. "But this is the covenant which I will make with the house of Israel after those days," declares the Lord, "I will put My law within them and on their heart I will write it; and I will be their God, and they shall be My people. They will not teach again, each man his neighbor and each man his brother, saying, 'Know the Lord,' for they will all know Me, from the least of them to the greatest of them," declares the Lord, "for I will forgive their iniquity, and their sin I will remember no more." (Jer. 31:31–34)

New covenant people have God's law written on their hearts, and what is in a person's heart controls how he or she lives. As the writer of Proverbs observed, "For as [a person] thinks in his heart, so is he" (Prov. 23:7, NKJV; cf. 2:10; 3:1; 4:4, 23; Pss. 40:8; 119:10–11; Matt. 6:21; 12:34–35; Rom. 6:17). Israel illustrated well the connection between knowing God and obeying Him. Even though the nation claimed to know Him, she demonstrated the emptiness of that claim by her continual disobedience (Ex. 32:9; Num. 14:11; 25:3; Deut. 9:7, 24; 32:16; Isa. 1:2, 4; 2:8; 29:13; Jer. 2:11–13; 3:6–8; 6:13; 8:5; 31:32; Ezek. 16:59; 33:31; Matt. 15:7–9; Acts 13:27; Rom. 10:3; 2 Cor. 3:13–15). Of course, the obedience that accompanies salvation is not a legalistic obedience, imposed externally or observed superficially and hypocritically; it is a gracious attitude of obedience that flows from the truth embraced internally, following the Holy Spirit's revealing of it through the Word. Even though believers still wrestle with sin (cf. Job 13:23; Ps. 19:13; Rom. 8:13; Heb. 12:1, 4), they can agree with Paul, who wrote,

I find then the principle that evil is present in me, the one who wants to do good. For I joyfully concur with the law of God in the inner man, but I see a different law in the members of my body, waging war against the law of my mind and making me a prisoner of the law of sin which is in my members. Wretched man that I am! Who will set me free from the body of this death? Thanks be to God through Jesus Christ our Lord! So then, on the one hand I myself with my mind am serving the law of God, but on the other, with my flesh the law of sin. (Rom. 7:21–25)

The word rendered **keep** (a form of the verb *tēreō*) stresses the idea of an observant, watchful obedience. It can also be translated "guard," which would in this context mean guarding **His commandments.** Since **keep** is a present, active subjunctive, it conveys the sense of believers continually safeguarding the commandments because they consider them precious (5:3; Ezra 7:10; Pss. 19:7–8; 119:1, 34, 77, 97, 113, 165; Rom. 7:22). John did not want his readers to settle for a marginal or minimal standard of righteousness. Rather, the apostle emphasized an extensive obedience that stems from a genuine reverence for God's commands (Ps. 119:66, 172; cf. Acts 17:11; James 1:25).

Commandments is from *entolē* ("injunction," "order," or "command"), not *nomos* ("law"). The term refers not to the Mosaic law, but to the precepts and directives of Christ (cf. Matt. 28:19–20). But of course the moral and spiritual precepts the Lord taught were consistent with those revealed to Moses (cf. Matt. 5:17–18; John 5:46), all reflective of God's immutable nature.

Under the new covenant God accepts believers' loving and sincere, albeit imperfect obedience (cf. 1 Kings 8:46; Prov. 20:9) and forgives their disobedience (cf. Pss. 65:3; 103:3; Isa. 43:25). By His grace they display a consistent, heartfelt devotion to the mind of Christ (1 Cor. 2:16; cf. Hos. 6:6) as revealed in the Word (Pss. 1:1–2; 112:1; 119:1–2; Isa. 48:17–18; Luke 11:28). That willing obedience to Scripture in daily living is a reliable indicator both to self and others that one has come to a saving knowledge of Jesus Christ (cf. Matt. 7:21; John 8:31; 14:21). It differentiates the unregenerate from the regenerate; Paul called the unregenerate "sons of disobedience" (Eph. 2:2), whereas Peter identified the regenerate "as obedient children" (1 Peter 1:14).

God-honoring obedience is really reflective of genuine love; as John wrote later in this epistle, "we love God and observe His commandments. For this is the love of God, that we keep His commandments; and His commandments are not burdensome" (5:2*b*–3). But this principle was not new to John, as he had heard it from Jesus years earlier in the upper room and recorded it in his gospel:

"If you love Me, you will keep My commandments." (John 14:15)

"He who has My commandments and keeps them is the one who loves Me; and he who loves Me will be loved by My Father, and I will love him and will disclose Myself to him." (14:21)

"If anyone loves Me, he will keep My word; and My Father will love him, and We will come to him and make Our abode with him. He who does not love Me does not keep My words; and the word which you hear is not Mine, but the Father's who sent Me." (14:23–24)

"If you keep My commandments, you will abide in My love; just as I have kept My Father's commandments and abide in His love." (15:10)

THE TEST APPLIED

The one who says, "I have come to know Him," and does not keep His commandments, is a liar, and the truth is not in him; but whoever keeps His word, in him the love of God has truly been perfected. By this we know that we are in Him: (2:4–5)

In keeping with the nickname Boanerges ("sons of thunder") that Jesus gave him and his brother James, John thunders at those who claim to **have come to know** Christ but do **not keep His commandments.** As he had earlier done in 1:6, "If we say that we have fellowship with Him and yet walk in the darkness, we lie and do not practice the truth," John warns that their claim to fellowship is completely unfounded. Anyone who makes such a claim and lives in disobedience **is a liar.** The apostle's epithet boldly exposes the danger of self-deception concerning salvation, which is damning to those who fail to realize their blindness, repent of their sins, and embrace the truth (cf. Gal. 6:7; Titus 3:3).

Plainly, those in God's kingdom hear His voice and obey it. Jesus told Pontius Pilate, "Everyone who is of the truth hears My voice" (John 18:37c; cf. 1 John 3:18–19). In sharp contrast, those who do not obey His commands demonstrate that **the truth is not in** them. John therefore exposed the empty pretense of those who assumed they had ascended to a higher level of "divine truth." For such false teachers, present with the readers, their so-called knowledge elevated them above prosaic earthly matters and rendered unnecessary any concern for moral conduct or godly living. But as James declared, "Even so faith, if it has no works, is dead, being by itself. . . . For just as the body without the spirit is dead, so also faith without works is dead" (James 2:17, 26; cf. Eph. 2:10; Heb. 12:14; 1 Peter 1:14–16). Those whose faith is genuine will obey the truth.

Verse 5 then applies the test for assurance positively. Whoever sincerely and lovingly **keeps His word, in him the love of God has**

truly been perfected. It is best to understand the phrase translated **the love of God** as an objective genitive, meaning **the love** *for* **God.** John describes the genuine love believers have for God as **perfected,** not in the sense of finished perfection, but salvation accomplishment. In fact, this Greek verb *teteleiōtai* is translated "accomplished" in John 4:34; 5:36; and 17:4. It can even mean "initiate." The supernatural granting of this love (Rom. 5:5) results in obedience to Scripture, and is not merely an emotional or mystical experience.

It is **by this** genuine love that believers **know that** they **are in Him.** The little phrase **in Him** [Christ] occurs many other places in the New Testament (vv. 8, 27–28; 3:6; 4:13; 5:20; 1 Cor. 1:5; 2 Cor. 5:21; Eph. 1:4, 7, 13; 4:21; Phil. 3:9; Col. 2:6–7, 10–11; 2 Thess. 1:12; cf. Col. 1:28) and indicates a central truth of the Christian faith. Commentator John Stott summarized the significance as follows:

> The whole context, and especially verse 6, suggests that the phrase *in him* again refers to Christ. To be "in Christ" is Paul"s characteristic description of the Christian. But John uses it too. To be (or to "abide" verse 6) "in" Him is equivalent to the phrase to "know" Him (3, 4) and to "love" Him (5). Being a Christian consists in essence of a personal relationship to God in Christ, knowing Him, loving Him, and abiding in Him as the branch abides in the vine (Jn. xv. I ff.). This is the meaning of "eternal life" (Jn. xvii. 3; i Jn. v. 20). (*The Epistles of John*, The Tyndale New Testament Commentaries [Grand Rapids: Eerdmans, 1964], 91. Italics in original.)

THE TEST EXEMPLIFIED

the one who says he abides in Him ought himself to walk in the same manner as He walked. (2:6)

The only person who can pass the test of obedience and realize full assurance is **the one who . . . abides in Him**—because Jesus Christ is the perfect role model for obeying the Father. In John 15:4–5 Jesus commanded,

> "Abide in Me, and I in you. As the branch cannot bear fruit of itself unless it abides in the vine, so neither can you unless you abide in Me. I am the vine, you are the branches; he who abides in Me and I in him, he bears much fruit, for apart from Me you can do nothing." (cf. vv. 10–11)

Believers draw spiritual life from the Lord Jesus Christ, even as branches do from a vine. To abide in Christ is to remain in Him—not a temporary, superficial attachment, but a permanent, deep connection (cf. Luke 9:23; John 6:53–65; Phil. 1:6; 2:11–13). Such authentic abiding in the Savior characterizes those who "continue in the faith firmly established and steadfast, and not moved away from the hope of the gospel that [they] have heard" (Col. 1:23; cf. 2:7; Eph. 3:17), because they are truly regenerate—new creatures who possess irrevocable eternal life.

John made it perfectly clear that those who claim to abide in Christ must **walk in the same manner as He walked. Walk** is a metaphor for daily conduct by believers (1:7; John 8:12; 12:35; Rom. 6:4; 8:4; 1 Cor. 7:17; 2 Cor. 5:7; Gal. 5:16; Eph. 2:10; 4:1; 5:2, 8; Col. 1:10; 2:6; 1 Thess. 2:12; 4:1; 2 John 6; cf. Mark 7:5). The Lord Himself perfectly exemplified this principle during His earthly ministry. In every way He obeyed His Father's will:

> "For I have come down from heaven, not to do My own will, but the will of Him who sent Me." (John 6:38)

> "And He who sent Me is with Me; He has not left Me alone, for I always do the things that are pleasing to Him." (John 8:29)

> "For this reason the Father loves Me, because I lay down My life so that I may take it again. No one has taken it away from Me, but I lay it down on My own initiative. I have authority to lay it down, and I have authority to take it up again. This commandment I received from My Father." (John 10:17–18)

> "So that the world may know that I love the Father, I do exactly as the Father commanded Me." (John 14:31)

Obviously, believers' obedience will not be perfect, as Jesus' was. Nonetheless, He established the perfect pattern they are to follow. If anyone claims to know Him and abide in Him, it will be evident in his life. He will walk in the light—in the realm of truth and holiness—and guard (obey) His commandments because of his passionate love for the truth and the Lord of the truth. Therein lies the key to real assurance of salvation.

A New Kind of Love
(1 John 2:7–11)

6

Beloved, I am not writing a new commandment to you, but an old commandment which you have had from the beginning; the old commandment is the word which you have heard. On the other hand, I am writing a new commandment to you, which is true in Him and in you, because the darkness is passing away and the true Light is already shining. The one who says he is in the Light and yet hates his brother is in the darkness until now. The one who loves his brother abides in the Light and there is no cause for stumbling in him. But the one who hates his brother is in the darkness and walks in the darkness, and does not know where he is going because the darkness has blinded his eyes. (2:7–11)

Love is the preeminent mark of a genuine believer. Love for God is the benchmark of one's relationship to Him, and love for other people is the epitome of human relationships. The New Testament repeatedly sets forth the supremacy of love. Jesus cited two Old Testament verses (Deut. 6:5; Lev. 19:18) as proof that to love God and man is to fulfill the supreme commandment of the law:

But when the Pharisees heard that Jesus had silenced the Sadducees, they gathered themselves together. One of them, a lawyer, asked Him a question, testing Him, "Teacher, which is the great commandment in the Law?" And He said to him, "'You shall love the Lord your God with all your heart, and with all your soul, and with all your mind.' This is the great and foremost commandment. The second is like it, 'You shall love your neighbor as yourself.' On these two commandments depend the whole Law and the Prophets." (Matt. 22:34–40; cf. 7:12; Rom. 13:10; 1 Tim. 1:5)

In a majestic and lyrical passage in his first letter to the Corinthians, the apostle Paul argued for the superiority of love over spiritual gifts:

But earnestly desire the greater gifts. And I show you a still more excellent way. If I speak with the tongues of men and of angels, but do not have love, I have become a noisy gong or a clanging cymbal. If I have the gift of prophecy, and know all mysteries and all knowledge; and if I have all faith, so as to remove mountains, but do not have love, I am nothing. And if I give all my possessions to feed the poor, and if I surrender my body to be burned, but do not have love, it profits me nothing. Love is patient, love is kind and is not jealous; love does not brag and is not arrogant, does not act unbecomingly; it does not seek its own, is not provoked, does not take into account a wrong suffered, does not rejoice in unrighteousness, but rejoices with the truth; bears all things, believes all things, hopes all things, endures all things. Love never fails; but if there are gifts of prophecy, they will be done away; if there are tongues, they will cease; if there is knowledge, it will be done away. For we know in part and we prophesy in part; but when the perfect comes, the partial will be done away. When I was a child, I used to speak like a child, think like a child, reason like a child; when I became a man, I did away with childish things. For now we see in a mirror dimly, but then face to face; now I know in part, but then I will know fully just as I also have been fully known. But now faith, hope, love, abide these three; but the greatest of these is love. (1 Cor. 12:31–13:13; cf. Matt. 5:44–45; John 13:34–35; 15:9; Eph. 4:32; Phil. 2:1–4; Col. 3:14; Heb. 10:24; 1 Peter 4:8; 1 John 4:8, 17–19)

Because love is the saint's highest moral duty toward others, it is not only the ultimate mark of genuine salvation, but also provides the supreme assurance of that reality.

In this passage John reiterates the theme of light versus darkness that he had introduced earlier (cf. 1:5–7). Light represents the kingdom of Christ and eternal life (Luke 2:32; John 1:4, 9; 8:12; 12:46; 2 Cor. 4:4b; 1 Peter 2:9; cf. Ps. 36:9; Prov. 4:18; John 3:20–21; Eph. 5:13), and darkness represents the kingdom of Satan and eternal death (Prov. 2:13; Matt. 8:12; 22:13; Acts 26:18; Eph. 5:11; 6:12; Col. 1:13; 1 Thess. 5:5; 2 Peter 2:4; Jude 6;

cf. Isa. 59:9–10). Though a form of the word *love* appears only once in this section, love is clearly John's theme as he emphasizes its primacy as a moral test to verify salvation (cf. 3:10–11, 16–18, 23; 4:7–12, 16–21; 5:1–3; 2 John 5–6). The passage describes love as an old commandment, a new commandment, and a way of life.

LOVE AS AN OLD COMMANDMENT

Beloved, I am not writing a new commandment to you, but an old commandment which you have had from the beginning; the old commandment is the word which you have heard. (2:7)

Throughout the centuries preachers, teachers, and commentators have called John "the apostle of love." His love to fellow believers to whom he wrote often expressed itself by the familiar term **beloved** (cf. 3:2, 21; 4:1, 7; 3 John 2). That title was so appropriate in this epistle, which affirms love as the benchmark of true salvation.

In a play on words, extended into verse 8, John wrote that the commandment to love was not a **new commandment** in one sense, but actually **an old commandment.** It had been taught throughout the biblical text. Whether they were Jews or Gentiles, John's readers would **have heard** from the Old Testament about the concept of loving one another (1 Sam. 20:17, 41–42; cf. Gen. 45:15; Ps. 133:1–2). In the Pentateuch, God established the law of love in unmistakable terms: "You shall not take vengeance, nor bear any grudge against the sons of your people, but you shall love your neighbor as yourself; I am the Lord" (Lev. 19:18).

Instructing the Romans concerning brotherly love, Paul quoted the Decalogue and Leviticus 19:18:

> Owe nothing to anyone except to love one another; for he who loves his neighbor has fulfilled the law. For this, "You shall not commit adultery, you shall not murder, you shall not steal, you shall not covet," and if there is any other commandment, it is summed up in this saying, "You shall love your neighbor as yourself." Love does no wrong to a neighbor; therefore love is the fulfillment of the law. (Rom. 13:8–10; cf. John 13:34–35; 1 Cor. 14:1; Phil. 1:9; Col. 3:14; 1 Thess. 4:9; 1 Tim. 2:15; Heb. 6:10; 1 Peter 1:22; 4:8; 1 John 3:23; 4:7, 21)

There is an inseparable link between obedience and loving God and one's neighbor; thus Paul declares that "love is the fulfillment of the law."

The truth that they were to love one another was something his readers would **have had from the beginning.** The **beginning** in view here is not the creation or God's giving of the Law to Moses, but **the beginning** of their Christian lives (cf. 2:24; 3:11; 2 John 6). This was taught them from the start, not merely by some recent innovation from John. **The word** concerning love **which** they **heard** was **the old commandment,** the Old Testament teaching on love, which Jesus had already reiterated (Matt. 22:34–40; Mark 12:28–34; cf. Matt. 5:43–48; Luke 6:27–36). When John's readers became Christians, they would have committed themselves to obey God's law, love Him, and love others, all of which Jesus taught and exemplified during His earthly ministry (Matt. 5:1–7:27; 16:24–27; 19:16–26; 28:18–20; Luke 10:29–37; 14:25–35; John 4:21–24; 6:26–58; 8:12, 31–32; 12:23–26; 13:1, 12–17; 15:1–17; 21:15–19; cf. John 7:37–38; 10:11–18; 11:25–26). John's teaching was thus part of the ethical instruction throughout all divine revelation and such as his readers had heard from the beginning of their Christian lives. Obedience to that instruction was a test of the reality of their conversion and a central element in the general submission of all who are in Jesus Christ and willingly bow to His lordship (Matt. 7:21–23; Luke 6:46; 9:22–26; Acts 4:19–20; 5:29; Rom. 6:17; 1 Peter 1:2, 14; cf. Eccl. 12:13; James 1:25).

Love as a New Commandment

On the other hand, I am writing a new commandment to you, which is true in Him and in you, because the darkness is passing away and the true Light is already shining. (2:8)

On the surface, **I am** appears to contradict John's previous "I am not" (v. 7). But a closer look clearly reveals that John was using this seeming contradiction to clarify how the old commandment to love is at the same time not new and yet new. There is a sense in which John was **writing a new** (*kainos*) **commandment.** *Kainos* (used in both vv. 7 and 8) defines something that is fresh in essence and quality while not necessarily chronologically new (*kairos*).

The commandment's newness is not found in the words, but in the illustration of love, described in the expression, **which is true in Him.** Even though the Old Testament taught the duty to love, never before had perfect love been so plainly manifested as it was in the incarnate Christ (John 13:1; 15:13; Acts 10:38; 2 Cor. 8:9; cf. Isa. 40:11; Matt. 4:23–24; 11:28–30; 23:37–39; Luke 19:41). So the newness is not in the command to love, but in the perfect manifestation of love in the person of Christ. This is one of many ways in which the Son of God incarnate revealed the nature of God in a fullness not before manifest (cf. John 1:14–15; Col. 2:9).

The Lord magnificently illustrated this truth in the upper room just hours before His death. His promises that night to the apostles that He would prepare a place in heaven for them (John 14:1–4), that His peace would be with them (John 14:27), that He would send the Holy Spirit to them (John 14:25–26; 15:26; 16:7–15), and that by abiding in Him they would bear much fruit (John 15:1–11) were reflections of His divine love. But He displayed love most graciously in His humbling service to them. John 13:1–17 records what happened:

> Now before the Feast of the Passover, Jesus knowing that His hour had come that He would depart out of this world to the Father, having loved His own who were in the world, He loved them to the end. During supper, the devil having already put into the heart of Judas Iscariot, the son of Simon, to betray Him, Jesus, knowing that the Father had given all things into His hands, and that He had come forth from God and was going back to God, got up from supper, and laid aside His garments; and taking a towel, He girded Himself. Then He poured water into the basin, and began to wash the disciples' feet and to wipe them with the towel with which He was girded. So He came to Simon Peter. He said to Him, "Lord, do You wash my feet?" Jesus answered and said to him, "What I do you do not realize now, but you will understand hereafter." Peter said to Him, "Never shall You wash my feet!" Jesus answered him, "If I do not wash you, you have no part with Me." Simon Peter said to Him, "Lord, then wash not only my feet, but also my hands and my head." Jesus said to him, "He who has bathed needs only to wash his feet, but is completely clean; and you are clean, but not all of you." For He knew the one who was betraying Him; for this reason He said, "Not all of you are clean." So when He had washed their feet, and taken His garments and reclined at the table again, He said to them, "Do you know what I have done to you? You call Me Teacher and Lord; and you are right, for so I am. If I then, the Lord and the Teacher, washed your feet, you also ought to wash one another's feet. For I gave you an example that you also should do as I did to you. Truly, truly, I say to you, a slave is not greater than his master, nor is one who is sent greater than the one who sent him. If you know these things, you are blessed if you do them.

The Lord's selfless, humble act was in keeping with Paul's portrait of Christ in his letter to the Philippians:

> He existed in the form of God, [but] did not regard equality with God a thing to be grasped, but emptied Himself, taking the form of a bond-servant, and being made in the likeness of men. Being found in appearance as a man, He humbled Himself by becoming obedient to the point of death, even death on a cross. (Phil. 2:6–8)

Christ's ministry in the upper room manifested the heart of God—perfect love, perfect sacrifice (Isa. 53:3–12; Eph. 5:2; Heb. 9:12), and perfect humility (Luke 22:27).

But the commandment to love not only has a new expression because of love's powerful display in Christ's life and ministry; it is also fresh because of its manifestation in the lives of believers. It is a glorious demonstration of what it means to be a new creation in Christ (2 Cor. 5:17). If anything defines this love from the human side, it is humility. Sinners are radically humbled (cf. James 4:6–10) to the point of self-hate (Luke 14:26) and self-denial (Matt. 16:24–27), so as to be like the penitent tax collector in Luke 18:13–14:

> But the tax collector, standing some distance away, was even unwilling to lift up his eyes to heaven, but was beating his breast, saying, "God, be merciful to me, the sinner!" I tell you, this man went to his house justified rather than the other; for everyone who exalts himself will be humbled, but he who humbles himself will be exalted.

At salvation, the Holy Spirit takes up residence in the believer's life (John 14:16–17; Rom. 8:9, 14; 1 Cor. 6:19; Eph. 1:13–14; 2 Tim. 1:14; 1 John 2:27; 3:24; 4:13) and sustains the original humility, out of which He produces spiritual fruit (Gal. 5:22–23), the most important of which is love. The apostle Paul affirmed the presence of this love in believers when he wrote to the Romans, "the love of God has been poured out within our hearts through the Holy Spirit who was given to us" (5:5), and when he wrote to the Thessalonians that "as to the love of the brethren, you have no need for anyone to write to you . . . for indeed you do practice it toward all. . . . But we urge you, brethren, to excel still more" (1 Thess. 4:9–10).

The new commandment or manifestation of love has come **because the darkness is passing away and the true Light is already shining.** Obviously, the true **Light** is Jesus Christ (John 8:12), who has come and inaugurated His kingdom (Zech. 9:9; Matt. 21:5; John 12:12–15; Heb. 1:8–9; 12:28; cf. Ps. 24:7–10), in which He (and this new dimension of love) **is already shining** (cf. Eph. 3:16–19). With the inauguration of Messiah's spiritual kingdom, **the true Light** began shining and overcoming **the darkness** of Satan's kingdom (Rom. 16:20; Col. 2:15; Heb. 2:14; 1 John 3:8; cf. Eph. 6:11–16). Right now the light coexists with the darkness, but *the* Light and the divine love He bears will increasingly dispel the darkness (cf. 1 John 2:17*a*), shine ever brighter during Christ's millennial reign, and eventually rule supremely throughout eternity. Thus, it is only because believers have been "rescued . . . from the domain of darkness, and transferred . . . to the kingdom of His beloved Son," the Light, that this new commandment is a reality in their lives (Col. 1:13).

Love as a Way of Life

The one who says he is in the Light and yet hates his brother is in the darkness until now. The one who loves his brother abides in the Light and there is no cause for stumbling in him. But the one who hates his brother is in the darkness and walks in the darkness, and does not know where he is going because the darkness has blinded his eyes. (2:9–11)

In this concluding portion of the passage, John applies the test of supernatural love to those who claim to be Christians. Its presence is a sure indicator of transformation, salvation, and divine life. The false teachers of John's day arrogantly claimed a higher knowledge of the divine nature and communion with deity, but it produced only proud disdain for unenlightened, common people. But the Christians, most of whom were slaves or members of the working class (cf. 1 Cor. 1:26–29), were the truly enlightened who demonstrated their true knowledge of God as they not only loved one another, but reached out in love to those lost in sin's darkness (cf. Matt. 5:44; Luke 6:27, 35).

It is a meaningless boast for someone to say **he is in the Light** (cf. Matt. 7:21–23; James 1:22; 2:14–26; 1 John 1:6); if he (or she) **hates** his **brother**—meaning that he does not love saints selflessly as God does — he is not in the divine kingdom of light but remains **in the darkness until now.** On the other hand, **the one who loves his brother abides in the Light and there is no cause for stumbling in him.** Those who love and obey God's Word and express selfless love to fellow believers are truly transformed; they are not going to cause others to fall. In the New Testament, **stumbling** refers to sinning (cf. Matt. 5:29–30; 13:41; 18:6, 8–9; Luke 17:2; John 16:1; 1 Cor. 8:13; Rev. 2:14). John used the term to explain that the person who truly loves others—as a reflection of his love for Christ—will not cause them to sin (cf. Rom. 13:8–10) or reject the gospel. So there is a love that proves salvation, as the Son of God said, "A new commandment I give to you, that you love one another, even as I have loved you, that you also love one another. By this all men will know that you are My disciples, if you have love for one another" (John 13:34–35).

John emphatically reiterates that anyone who **hates his brother is in the darkness and walks** [follows a normal course of life] **in the darkness.** Such people **do not know where** they are **going** [cf. John 12:35] **because the darkness has blinded** their **eyes.** They are like those who are completely blind and grope around to determine where they are (cf. Gen. 19:11; Acts 13:11–12). Such loveless people are clearly outside the kingdom of Light (cf. Matt. 5:21–22; 1 John 3:15) and void of spiritual life. John described such claimants earlier as liars:

This is the message we have heard from Him and announce to you, that God is Light, and in Him there is no darkness at all. If we say that we have fellowship with Him and yet walk in the darkness, we lie and do not practice the truth. (1:5–6)

Unconverted sinners, devoid of love and living in spiritual darkness, cannot possibly fulfill Jesus' well-known love command (see again John 13:34–35), which He originally gave to the apostles in the upper room. Neither can they express the kind of sacrificial love Jesus showed when He washed the apostles' feet (John 13:3–15), nor what He referred to later that evening when He declared, "Greater love has no one than this, that one lay down his life for his friends" (John 15:13; cf. 1 John 3:16).

On the other hand, obedience to that commandment is a valid test for each believer's genuineness. Such obedience provides a distinct contrast to those who are without love and persist in walking in darkness. Believers who manifest the new kind of love first taught by Jesus and reiterated by John truly obey the Lord's command in the Sermon on the Mount, "Let your light shine before men in such a way that they may see your good works, and glorify your Father who is in heaven" (Matt. 5:16; cf. Eph. 5:8; Phil. 2:15; 1 Peter 2:9).

The Stages of Spiritual Growth (1 John 2:12–14)

7

I am writing to you, little children, because your sins have been forgiven you for His name's sake. I am writing to you, fathers, because you know Him who has been from the beginning. I am writing to you, young men, because you have overcome the evil one. I have written to you, children, because you know the Father. I have written to you, fathers, because you know Him who has been from the beginning. I have written to you, young men, because you are strong, and the word of God abides in you, and you have overcome the evil one. (2:12–14)

One essence of life is growth. This is true in both the physical realm and in the spiritual realm. Just as living seeds grow into mature plants and infants grow into mature adults, so new Christians grow into Christlikeness. When growth is hindered in the physical realm, either by malnutrition, disease, or birth defects, the results can be tragic. But it is an even greater tragedy when believers fail to grow and mature spiritually. After all, immature Christians cannot fully appreciate all the blessings and privileges that God has reserved for them, nor serve Him with the usefulness He desires (John 15:4–5; 17:21; Rom. 5:2; 8:28, 34; 9:23; 2 Cor. 4:15–17;

Eph. 2:19; 3:12, 20; Phil. 4:7; Heb. 7:25; James 1:17; 2 Peter 1:4; cf. Pss. 18:2; 27:1; 46:11; 48:14; Isa. 40:11).

Like physical growth, spiritual growth ultimately depends on God's power, but it also requires the element of human responsibility. All scriptural calls to obedience make that obvious. In fact, the New Testament repeatedly echoes the call for Christians to "work out your salvation with fear and trembling" (Phil. 2:12). Peter commanded believers to "grow in the grace and knowledge of our Lord and Savior Jesus Christ" (2 Peter 3:18*a*), while Paul exhorted them to "be imitators of God, as beloved children" (Eph. 5:1). Paul also set forth spiritual growth's ultimate goal:

> Brethren, I do not regard myself as having laid hold of it yet; but one thing I do: forgetting what lies behind and reaching forward to what lies ahead, I press on toward the goal for the prize of the upward call of God in Christ Jesus. (Phil. 3:13–14; cf. Rom. 8:29)

He understood that "the goal for the prize of the upward call of God" is to become like "Christ Jesus" (cf. Phil. 2:5; 3:10). The apostle John reiterated that same truth when he wrote, "The one who says he abides in Him ought himself to walk in the same manner as He walked" (1 John 2:6). As those who love the Lord, believers are to continually pursue holiness "like the Holy One who called [them]" (1 Peter 1:15). Thankfully, God has provided His church with gifted men to help believers as they grow in that pursuit:

> And He gave some as apostles, and some as prophets, and some as evangelists, and some as pastors and teachers, for the equipping of the saints for the work of service, to the building up of the body of Christ; until we all attain to the unity of the faith, and of the knowledge of the Son of God, to a mature man, to the measure of the stature which belongs to the fullness of Christ. (Eph. 4:11–13; cf. vv. 15–16; 3:16–20; Rom. 8:29; 2 Cor. 3:18; Gal. 4:19; 1 Peter 2:2)

Every biblical command toward sanctification assumes the necessary obedience of the ones commanded. That makes it clear that believers have a duty to faithfully and obediently use the means of grace to grow to maturity.

In discussing spiritual growth, it is important to address several misconceptions that must be carefully avoided. First, spiritual growth does not determine the believer's standing in grace before God. That issue is finally and completely settled when sinners trust in the atoning work of Jesus Christ and have His righteousness imputed to them (Rom. 3:21–26;

4:5–8; 1 Cor. 1:30; 2 Cor. 5:21; Gal. 3:13; Phil. 3:9; Col. 2:10; 1 Peter 2:24). At the moment of conversion, Christ's own sacrifice for sin is applied to the believing sinner and His own righteousness credited to the penitent so that God's wrath is turned away, all sin is paid for and pardoned, and the believer is accepted by God in Christ Jesus. The resultant standing is fixed and irrevocable, and it settles forever believers' heavenly destiny.

Second, spiritual growth does not affect God's love for believers. He does not love the mature saints more than the less mature. (The reason for this is that His love is not based on the individual merit of any person [Rom. 5:8].) The Lord Jesus Christ loves all the elect perfectly. Even on the night before the crucifixion, the apostles demonstrated immaturity and pride (they were arguing about who would be the greatest in the kingdom [Luke 22:24; cf. Matt. 20:20–24; Mark 9:34]), being insensitive to their Lord who was already in the looming shadow of the cross. Still, John writes that in their worst behavior, the Lord continued to love them "to the end," that is, to perfection, or to the maximum of His love (John 13:1).

Third, spiritual growth is not measured by the calendar (cf. Heb. 5:11–14). People who have been believers for many years are often less mature than others who have been believers for a much shorter time. This may be the result of inadequate study or instruction in the Word (cf. Eph. 4:11–15), or fleshly disobedience and unfaithful application of sound teaching (1 Cor. 3:1–3).

Fourth, spiritual growth is unrelated to the amount of theological information believers know. Some Christians have an adequate or even exceptional amount of biblical and theological knowledge, and yet are shockingly immature spiritually. That is a dangerous position to be in, because the more biblical information one receives but does not apply, the more deceived he becomes about his own spiritual condition (cf. Rom. 2:17–29; Heb. 5:12–14). The same sun that melts the wax hardens the clay. Constant disobedience produces indifference and a subdued conscience, stunting spiritual growth.

Fifth, spiritual growth has nothing to do with outwardly successful ministry activity. Some of the busiest people in the church are unskilled in the truth and immature in the wisdom that comes from above (James 3:17–18). Even prominent spiritual leaders can display an appalling lack of biblical wisdom. Great temporal success, a high level of influence, heading a large organization, or generating much financial support is not an indicator of genuine spiritual maturity. In fact, sometimes the opposite is true. For Paul, weakness, suffering, persecution, and poverty (2 Cor. 6:3–10; 11:23–33; 12:9–10; Phil. 4:11–13; cf. 1 Tim. 6:6–10) were the true signs of his maturity in the Lord.

Finally, spiritual growth is not mystical, sentimental, or psychological. It does not stem from a once-for-all act of spiritual rededication, religious decision, or an emotional experience that produces good feelings. Rather, as physical growth results from the process of taking in food, so also spiritual growth results from the process of taking in God's truth (His Word), believing it, and applying it (John 5:24, 39; 6:63; 8:31–32; Acts 17:11; Rom. 15:4; 1 Thess. 2:13; 4:1–2; 1 Tim. 4:5–6; James 1:22–25). Responding to Satan's temptation, Jesus quoted Moses' words from Deuteronomy 8:3: "It is written, 'Man shall not live on bread alone, but on every word that proceeds out of the mouth of God'" (Matt. 4:4). Paul's letters define spiritual growth as being "transformed by the renewing of your mind" (Rom. 12:2); "perfecting holiness in the fear of God" (2 Cor. 7:1); "press[ing] on toward the goal" (Phil. 3:14); "being built up in Him and established in your faith" (Col. 2:7); and "pursu[ing] righteousness, godliness, faith, love, perseverance and gentleness" (1 Tim. 6:11). And Peter commanded his readers, in 1 Peter 2:2, to "long for the pure milk of the word, so that by it you may grow in respect to salvation."

The apostle John, under the inspiration of the Holy Spirit, placed this paragraph here to give assurance and comfort to his readers that they were the true children of God, unlike the false teachers and counterfeit believers who threatened them. In view of the doctrinal and practical tests that John had already presented—the test about belief in Christ, the test about recognition of sin, the tests for obedience and love —the apostle wanted to confirm the authenticity of his readers' salvation. This paragraph underscores his subsequently stated purpose for the entire letter: "These things I have written to you who believe in the name of the Son of God, so that you may know that you have eternal life" (1 John 5:13; cf. 1:4).

Obviously, not all original or current readers of this letter were or are at equal stages of spiritual maturity. Some are spiritual infants while others are spiritual adults. In order to effectively encourage all recipients, John began this very definitive section with a general reassurance, after which he gave specific assurance to those at each general stage of spiritual growth: little children, young men, and fathers.

GENERAL REASSURANCE

I am writing to you, little children, because your sins have been forgiven you for His name's sake. (2:12)

John knew that the people to whom he was **writing** were believers and that their **sins** had **been forgiven**. In this verse, and in the verses that follow, the apostle said "I am writing to you" or "I have written to you" six times, in order to emphatically state that his message was limited to his readers, the ones who truly were part of God's family.

The word translated **little children** (*teknia*) means "born ones," speaking of offspring in a general sense without regard for age. It is commonly used in the New Testament to describe believers as the **children** of God (John 13:33; 1 John 2:1, 28; 3:7, 18; 4:4; 5:21; cf. Gal. 4:19, 28). By using this term, the apostle was addressing all who were true offspring of God, at any level of spiritual maturity. His focus was on all who mourned over their sinful condition (Matt. 5:4), trusted Jesus Christ as their only Lord and Savior (Acts 16:31), had their lives transformed by the Holy Spirit (Titus 3:5), lived in obedience to God's Word (Rom. 6:17), and showed sincere love for one another (1 Peter 1:22).

Only two spiritual families exist from God's perspective: children of God and children of Satan (cf. John 8:39–44). God's children do not love Satan's family or give their allegiance to the world he controls (cf. 1 John 2:15). Instead, they grow (though not all at the same rate or with equal consistency) in their love for the Lord, a love that will manifest itself in heartfelt obedience and service (cf. John 14:15).

The New Testament plainly states that all believers, no matter where they are on the spiritual growth continuum, have **been forgiven** of all their **sins** (1:7; Matt. 26:28; Luke 1:77; Acts 2:38; 3:19; 26:18; Col. 1:14; 2:13–14). In fact, this truth is foundational to the evangelistic mission of the church. Jesus told His apostles "that repentance for forgiveness of sins would be proclaimed in His name to all the nations" (Luke 24:47). Peter declared to Cornelius and his companions, "Of Him [Christ] all the prophets bear witness that through His name everyone who believes in Him receives forgiveness of sins" (Acts 10:43; cf. 13:38–39). Paul attested: "In Him we have redemption through His blood, the forgiveness of our trespasses, according to the riches of His grace" (Eph. 1:7; cf. 4:32; 1 John 1:7; 3:5). Of course, this great reality of the forgiveness of sins was not new in the New Testament, but was firmly rooted in Old Testament teaching (cf. Pss. 32:1–2; 86:5; 103:12; 130:3–4; Isa. 1:18–19; 43:25; 44:22).

John concluded this sentence with the reminder that God grants forgiveness to believers, not because of their own worthiness or merit, but **for His name's sake.** That expression refers to God's glory (cf. Deut. 28:58; Neh. 9:5; Ps. 8:1; Isa. 42:8; 48:11), which is the overarching reason for everything He does (cf. Pss. 19:1; 25:11; 57:5; 79:8–9; 93:1; 104:31; 106:7–8; 109:21; 111:3; 113:4; 145:5, 12; Isa. 6:3; 48:9; Jer. 14:7–9; Hab. 2:14; Rom. 1:5). God forgives sinners because it pleases Him to glorify His name by manifesting His superabundant grace, mercy, and power. As those who have been given the gift of forgiveness, believers will forever praise and magnify God (cf. 2 Cor. 4:15; Rev. 5:11–13). Still, while on earth, they are at different stages of growth, with distinguishing characteristics.

ASSURANCE TO SPIRITUAL CHILDREN

I have written to you, children, because you know the Father. (2:13c)

The term rendered **children** (*paidia*) is different from the term rendered "little children" (*teknia*) in verse 12. As noted above, *teknia* refers to all the children of God. But *paidia* denotes more specifically young **children,** those still under parental instruction. Such children are ignorant and immature and in need of care and guidance.

Immature spiritual children are those who **know the Father** (Ps. 9:10; cf. John 10:4, 14; Rom. 8:15; Gal. 4:6) in the same way as an infant has little more than a basic knowledge of his or her parents. The distinguishing characteristic of babes in Christ is that they are consumed with their new-found relationship to the God and Savior they have come to know savingly (e.g., Luke 19:5–6), and with the resulting joy and peace of that knowledge. But they are still infants, who have yet to feast on the nourishing spiritual meat of sound doctrine (cf. Heb. 5:12–13).

As with physical babes, the ignorance of spiritual children makes them prone to weaknesses and highly susceptible to dangers. They are all too often motivated by fleshly desires and lack discernment to avoid what is harmful and pursue what is beneficial. They often naively attach themselves to their spiritual heroes or favorite teachers, for which Paul reprimanded the Corinthians: "For when one says, 'I am of Paul,' and another, 'I am of Apollos,' are you not mere men?" (1 Cor. 3:4; cf. vv. 1–3, 5; 1:12–13). Spiritual children also lack discernment and are vulnerable to the allurements of deceivers and their heretical doctrines. That is why Paul warned the Ephesians,

> We are no longer to be children, tossed here and there by waves and carried about by every wind of doctrine, by the trickery of men, by craftiness in deceitful scheming; but speaking the truth in love, we are to grow up in all aspects into Him who is the head, even Christ. (Eph. 4:14–15; cf. 1 Cor. 16:13)

Mature believers can applaud new believers' exuberant love, their eager and sincere devotion to God, their attachment to new-found friends in Christ, and their often optimistic viewpoint toward their new Christian life. However, mature Christians must also warn the less mature against the danger of being led astray by false teachers and their demon-inspired doctrines (2 John 10–11).

ASSURANCE TO SPIRITUAL YOUNG MEN

I am writing to you, young men, because you have overcome the evil one. . . . I have written to you, young men, because you are strong, and the word of God abides in you, and you have overcome the evil one. (2:13*b*, 14*b*)

The second stage of spiritual growth takes believers from an emphasis on the basic relationship to an emphasis on biblical revelation. In contrast to spiritual children, who are primarily focused on devotion to God, spiritual **young men** have advanced to be concerned with clarity of doctrine.

Spiritual young men are marked by an understanding of Scripture truth (cf. Pss. 1:2; 119:11, 16, 97, 103, 105, 148; Acts 17:11; 20:32; 2 Tim. 3:15). They have outgrown the childish self-absorption with feelings and moved beyond the elementary struggles often associated with new Christians. They have a biblical worldview, their theology is largely in place, and they have a mature love for the truth and a desire to proclaim and defend it (cf. Eph. 6:17; 2 Tim. 2:15; Heb. 4:12).

Because the **word of God abides in** those at this stage, they are **strong** in doctrinal truth (Eph. 4:13–16; 1 Tim. 4:6; 2 Tim. 3:16–17; Titus 2:1; cf. Ps. 119:99). As a result, they **have** already **overcome the evil one.** After all, Satan's primary emphasis is not on tempting individuals to sin (cf. James 1:14), but on working through manifold false religious systems to deceive the world and lead most to damnation (2 Cor. 10:3–5; 11:13–15; Eph. 6:11–12; cf. 1 Tim. 4:1–2; 1 John 4:1, 3). The spiritual young men at this stage of maturity, however, are equipped through their understanding of Scripture to stand firm against his deceptive schemes (Eph. 6:11). Armed with the sound doctrine they have been taught, they are able to refute error and guard the truth.

ASSURANCE TO SPIRITUAL FATHERS

I am writing to you, fathers, because you know Him who has been from the beginning. . . . I have written to you, fathers, because you know Him who has been from the beginning. (2:13*a*, 14*a*)

The third stage of spiritual growth is when believers do not merely understand doctrine intellectually, but have come to **know** (from *ginōskā*, "to know by taking in knowledge; to come to know") **Him** (God), the source of the truth and the object of the worship and praise it produces. John asserts that reality in both verses 13 and 14, and

Paul echoes it in Philippians 3:10. Those who are spiritual **fathers** have meditated (cf. Josh. 1:8; Pss. 1:2; 19:14; 49:3; 77:11–12; 139:17–18; 143:5) on the depths of God's character to such an extent that they gain a deep knowledge of Him and worship Him intimately. In a sense, the most mature saints have come full circle, with the emphasis of their Christian lives again on their relationship with the eternal God **who has been from the beginning** (Pss. 90:2; 102:25–27; Rom. 1:20; Rev. 1:8; 16:5; 21:6; 22:13; cf. John 8:58). Only now that relationship is markedly fuller and richer because it is completely informed by and anchored to the comprehensiveness of biblical doctrine. Job, through his experience of severe trials, came to this deep knowledge of God. He affirmed, "Therefore I retract, and I repent in dust and ashes" (Job 42:6), and thereby actually repented of his incomplete, immature view of God held earlier in his life (cf. Job 36:3–4; Ps. 119:66; Prov. 1:7; 2:10; 9:10; Phil. 1:9; Col. 1:9–10; 2 Peter 1:3, 8).

The only way believers can progress on the continuum of spiritual growth—from children, to young men, to fathers—is through the life-giving, life-transforming application of the Word of God in their lives (2 Tim. 2:15; cf. Ezra 7:10). By reading, studying, memorizing, meditating on, and applying the Bible's truth in every situation, Christians are transformed into the image of God (cf. 2 Cor. 3:18) by the power of the Spirit (cf. Eph. 6:17; Col. 3:16; 2 Peter 1:19–21).

As they continue to grow in their sanctification, the goal of all believers must be to become spiritual fathers, characterized by an intimate communion with God. In His high priestly prayer for the apostles and all believers, Christ prayed,

> For their sakes I sanctify Myself, that they themselves also may be sanctified in truth. I do not ask on behalf of these alone, but for those also who believe in Me through their word; that they may all be one; even as You, Father, are in Me and I in You, that they also may be in Us, so that the world may believe that You sent Me. The glory which You have given Me I have given to them, that they may be one, just as We are one; I in them and You in Me, that they may be perfected in unity, so that the world may know that You sent Me, and loved them, even as You have loved Me. Father, I desire that they also, whom You have given Me, be with Me where I am, so that they may see My glory which You have given Me, for You loved Me before the foundation of the world. O righteous Father, although the world has not known You, yet I have known You; and these have known that You sent Me; and I have made Your name known to them, and will make it known, so that the love with which You loved Me may be in them, and I in them. (John 17:19–26)

Jesus desired that believers would know God not in a superficial way, nor in an academic sense only, but with supernatural intimacy, made possible only by lifetime obedience to Him and His Word.

John's description of the stages of spiritual growth also challenges believers to "excel still more" (1 Thess. 4:10) in their Christian walks. Spiritual children must move beyond their initial delight in the Father's love to a sound knowledge of biblical truth. Young men must not rest in their knowledge of biblical truth, but press on to know deeply the God from whom all truth comes and to whom all truth points. And even fathers must continue to expand and deepen their knowledge of the eternal God. As long as saints live on this earth, they are bound to obey the mandate to "grow in the grace and knowledge of our Lord and Savior Jesus Christ" (2 Peter 3:18*a*).

The Love
God Hates
(1 John 2:15–17)

8

Do not love the world nor the things in the world. If anyone loves the world, the love of the Father is not in him. For all that is in the world, the lust of the flesh and the lust of the eyes and the boastful pride of life, is not from the Father, but is from the world. The world is passing away, and also its lusts; but the one who does the will of God lives forever. (2:15–17)

As he came to the end of his earthly life and reflected on his many years of faithful ministry, the apostle Paul wrote,

> For I am already being poured out as a drink offering, and the time of my departure has come. I have fought the good fight, I have finished the course, I have kept the faith; in the future there is laid up for me the crown of righteousness, which the Lord, the righteous Judge, will award to me on that day; and not only to me, but also to all who have loved His appearing. (2 Tim. 4:6–8)

Having ministered boldly and obediently, Paul was eager to see his Savior and receive his eternal reward. Yet at the same time Paul was acutely concerned about those whom he would leave behind (cf. Phil. 1:21–24).

One such individual was Timothy, Paul's close ministry companion and son in the faith (1 Tim. 1:2; 2 Tim. 2:1). And while Paul was confident in the spiritual integrity of his disciple (2 Tim. 1:5), he also knew that Timothy, as a young man (cf. 1 Tim. 4:12), was vulnerable to certain temptations. For that reason, in his final epistle, the apostle exhorted his young protégé to remain strong and courageous:

> I remind you to kindle afresh the gift of God which is in you through the laying on of my hands. For God has not given us a spirit of timidity, but of power and love and discipline. Therefore do not be ashamed of the testimony of our Lord or of me His prisoner, but join with me in suffering for the gospel according to the power of God.... Retain the standard of sound words which you have heard from me, in the faith and love which are in Christ Jesus. Guard, through the Holy Spirit who dwells in us, the treasure which has been entrusted to you. (2 Tim. 1:6–8, 13–14)

Paul continued by reminding Timothy of the astonishing and sobering reality that many had already deserted him: "You are aware of the fact that all who are in Asia turned away from me, among whom are Phygelus and Hermogenes" (2 Tim. 1:15). But perhaps the most notorious defector among Paul's associates appears in 2 Timothy 4:10: "Demas, having loved this present world, has deserted me and gone to Thessalonica." Demas had likely been a coworker with Paul for many years and had ministered with such noble colleagues as Crescens, Titus, Luke, Mark, Tychicus (vv. 10–12), Epaphras, and Aristarchus (Col. 4:12–14; Philem. 23–24). Yet despite having long been in the presence of such formidable men of God—preachers of the Word, authors of Scripture, church planters, faithful servants, men of prayer, and men who suffered for the gospel—Demas utterly abandoned Paul and the members of his team.

Second Timothy 4:10 plainly states the reason for Demas's defection: he "loved this present world." He loved the world system, with its sin, human wisdom, and satanic deceptions, more than he loved God's kingdom. Demas's life exhibited characteristics of both the shallow, rocky soil, in which the seed of the Word flourished briefly but withered and died in the face of tribulation and persecution; and the thorny soil, in which the seed was smothered under the cares of the world and the deceitfulness of wealth (see Jesus' parable in Matt. 13:3–23). While Paul willingly anticipated martyrdom for his faith, Demas decided that he was unwilling to pay a similar price. Therefore he forsook his co-laborers and went "to Thessalonica," a large, cosmopolitan city on the main east-west trade route of Asia Minor that offered all the materialistic, immoral, and philosophical allurements of the world he loved. In so doing, Demas proved he was never a lover of God.

Demas was guilty of spiritual harlotry, the kind of sin against which James strongly warned some of his readers: "You adulteresses, do you not know that friendship with the world is hostility toward God? Therefore whoever wishes to be a friend of the world makes himself an enemy of God" (James 4:4). James's figurative language recalled the familiar Old Testament imagery of Israel's spiritual adultery (cf. 2 Chron. 21:11–15; Jer. 2:20–25; 3:1–14; Hos. 1:2; 4:15; 9:1).

By committing spiritual harlotry, Demas made himself "an enemy of God," another familiar Old Testament concept (cf. Deut. 32:41; Pss. 21:8–9; 68:21; 72:9; Nah. 1:2). He did so by returning to the life he had hypocritically suppressed for a few years while traveling with Paul and the others.

Demas's tragic example provides an unambiguous biblical illustration of the love God hates. The perfect love of God is a theme that runs throughout Scripture (Deut. 7:7–8; 10:15; Pss. 25:6; 26:3; 36:7, 10; 40:11; 63:3; 69:16; 92:2; 103:4; 119:88; 138:2; 143:8; Isa. 63:7; Jer. 31:3; Hos. 2:19; Zeph. 3:17) and appears with particular emphasis in the New Testament (Rom. 5:5, 8; 8:39; 2 Cor. 13:11; Eph. 2:4–5; 2 Thess. 2:16; Titus 3:4; Jude 21), especially in this epistle (2:5; 3:1; 4:7–21) and elsewhere in John's writings (John 3:16; 5:42; 11:5, 36; 13:1–2; 14:21, 23; 15:9–10, 12; 16:27; 17:23–24; 19:26; cf. 2 John 3, 6). Yet because God loves perfectly, He also hates perfectly. As the Holy One (cf. 2 Kings 19:22; Ps. 71:22; Prov. 30:3; Isa. 1:4; 40:25), He loves all that is righteous, holy, and in line with His will and glorious purpose (cf. Ex. 15:11; 1 Sam. 2:2; Pss. 22:3; 47:8; 99:3, 5; 145:17; Isa. 6:3; 57:15; Rev. 4:8; 15:4). What this means, of course, is that He simultaneously hates whatever threatens or opposes those things (Deut. 29:20, 27–28; 32:19–22; Pss. 2:2–5; 7:11; 21:8–9; Nah. 1:2–3; Zeph. 1:14–18; Rom. 1:18; Col. 3:6; Rev. 11:18; cf. Matt. 13:41; 25:41; 1 Cor. 6:9–10; 2 Thess. 1:8; Rev. 21:27).

The absolutely perfect love of God likewise demands that those who love Him share His hatred of all that is opposed to Him. The psalmist exhorted, "Hate evil, you who love the Lord" (97:10; cf. Prov. 8:13); and, "From Your precepts I get understanding; therefore I hate every false way" (119:104; cf. vv. 128, 163; 139:21–22). Solomon outlined more specifically some of those false and evil ways:

> There are six things which the Lord hates, yes, seven which are an abomination to Him: haughty eyes, a lying tongue, and hands that shed innocent blood, a heart that devises wicked plans, feet that run rapidly to evil, a false witness who utters lies, and one who spreads strife among brothers. (Prov. 6:16–19; cf. Amos 5:21; Mal. 2:16; Rev. 2:6)

God hates all those things because they are utterly inconsistent with His holy nature and glory.

This short but familiar passage in John's first letter describes a major object of God's hatred—the world and those who love it. In the midst of John's series of doctrinal and moral tests regarding the assurance of salvation (4:13), the apostle inserted a command not to love the world. His admonition, which is part of the moral test, divides into two main elements: the command not to love the world, and reasons believers are not to love the world.

THE COMMAND NOT TO LOVE THE WORLD

Do not love the world nor the things in the world. (2:15*a*)

By examining its use in a particular biblical context, and properly comparing Scripture with Scripture, one can understand the various meanings of the term **world.** In this verse it is clear what John is *not* referring to. First, he is not speaking of the physical world, or the created order. John would not have commanded his readers to hate something that God in Genesis 1:31 pronounced was originally "very good." Even though creation is marred by the fall (cf. Genesis 3), nature's physical beauties still reflect God's glory and demand praise. The psalmist expressed this principle eloquently:

> The heavens are telling of the glory of God; and their expanse is declaring the work of His hands. Day to day pours forth speech, and night to night reveals knowledge. There is no speech, nor are there words; their voice is not heard. Their line has gone out through all the earth, and their utterances to the end of the world. In them He has placed a tent for the sun, which is as a bridegroom coming out of his chamber; it rejoices as a strong man to run his course. Its rising is from one end of the heavens, and its circuit to the other end of them; and there is nothing hidden from its heat. (Ps. 19:1–6; cf. 104:1–32; Acts 14:15–17; 17:23–28; Rom. 1:20)

Second, John would not have commanded believers to hate the **world** of humanity. That is because God loves people in the world and sent His Son to be the propitiation for their sin (see 2:2; 4:9–10, 14; cf. John 3:16; 2 Cor. 5:19; 1 Tim. 2:3–6; Titus 2:11–14; 3:4–5).

The world and its **things,** which John warned his readers **not** to **love,** is the invisible, spiritual system of evil. It is the *kosmos* ("world order," "realm of existence," "way of life") governed by Satan; as Paul reminded the Ephesians, "You formerly walked according to the course of this world, according to the prince of the power of the air, of the spirit that is now working in the sons of disobedience" (Eph. 2:2). Later in this letter John wrote: "the whole world lies in the power of the evil one" (5:19; cf. 4:1–5; John 12:31). The "world" here refers to the same evil system that Jesus referred to when He said, "If the world hates you, you know that it has hated Me before it hated you" (John 15:18; cf. 17:14). So, it was not humanity in general or the created order that hated Christ, but rather the wicked, corrupt (2 Peter 2:19), demonic ideologies and enterprises that stimulate fallen humanity (cf. Matt. 13:19, 38; 2 Cor. 2:11; 4:4; 11:14; 1 Thess. 2:18; 2 Thess. 2:9; Rev. 16:14). In keeping with this understanding, the apostle Paul correctly viewed the world as engaged in a massive spiritual war against the kingdom of God:

> For though we walk in the flesh, we do not war according to the flesh, for the weapons of our warfare are not of the flesh, but divinely powerful for the destruction of fortresses. We are destroying speculations and every lofty thing raised up against the knowledge of God, and we are taking every thought captive to the obedience of Christ. (2 Cor. 10:3–5; cf. Eph. 6:11–13)

"Speculations" means ideologies or belief systems, ranging from primitive, animistic systems to sophisticated, complex world religions, philosophies, political theories, or any unbiblical worldviews. They represent all unbelieving ideas and dogmas that, often from an elitist standpoint, rise up against the true knowledge of God. In response, believers are commanded to confront and destroy the world's spiritual lies and false speculations with the truth. Paul thus identifies the world as the full spectrum of beliefs and inclinations that oppose the things of God, and John implicitly echoes that definition. When a person becomes a Christian, he or she is no longer a slave to the world system. Christians have been "rescued . . . from the domain of darkness, and transferred . . . to the kingdom of His beloved Son" (Col. 1:13; cf. 2 Cor. 6:17–18; Eph. 5:6–12).

REASONS BELIEVERS ARE NOT TO LOVE THE WORLD

If anyone loves the world, the love of the Father is not in him. For all that is in the world, the lust of the flesh and the lust of the eyes and the boastful pride of life, is not from the Father, but is from the world. The world is passing away, and also its lusts; but the one who does the will of God lives forever. (2:15b–17)

The kingdom of the world and the kingdom of God are inherently incompatible (cf. 4:5–6; 5:4–5; John 15:19; Gal. 6:14). The two are mutually exclusive and opposed to one another. They are antithetical, and cannot peacefully coexist. True Christians therefore will not be characterized by a habitual love for the world, nor will worldly people demonstrate a genuine affection for the gospel and its Lord (John 3:20; Acts 7:51; 13:8–10; 17:5, 13; Rom. 8:7; Col. 1:21; 1 Thess. 2:14–16).

Clearly, there is an unmistakable line of demarcation between the things of God and the things of the world. The ongoing moral and ethical deterioration of contemporary culture makes this obvious. Even brief consideration provides a lengthy list of cultural agendas that are aggressively hostile to biblical Christianity: an attack on the traditional family by feminism; an active promotion of sexual promiscuity and homosexuality; an increasing acceptance of violence; an emphasis on materialism and hedonism by the secular media; a steady decline in standards of personal integrity and business ethics; an undermining of right and wrong by postmodern relativism; and so on.

In order to support his admonition, John does not offer a long list of specifics or detailed illustrations. Instead, he presents three general reasons believers must not love the world: because of who they are, because of what the world does, and because of where the world is going.

BECAUSE OF WHO BELIEVERS ARE

If anyone loves the world, the love of the Father is not in him. (2:15b)

Because believers are forgiven (Pss. 86:5; 130:3–4; Isa. 1:18; Matt. 26:28; Luke 1:77; Eph. 1:7; 4:32; Col. 1:14; 2:13–14; 3:13; 1 John 2:12), have a true knowledge of God (2 Cor. 2:14; 4:6; Eph. 4:13; Col. 1:9–10), have the Word of God abiding in them (Ps. 119:11; Col. 3:16), have overcome Satan (James 4:7; 1 John 4:4), and have an increasingly intimate relationship with the Father (1 John 2:12–14), they cannot love the world. **Anyone** who **loves the world** demonstrates that **the love of the Father is not in him.** Like Demas, such spiritual defectors manifest that any previous claim to know and love God was nothing but a lie (2:19).

Nonetheless, the basic identity of believers as God's children does not make them immune to the world's allure. Because they are still fallen sinners—though saved by grace—true followers of Christ are tempted through their remaining flesh by the world's behaviors and enterprises (Matt. 26:41; 1 Cor. 10:13; Gal. 6:1; Eph. 6:16; James 1:12–14; 1 Peter 5:8–9).

Whether the temptation comes from worldly priorities, worldly amusements, worldly riches, or worldly lusts, believers desire to resist the world's effort to seduce them. As Jesus warned His listeners, "No servant can serve two masters; for either he will hate the one and love the other, or else he will be devoted to one and despise the other. You cannot serve God and wealth" (Luke 16:13; cf. Matt. 6:19–21, 24).

BECAUSE OF WHAT THE WORLD DOES

For all that is in the world, the lust of the flesh and the lust of the eyes and the boastful pride of life, is not from the Father, but is from the world. (2:16)

The meaning of **all that is in the world** and **is from the world** appears in the three qualifying descriptions of sin's categories. Sin is the dominant reality in the world, and launching from this verse it is helpful to look more extensively at sin, by definition called "lawlessness" (1 John 3:4)—any violation of God's perfect and holy law. Whereas the law of God encompasses all that is righteous (Pss. 19:7; 119:142; Isa. 42:21; cf. Josh. 1:7–8; Ps. 119:18; Neh. 8:9, 18; Isa. 51:4; Matt. 22:36–40; Acts 28:23; Rom. 3:21; James 1:25), sin encompasses all that is unrighteous (Prov. 24:9; Matt. 15:19; 1 John 5:17; cf. Gen. 6:5).

Although it manifests itself in external actions, the roots of sin go much deeper, embedded in the very fabric of the depraved human heart. Sin permeates the fallen mind, internally defiling the sinner in every aspect of his being (cf. Matt. 15:18–20). Thus, the Old Testament likens sin to a deadly plague (1 Kings 8:38, NKJV) or filthy garments (Zech. 3:3–4; cf. Isa. 64:6). Sin is so foul that God hates it (Prov. 15:9) and sinners hate themselves (Ezek. 6:9) because of their inherent wickedness.

Sin is by nature both rebellious and ungrateful—so much so that if possible it would dethrone God in favor of sinners (cf. Ps. 12:4; Jer. 2:31; 44:17). Its attitude is that of Absalom, who when forgiven by his father, King David, nevertheless immediately plotted to overthrow him (2 Sam. 14:33–15:12). Romans 1:21*a* says of the ungodly, "Even though they knew God, they did not honor Him as God *or give thanks*" (emphasis added; cf. 2 Tim. 3:2).

Sin is also humanly incurable. Sinners have no capacity in and of themselves to remedy their sin (Rom. 8:7–8; 1 Cor. 2:14; Eph. 2:1). The prophet Isaiah described Israel's incurably sinful condition:

> Alas, sinful nation, people weighed down with iniquity, offspring of evildoers, sons who act corruptly! They have abandoned the Lord, they have despised the Holy One of Israel, they have turned away from Him.

Where will you be stricken again, as you continue in your rebellion? The whole head is sick and the whole heart is faint. From the sole of the foot even to the head there is nothing sound in it, only bruises, welts and raw wounds, not pressed out or bandaged, nor softened with oil. (Isa. 1:4–6)

Sin is like a terminal illness, or hereditary condition, about which sinners can do nothing in their own strength. God demanded of Israel, "Can the Ethiopian change his skin or the leopard his spots? Then you also can do good who are accustomed to doing evil" (Jer. 13:23; cf. Job 14:4; Matt. 7:16–18).

Finally, sin is universal. David wrote, "They have all turned aside, together they have become corrupt; there is no one who does good, not even one" (Ps. 14:3; cf. Isa. 53:1–3; Eccl. 7:20; Rom. 3:10–12; 5:12). Thus all people, left to their own devices, choose to sin:

This is the judgment, that the Light has come into the world, and men loved the darkness rather than the Light, for their deeds were evil. For everyone who does evil hates the Light, and does not come to the Light for fear that his deeds will be exposed. (John 3:19–20; cf. Ps. 7:14; Prov. 4:16; Isa. 5:18; Jer. 9:5)

It is because people are sinful that evil overpowers fallen mankind (cf. Gen. 6:5; John 8:34; Rom. 6:20a), such that all that unregenerate people can think about and do are sinful things, because sin so utterly dominates their minds, wills, and affections. It is because of sin that they are under Satan's control, as slaves to the prince of darkness (cf. Eph. 2:2). It is because of sin that the unredeemed remain under the wrath of God, destined for eternal hell unless they repent (Ps. 9:17; Matt. 3:7, 10, 12; 7:13; 13:40–42; 25:41, 46; Luke 13:3; John 3:36; Rom. 1:18; 2:5; Col. 3:6; Rev. 6:17; 19:15; 20:11–15). And it is because of sin that people are subject to all the miseries of this life. As Eliphaz the Temanite, one of Job's friends, remarked, "Man is born for trouble" (Job 5:7a). And Solomon reminded his readers of the emptiness and meaninglessness that sin causes, "I have seen all the works which have been done under the sun, and behold, all is vanity and striving after wind" (Eccl. 1:14; cf. vv. 2, 8; Isa. 48:22; Rom. 8:20).

It is also crucial to rightly understand the nature of sin's origin in human behavior. While it is true that temptation comes from Satan's system (cf. Eph. 6:12; 1 Peter 5:8–9) through the world, sinful behavior cannot ultimately be blamed on external influences. The sinner himself is responsible for his sinful actions, which spring from his own wicked desires (James 1:13–16). Sin, then, abides in all human hearts, as Jesus clearly taught:

After He called the crowd to Him again, He began saying to them, "Listen to Me, all of you, and understand: there is nothing outside the man which can defile him if it goes into him; but the things which proceed out of the man are what defile the man. If anyone has ears to hear, let him hear." When he had left the crowd and entered the house, His disciples questioned Him about the parable. And He said to them, "Are you so lacking in understanding also? Do you not understand that whatever goes into the man from outside cannot defile him, because it does not go into his heart, but into his stomach, and is eliminated?" (Thus He declared all foods clean.) And He was saying, "That which proceeds out of the man, that is what defiles the man. For from within, out of the heart of men, proceed the evil thoughts, fornications, thefts, murders, adulteries, deeds of coveting and wickedness, as well as deceit, sensuality, envy, slander, pride and foolishness. All these evil things proceed from within and defile the man." (Mark 7:14–23; cf. Gen. 6:5; Jer. 17:9; James 1:13–15)

The Lord's words illustrate the doctrine of original sin; all sin stems from mankind's fallen nature, and that nature derives from Adam and Eve's initial disobedience (Genesis 3; cf. Pss. 51:5; 58:3; Eph. 2:3; 4:17–19; Col. 2:13*a*). Since then, it has been an integral part of everyone who has lived (Rom. 5:12–21).

Understanding the serious danger sin poses, the apostle John summarized the avenues the world uses to incite sin: **the lust of the flesh, the lust of the eyes,** and **the boastful pride of life.** Though briefly stated, those three designations are of profound importance.

The lust of the flesh refers to the debased, ignoble cravings of evil hearts. **The flesh** denotes humanness and its sinful essence. The word translated **lust** (*epithumia*) is a common New Testament term denoting both positive and negative desires (Luke 22:15; Rom. 1:24; Phil. 1:23; Col. 3:5; 1 Thess. 2:17; 2 Tim. 2:22; Titus 3:3; James 1:14–15; 2 Peter 1:4; cf. Matt. 5:28; Gal. 5:17; Heb. 6:11; James 4:2). Here it refers negatively to the sensual impulses from the world that draw people toward transgressions. The expression **lust of the flesh** brings to mind primarily sexual sins, but, while they are included in its definition, the phrase is certainly not limited to that meaning.

The base desire of the human heart perverts and distorts all normal desires (Jer. 17:9), sending them into a relentless, slavish pursuit of evil that exceeds the proper limits of what is good, reasonable, and righteous —any attitude, speech, or action that opposes God's law (cf. Rom. 7:5; 8:7). Those lusts include all the immoral excesses about which Paul warned the Galatians:

> Now the deeds of the flesh are evident, which are: immorality, impurity, sensuality, idolatry, sorcery, enmities, strife, jealousy, outbursts of anger, disputes, dissensions, factions, envying, drunkenness, carousing, and things like these, of which I forewarn you, just as I have forewarned you, that those who practice such things will not inherit the kingdom of God. (Gal. 5:19–21; cf. Rom. 1:24–32; 1 Cor. 6:9–10)

Those sinful attitudes and actions are primary characteristics of the world system and are irresistibly appealing to the corruption of the unconverted soul.

The world also entices sinners to thoughts and actions contrary to God's will through **the lust of the eyes.** Eyes are gifts from God (cf. Prov. 20:12; Eccl. 11:7) that enable people to see His beautiful creation and excellent works (cf. Pss. 8:3–4; 19:1; 33:5; 104:24; Isa. 40:26; Rom. 1:20). However, as they let in light, so they are open windows for temptation to enter; thus sin perverts the use of the eyes (cf. Prov. 27:20; Eccl. 1:8; 4:8) and plunges people into dissatisfaction, covetousness, and idolatry (cf. Pss. 106:19–20; 115:4; Eccl. 5:10). Lot's wife misused her eyes, and God killed her as a result (Gen. 19:17, 26). Achan plundered the forbidden goods he saw, which also led to his death (Josh. 7:18–26; 22:20). From his rooftop David saw Bathsheba bathing, subsequently committed adultery with her, and paid severely for his sin the remainder of his life (2 Sam. 11:1–5; 12:1–20; Ps. 51:1–17). Because of such potential consequences, it is imperative for believers to guard their eyes (cf. Job 31:1; Ps. 101:3; 119:37). Jesus' graphic hyperbole underscores the necessity of avoiding the lust of the eyes.

> "You have heard that it was said, 'You shall not commit adultery'; but I say to you that everyone who looks at a woman with lust for her has already committed adultery with her in his heart. If your right eye makes you stumble, tear it out and throw it from you; for it is better for you to lose one of the parts of your body, than for your whole body to be thrown into hell." (Matt. 5:27–29)

The third human element that provides an avenue into the soul for temptation is **the boastful pride of life.** Such **pride** is the arrogance (cf. 1 Sam. 2:3; 17:4–10, 41–45; Pss. 10:3; 75:4; Prov. 25:14; Jer. 9:23; Rom. 1:30; James 3:5; 4:16) that arguably motivates all other sin, including the lust of the flesh and eyes, as it seeks to elevate self above everyone else (cf. Ps. 10:2, 4; Prov. 26:12; Dan. 5:20; Luke 18:11–12; Rom. 12:3, 16). Pride is the corruption of the noblest parts of man's essence (cf. Ps. 10:2–6, 11; Prov. 16:18–19), his rationality and spirit that were created for him by God (Gen. 1:26–27). Instead of accepting that reality with appropriate humility and gratitude to God, sinners exalt themselves and seek fulfillment in things that glorify the creature rather than the Creator (Rom. 1:22–25).

In **the flesh** (sensuality), humanity functions according to the base desires of animals (cf. Ex. 32:1–9, 19–20, 25). With **the eyes** (covetousness), individuals seek to have more than others (cf. Luke 12:16–21). Through **pride,** humanity defies God and arrogantly attempts to dethrone the Sovereign of the universe (cf. Gen. 11:2–4). That threefold matrix of temptation, however, is more than a theological abstraction. Two of the most foundational and pivotal passages in Scripture, Genesis 3:1–7 and Luke 4:1–13, support concretely and historically how Satan has attacked via those avenues.

> Now the serpent was more crafty than any beast of the field which the Lord God had made. And he said to the woman, "Indeed, has God said, 'You shall not eat from any tree of the garden'?" The woman said to the serpent, "From the fruit of the trees of the garden we may eat; but from the fruit of the tree which is in the middle of the garden, God has said, 'You shall not eat from it or touch it, or you will die.'" The serpent said to the woman, "You surely will not die! For God knows that in the day you eat from it your eyes will be opened, and you will be like God, knowing good and evil." When the woman saw that the tree was good for food, and that it was a delight to the eyes, and that the tree was desirable to make one wise, she took from its fruit and ate; and she gave also to her husband with her, and he ate. Then the eyes of both of them were opened, and they knew that they were naked; and they sewed fig leaves together and made themselves loin coverings. (Gen. 3:1–7)

> Jesus, full of the Holy Spirit, returned from the Jordan and was led around by the Spirit in the wilderness for forty days, being tempted by the devil. And He ate nothing during those days, and when they had ended, He became hungry. And the devil said to Him, "If You are the Son of God, tell this stone to become bread." And Jesus answered him, "It is written, 'Man shall not live on bread alone.'" And he led Him up and showed Him all the kingdoms of the world in a moment of time. And the devil said to Him, "I will give You all this domain and its glory; for it has been handed over to me, and I give it to whomever I wish. Therefore if You worship before me, it shall all be Yours." Jesus answered him, "It is written, 'You shall worship the Lord your God and serve Him only.'" And he led Him to Jerusalem and had Him stand on the pinnacle of the temple, and said to Him, "If You are the Son of God, throw Yourself down from here; for it is written, 'He will command His angels concerning You to guard You,' and, 'on their hands they will bear You up, so that You will not strike Your foot against a stone.'" And Jesus answered and said to him, "It is said, 'You shall not put the Lord your God to the test.'" When the devil had finished every temptation, he left Him until an opportune time. (Luke 4:1–13)

In both cases Satan utilized the same threefold temptation to attack his target. Adam and Eve succumbed in Genesis 3:6, plunging the human race into sin: "When the woman saw that the tree was good for food, and that it was a delight to the eyes, and that the tree was desirable to make one wise, she took from its fruit and ate; and she gave also to her husband with her, and he ate." The devil appealed to Eve's desire for food (**lust of the flesh**), her desire to have something attractive (**lust of the eyes**), and her desire to have wisdom (**pride of life**). Adam accepted the same enticements without protest and ate the fruit his wife gave him, and Satan's kingdom gained its initial foothold on earth.

In the second account, Satan used a similar approach as he sought to derail Jesus' redemptive mission (cf. Matt. 16:21–23; John 13:21–30). He appealed to the Lord's humanity (His hunger for bread), His eyes (His appreciation of the world's splendor), and His perceived pride (His jumping from the temple's pinnacle would have presumed on God's protection and gained extra prestige when He landed safely). But all three of the Devil's sinister approaches were unsuccessful as the Lord refuted each appeal by quoting Old Testament truth (Deut. 8:3; 6:13, 16; cf. 10:20).

It is not surprising, then, to see that the world, under Satan's leadership, continues to assault sinners through those same three pathways of temptation. The Devil plays on the corruptibility of the fallen human heart to achieve the maximum impact for evil and chaos in the world. But believers are not slaves to the diabolical, corrupt world system (Rom. 6:5–14; James 4:7; 1 Peter 5:8–9; 1 John 4:1–6). Like their Lord who has redeemed them, they possess the ability to successfully resist the temptations of this world (cf. Rom. 8:1–13; James 4:7).

BECAUSE OF WHERE THE WORLD IS GOING

The world is passing away, and also its lusts; but the one who does the will of God lives forever. (2:17)

The third reason believers are not to love **the world** is because it **is passing away.** The principle of spiritual death that permeates the world is the exact opposite of the principle of spiritual life, which operates in God's kingdom. Thus, the living dead in the world are destined for eternal death in hell, but Christians are destined for eternal life in heaven (Matt. 13:37–50; 25:31–46; cf. Matt. 5:12a; Luke 10:20; Heb. 12:22–23; 1 Peter 1:3–5).

The verb translated **is passing away** is a present tense form of *paragō* ("to disappear"). The present tense indicates that the world is already in the process of self-destruction (1 Cor. 7:31b; 1 Peter 4:7a; cf. James

1:10; 4:14; 1 Peter 1:24). The entire system contains the seeds of its own dissolution (cf. Rom. 8:20–21). (God will destroy the physical universe at the end of the millennium and just prior to the second coming of Jesus Christ [2 Peter 3:10], but that is not what John had in view here.) John looked ahead to the destruction of the satanic world system and all those who cling to its **lusts**—its ideologies that oppose God and Christ (2 Cor. 10:3–5; 2 Peter 2:1–17; Jude 12–15; Rev. 18:21–24; cf. 19:11–21; 20:7–10). They are all hurtling rapidly toward eternal damnation, as Paul wrote concerning the ungodly who persecuted the Thessalonian believers:

> For after all it is only just for God to repay with affliction those who afflict you, and to give relief to you who are afflicted and to us as well when the Lord Jesus will be revealed from heaven with His mighty angels in flaming fire, dealing out retribution to those who do not know God and to those who do not obey the gospel of our Lord Jesus. These will pay the penalty of eternal destruction, away from the presence of the Lord and from the glory of His power, when He comes to be glorified in His saints on that day, and to be marveled at among all who have believed—for our testimony to you was believed. (2 Thess. 1:6–10)

Paul did not say that those unrepentant members of the world would cease to exist (that would be the unbiblical doctrine of annihilationism), but that they would undergo an everlasting punishment in hell (cf. Matt. 25:46; Mark 9:43–49; Rev. 20:15). The world's process of self-destruction will only accelerate and grow worse in the coming years (cf. 2 Tim. 3:13) until the Lord returns.

On the other hand, the **one who does the will of God,** who savingly trusts and obeys Christ, has nothing to fear concerning the world's destruction (1 Thess. 1:10; 5:9). It is God's will that people believe the gospel, repent of their sin, and embrace Jesus Christ as Lord and Savior (Mark 1:15; John 6:29; 1 Tim. 2:4–6). John earlier had heard these words of Jesus: "For this is the will of My Father, that everyone who beholds the Son and believes in Him will have eternal life" (John 6:40*a*). Each person who has obeyed that teaching is a Christian and **lives forever** (Luke 6:46–48; John 8:51; 10:27; 14:21; 15:10; James 1:22–25; 1 John 2:5; 3:24; cf. Pss. 25:10; 111:10).

The apostle Paul is a sterling example of one who learned what it means to love the things of God rather than the things of the world. In Philippians 3:3–11 he recounts his transformation:

> For we are the true circumcision, who worship in the Spirit of God and glory in Christ Jesus and put no confidence in the flesh, although I myself might have confidence even in the flesh. If anyone else has a mind to put confidence in the flesh, I far more: circumcised the eighth

day, of the nation of Israel, of the tribe of Benjamin, a Hebrew of Hebrews; as to the Law, a Pharisee; as to zeal, a persecutor of the church; as to the righteousness which is in the Law, found blameless. But whatever things were gain to me, those things I have counted as loss for the sake of Christ. More than that, I count all things to be loss in view of the surpassing value of knowing Christ Jesus my Lord, for whom I have suffered the loss of all things, and count them but rubbish so that I may gain Christ, and may be found in Him, not having a righteousness of my own derived from the Law, but that which is through faith in Christ, the righteousness which comes from God on the basis of faith, that I may know Him and the power of His resurrection and the fellowship of His sufferings, being conformed to His death; in order that I may attain to the resurrection from the dead. (cf. Acts 9:1–22; 26:4–23)

Like Paul, believers must persevere in sanctification and righteousness by "forgetting what lies behind and reaching forward to what lies ahead . . . toward the goal for the prize of the upward call of God in Christ Jesus" (Phil. 3:13b–14). By doing this they will demonstrate that they love what God loves and hate what He hates. They will clearly no longer be devoted to the unbelieving world system and will shun its continuous appeal to sin, which comes through **the lust of the flesh and the lust of the eyes and the boastful pride of life.**

Antichrists and Christians (1 John 2:18–27)

9

Children, it is the last hour; and just as you heard that antichrist is coming, even now many antichrists have appeared; from this we know that it is the last hour. They went out from us, but they were not really of us; for if they had been of us, they would have remained with us; but they went out, so that it would be shown that they all are not of us. But you have an anointing from the Holy One, and you all know. I have not written to you because you do not know the truth, but because you do know it, and because no lie is of the truth. Who is the liar but the one who denies that Jesus is the Christ? This is the antichrist, the one who denies the Father and the Son. Whoever denies the Son does not have the Father; the one who confesses the Son has the Father also. As for you, let that abide in you which you heard from the beginning. If what you heard from the beginning abides in you, you also will abide in the Son and in the Father. This is the promise which He Himself made to us: eternal life. These things I have written to you concerning those who are trying to deceive you. As for you, the anointing which you received from Him abides in you, and you have no need for anyone to teach you; but

as His anointing teaches you about all things, and is true and is not a lie, and just as it has taught you, you abide in Him. (2:18–27)

Ever since the moment Satan and his demonic forces rebelled against heaven, there has been a supernatural, God-opposing, evil power throughout the universe ("the world" of 2:15–17). From its earliest chapters, the Bible shows that the Evil One (cf. 2:13, 14) and all who function in his kingdom (Eph. 2:2–3; Col. 1:13) have constantly opposed God's plan (e.g., the fall [Gen. 3]; the flood [Gen. 6:1–13]; the tower of Babel [Gen. 11:1–9]; Satan's affliction of Job [Job 1:6–2:7]). As the original architect of the anti-God agenda, the Devil has always been the prime example of the antichrist spirit and the energizer of the innumerable antichrists who have followed his lead.

Though the term *antichrist* occurs only in John's letters, the concept it expresses appears repeatedly throughout Scripture (cf. Dan. 7:7f.; 9:26–27; 11:36–39; Matt. 24:15; Mark 13:6; 2 Thess. 2:3, 8; Rev. 11:7; 13:1–10, 18; 17:1–18). It is a compound word that transliterates the Greek word *antichristos,* from *christos* ("Christ") and *anti* ("against," or "in the place of"). The term denotes anyone who opposes Christ, seeks to supplant Him (Matt. 24:24; Mark 13:21–22), or falsely represents Him. Such opposition always offers distorted and aberrant views about the nature of Christ (cf. 2 John 7); for example, reflected in John's definitive statement that "every spirit that does not confess Jesus is not from God; this is the spirit of the antichrist" (1 John 4:3*a*).

Scripture clearly teaches that during the future seven-year tribulation period (Mark 13:19), one man will emerge as the ultimate Antichrist. Through the centuries, there has been much study and speculation, by both scholars and lay persons, concerning who this final Antichrist will be. People have proposed numerous historical figures, including Nero and other Roman emperors, Muhammad, various popes, Napoleon Bonaparte, Benito Mussolini, and Adolf Hitler. Such ill-advised speculation has always proved futile. When the apostle John wrote this letter, he said many antichrists had already arisen in the brief sixty years since Pentecost, and countless more have plagued the church until now.

In this passage, John reiterates his earlier doctrinal tests (the proper assessment of man's sinfulness and the correct evaluation of Christ's nature as the God-man) and moral tests (love for Christ and others, and obedience to the Word). The purpose of these tests, as stated by John in 5:13, was to help his readers assess their true standing before God—whether or not they were saved. The apostle understood that a wrong view of Christ, if not repented of and corrected, would lead to eternal damnation (cf. John 8:24). Such terrifying consequences make the issue black and white, which is why John presented it with such directness: false professors of the faith deny the truth about Christ, revealing themselves to be antichrists; true professors, on the other hand, affirm —along with the other marks—the truth about Christ, revealing themselves to be genuine children of God.

THE CHARACTERISTICS OF ANTICHRISTS

Children, it is the last hour; and just as you heard that antichrist is coming, even now many antichrists have appeared; from this we know that it is the last hour. They went out from us, but they were not really of us; for if they had been of us, they would have remained with us; but they went out, so that it would be shown that they all are not of us. . . . Who is the liar but the one who denies that Jesus is the Christ? This is the antichrist, the one who denies the Father and the Son. Whoever denies the Son does not have the Father; the one who confesses the Son has the Father also. . . . These things I have written to you concerning those who are trying to deceive you. (2:18–19, 22–23, 26)

The combination of deceptive hypocrisy and demonic heresies made the antichrist teachers doubly dangerous as they intentionally tried to creep into the church unnoticed, before hatching their destructive schemes (cf. Jude 4). In order to warn his readers, John began this section with a brief introduction of the antichrists followed by a description of their characteristics.

THE INTRODUCTION OF ANTICHRISTS

Children, it is the last hour; and just as you heard that antichrist is coming, even now many antichrists have appeared; from this we know that it is the last hour. (2:18)

Again John addressed his readers as **children** (*paidia;* cf. 2:13), identifying them as those who belonged to the family of God, and those whom their Father desired to warn that there was impending danger. It is essential that Christians, especially those who are less spiritually mature and hence most vulnerable, understand the serious threat that antichrists pose.

Further underscoring the urgency of the subject, John reminded his readers that **it is the last hour.** The phrase literally reads, "last hour it is," the word order making it an emphatic expression. **The last hour** refers to the present evil age, one of only two ages—along with the age to come—that the New Testament outlines (cf. Matt. 12:32; Mark 10:30; Eph. 1:21; Heb. 6:5). **The last hour** began at the first coming of Jesus Christ (cf. 1 Cor. 10:11; Gal. 4:4; Heb. 1:1–2; 9:26; 1 Peter 1:20), and will end when He returns. (The age to come encompasses all of the future, including the millennial kingdom, the thousand-year earthly reign of Christ when righteousness will prevail in the world [Isa. 9:6–7; 11:2, 6–9; 30:23–26; 35:2–6; 45:22–24; 65:18–23; 66:13; Ezek. 34:25; 47:12; Joel 2:28–32; Amos 9:13; Zech. 14:16–21; 1 Cor. 15:24–28; Rev. 20:4; cf. 2 Sam. 7:16; Matt. 19:28; Rev. 3:21; 5:10].)

Christ's arrival aroused Satan's opposition to an intensity not seen before or since, resulting in the rise of **many antichrists.** After three years of relentless hostility toward Him (cf. Acts 4:26–28), His enemies finally had Him nailed to the cross. That same malignant antichrist spirit has continued to flourish to this day (1 John 4:3).

This verse is the first New Testament use of the term *antichrist,* yet it is certainly not the first biblical introduction to the concept. As John himself pointed out, his readers had already heard **that antichrist is coming.** Since they knew about the coming of the Christ from the Old Testament prophecies, some may have known about antichrist from the same sources. The prophet Daniel foresaw a human leader, satanically energized, who will come to Jerusalem, enforce his will, exalt himself above all other people and gods, and wreak havoc and slaughter (Dan. 7–8; 9:26–27; 11). The final **Antichrist** will be an imposing, intimidating figure of superior intellect and oratorical skills, possessing advanced military and economic expertise, who becomes the leader of the world. He will be so convincing as an ally and deliverer that Israel will sign a pact with him to be her protector. Then he will turn against the nation and will occupy the throne in the sanctuary of the rebuilt temple, which for Israel will still symbolize the presence of God, and blasphemously present himself to the world as if he were God. (For additional details of Antichrist's actions, see Revelation 13, 17 and my commentary on those passages in *Revelation 12–22,* The MacArthur New Testament Commentary [Chicago: Moody, 2000], 35–65, 155–72; see also Rev. 6:2; 16:13; 19:20.)

The prophet Zechariah also foresaw the future Antichrist:

"For behold, I [God] am going to raise up a shepherd in the land who will not care for the perishing, seek the scattered, heal the broken, or sustain the one standing, but will devour the flesh of the fat sheep and tear off their hoofs. Woe to the worthless shepherd who leaves the flock! A sword will be on his arm and on his right eye! His arm will be totally withered and his right eye will be blind." (Zech. 11:16–17)

At the end of the age God will permit an evil shepherd (Antichrist) to arise, who will be the antithesis of the Good Shepherd. This man will be a false shepherd who does not love sheep but slaughters them to fill his insatiable hunger. Zechariah portrays him as a son of destruction devoted to violence and devastation. Though his arm represents his great strength and his eye his intelligence, he is doomed. God will destroy that Antichrist when His sword of vengeance falls on him.

John's readers surely would also have known about Jesus' Olivet Discourse, in which He made reference to the same Antichrist-related events as those already prophesied in the Old Testament:

> Therefore when you see the abomination of desolation which was spoken of through Daniel the prophet, standing in the holy place (let the reader understand), then those who are in Judea must flee to the mountains. Whoever is on the housetop must not go down to get the things out that are in his house. Whoever is in the field must not turn back to get his cloak. But woe to those who are pregnant and to those who are nursing babies in those days! But pray that your flight will not be in the winter, or on a Sabbath. For then there will be a great tribulation, such as has not occurred since the beginning of the world until now, nor ever will. Unless those days had been cut short, no life would have been saved; but for the sake of the elect those days will be cut short. Then if anyone says to you, "Behold, here is the Christ," or "There He is," do not believe him. For false Christs and false prophets will arise and will show great signs and wonders, so as to mislead, if possible, even the elect. Behold, I have told you in advance. (Matt. 24:15–25)

The recipients of John's letter most likely also would have been familiar with Paul's words, written four decades earlier, that clearly predicted the coming Antichrist. He instructed the Thessalonian believers as follows:

> Now we request you, brethren, with regard to the coming of our Lord Jesus Christ and our gathering together to Him, that you not be quickly shaken from your composure or be disturbed either by a spirit or a message or a letter as if from us, to the effect that the day of the Lord has come. Let no one in any way deceive you, for it will not come unless the apostasy comes first, and the man of lawlessness is revealed, the son of destruction, who opposes and exalts himself above every so-called god or object of worship, so that he takes his seat in the temple of God, displaying himself as being God. Do you not remember that while I was still with you, I was telling you these things? And you know what restrains him now, so that in his time he will be revealed. For the mystery of lawlessness is already at work; only he who now restrains will do so until he is taken out of the way. Then that lawless one will be revealed whom the Lord will slay with the breath of His mouth and bring to an end by the appearance of His coming; that is, the one whose coming is in accord with the activity of Satan, with all power

and signs and false wonders, and with all the deception of wickedness for those who perish, because they did not receive the love of the truth so as to be saved. For this reason God will send upon them a deluding influence so that they will believe what is false, in order that they all may be judged who did not believe the truth, but took pleasure in wickedness. (2 Thess. 2:1–12)

Paul declared that those climactic events would not occur until "the apostasy comes first." "Apostasy" is the transliteration of *apostasia* ("a falling away," "a forsaking," "a defection"). Theologically, it is the deliberate abandonment of a formerly professed position. But in this context the word denotes more than a mere general abandonment of God and Christ. Throughout redemptive history a certain general apostasy will always be occurring in the churches, in keeping with the ever-present Laodicean spirit (Rev. 3:14–16; cf. Heb. 10:25–31; 2 Peter 2:20–22). In fact, as time passes there will be an escalating defection from the truth:

> But the Spirit explicitly says that in later times some will fall away from the faith, paying attention to deceitful spirits and doctrines of demons, by means of the hypocrisy of liars seared in their own conscience as with a branding iron, men who forbid marriage and advocate abstaining from foods which God has created to be gratefully shared in by those who believe and know the truth. (1 Tim. 4:1–3; cf. Matt. 24:12; 2 Tim. 3:1–9; 2 Peter 2:1–3; Jude 4, 17–19)

However, Paul wrote to the Thessalonians about a unique, identifiable, historical *event—the* apostasy. Before the day of the Lord comes, there will be a climactic act of apostasy led by the man of lawlessness, or son of destruction. That man—the Antichrist—will openly defy God's rule and live without regard for His law (cf. 1 John 3:4). The only thing that "restrains him [the final Antichrist] now, so that in his time he will be revealed" (2 Thess. 2:6) is the Holy Spirit, whom God, in His perfect timing, will take out of the way. Thus Satan's man of sin and destruction cannot arrive apart from the divine timetable. (For a fuller discussion of 2 Thessalonians 2:1–12, see *1 & 2 Thessalonians,* The MacArthur New Testament Commentary [Chicago: Moody, 2002], 263–85.)

THE CHARACTERISTICS OF ANTICHRISTS

They went out from us, but they were not really of us; for if they had been of us, they would have remained with us; but they went out, so that it would be shown that they all are not of us. . . . Who is the liar but the one who denies that Jesus is the Christ? This is

the antichrist, the one who denies the Father and the Son. Whoever denies the Son does not have the Father; the one who confesses the Son has the Father also. . . . These things I have written to you concerning those who are trying to deceive you. (2:19, 22–23, 26)

Antichrists who infiltrate the church and mingle among true believers, attempting to destroy by spreading lies and deceptions, are clearly identifiable by three primary characteristics. First, they depart from the fellowship. They enter the church only to sabotage it through an often-sophisticated strategy of false teaching and lies. But eventually most depart, separating from true Christians, leaving a path of spiritual destruction in their wake, and inevitably taking some of the weak with them.

Some who remain are confused and left wondering if the false teachers and their "converts" took the real truth with them when they left. They might also find themselves asking why their professed brethren, if they had really been part of the true church, had so readily followed the antichrists. Such questions were apparently being asked by John's readers. And the apostle addressed all those doubts with the simple statement, **They went out from us, but they were not really of us.**

If those teachers and their adherents had possessed the true eternal life, John elaborated, **they would have remained with us.** God allowed—and still allows—liars, deceivers, and false teachers to come into the assembly of believers to purge it, **so that it would be shown that they all are not of** the fellowship. Those who defect give clear evidence of their true character and unregenerate condition. Thus, in His perfect plan, God uses false teachers to draw away false believers from the church, so they will not remain in the assembly as harmful and corrupting influences (cf. 1 Cor. 5:6; Gal. 5:9). He permits antichrists to do their sinister work in His own church for the ultimate good of His body (cf. Gen. 50:20). In a surprising way, He allowed a messenger from Satan to fracture the Corinthian church in order to wound the apostle Paul and produce in him greater humility, trust, and strength (2 Cor. 12:7–10). Of course, false teachers are fully responsible for their heinous actions, earning for themselves the severest eternal judgment (cf. Jude 13; 2 Peter 2:12). Nevertheless, in spite of their hatred for God, they serve His end to purify His people. Satan and all his demons, in the final analysis, serve the sovereign purposes of God.

Genuine believers need not fear some fatal influence from the activities of antichrists, because the children of God will always stay true to the faith and persevere to the end (John 10:27–30; Phil. 1:6; 1 Peter 1:5; Jude 24–25). Paul assured the Colossians that because they were reconciled to God they would not defect (Col. 1:21–23), and the writer of

Hebrews gave a similar assurance (Heb. 3:6, 14). On the other hand, those who oppose the truth or engage in apostasy (cf. Num. 16:1–35; 22–25; 1 Tim. 4:1–3; 2 Peter 2:1–9; Jude 10–13), or are not anchored in the truth (Matt. 7:26–27; Mark 4:17; Heb. 6:4–6), have no real salvation.

The second clearly recognizable characteristic of antichrists is that they deny the faith. Specifically in this context they fail John's Christological test. The spirit of antichrist is that of **the liar . . . who denies that Jesus is the Christ.** A right view of Jesus Christ—His person, work, and saving message—is an essential mark of genuine saving faith; no one can be saved who rejects the biblical revelation about Christ (John 8:24; cf. 1:12–13; 3:18, 36; Acts 4:12; Rom. 10:9–10; 1 Cor. 15:1–4). Nor is there hope for one who relies on some personal, speculative notion of who He is (cf. Matt. 16:13–14). Genuine salvation requires embracing Him as the anointed Messiah of God (John 1:43–49), affirming that He is the one and only God-man (1 Tim. 2:5; Titus 2:13), and obeying His gospel teachings (Mark 1:15; John 3:36; 15:10).

As elsewhere in this letter and in his gospel (1:3; 4:2–3, 9–10; cf. John 1:1, 14; 5:23; 10:30; 12:45; 14:7–10), John stresses the inseparable divine equality of **the Father and the Son,** noting that an **antichrist** is **one who denies** them both. He further emphasizes this point by asserting that **whoever denies the Son does not have the Father** (cf. 4:2–3). Despite their claims to the contrary, those who deny the deity of Jesus Christ do not know God (cf. Matt. 11:27; Luke 10:16; John 5:23; 15:23–24; 2 John 9).

Any denial, deviation, or distortion of the scriptural view of Jesus Christ—His incarnation (Matt. 1:18–25; John 1:14); that He is both Son of God (Mark 1:1) and Son of Man (John 9:35–37), the promised Prophet (Deut. 18:15, 18), Priest (Heb. 4:14–5:10), King (Isa. 9:7; John 12:12–15), and Redeemer (1 Cor. 1:30; Gal. 3:13; 4:4–5; cf. Isa. 59:20)—constitutes the spirit of antichrist.

An equally intolerable view, and one more common in John's day when incipient Gnosticism threatened the church, is to deny that Christ—born, living, dying, rising, and ascending as a real man—came in human flesh (cf. Phil. 2:5–9; Col. 2:9). In his second letter, John wrote, "Many deceivers have gone out into the world, those who do not acknowledge Jesus Christ as coming in the flesh. This is the deceiver and the antichrist" (v. 7). That heretical perception of Christ several decades later became a major tenet of Gnosticism. Its unbiblical philosophy envisioned a "Christ spirit," an ethereal but powerful supernatural being who descended on a man named Jesus at His baptism and left Him just before His death. Thus the "Christ spirit" was not fully human but only temporarily indwelt a man through whom that spirit, before departing, demonstrated extraordinary power and wisdom.

Third, antichrists by nature try to confuse the faithful. John warned his readers that he had **written to** them **concerning those who** were **trying to deceive** them. False teachers persist in trying to mislead the saints, but ultimately they cannot cause believers to abandon the faith. Regarding their futile efforts, Jesus said, "False Christs and false prophets will arise and will show great signs and wonders, so as to mislead, if possible, even the elect" (Matt. 24:24; cf. John 10:4–5). They can muddle the simplicity of believers' devotion to Christ (cf. Gal. 1:6–9; Col. 2:4–5, 16–19), tamper with their spiritual confidence (cf. 1 Tim. 6:3–5*a*), cause them to doubt the sufficiency of the Word (2 Tim. 3:16–17; cf. Col. 2:20–23) and be confused or uncertain about key doctrines (Gal. 3:1), but they cannot take away the faith that secures them to Christ or the eternal life that belongs to those who are truly elect and regenerate (John 10:27–29).

THE CHARACTERISTICS OF CHRISTIANS

But you have an anointing from the Holy One, and you all know. I have not written to you because you do not know the truth, but because you do know it, and because no lie is of the truth. . . . As for you, let that abide in you which you heard from the beginning. If what you heard from the beginning abides in you, you also will abide in the Son and in the Father. This is the promise which He Himself made to us: eternal life. . . . As for you, the anointing which you received from Him abides in you, and you have no need for anyone to teach you; but as His anointing teaches you about all things, and is true and is not a lie, and just as it has taught you, you abide in Him. (2:20–21, 24–25, 27)

Opposite antichrists are true Christians who are people committed to the truth. In his second letter, John wrote to the church, "I was very glad to find some of your children walking in truth" (v. 4*a*); and again in his third epistle he encouraged his readers with the following: "I have no greater joy than this, to hear of my children walking in the truth" (v. 4). The apostle's portrait of Christians as ones who walk in the truth (cf. 2 Cor. 4:2; Eph. 6:14; 1 Thess. 2:13) is in sharp distinction to the antichrists who propagate spiritual lies. In the end, there are two obvious reasons that believers are not led astray: they accept the faith, and they remain faithful to it.

CHRISTIANS ACCEPT THE FAITH

But you have an anointing from the Holy One, and you all know. I have not written to you because you do not know the truth, but because you do know it, and because no lie is of the truth. . . . As for you, the anointing which you received from Him abides in you, and you have no need for anyone to teach you; but as His anointing teaches you about all things, and is true and is not a lie, and just as it has taught you, you abide in Him. (2:20–21, 27)

The false teachers who threatened John's readers employed the terms for knowledge and anointing to describe their religious experience. They arrogantly saw themselves as possessing an elevated and esoteric form of divine knowledge, and as the recipients of a special, secret, transcendent anointing. That led them to believe they were privy to truth that the uninitiated lacked. John's response, which was both a rebuttal to the antichrists and a reassurance to the believers, was to assert that, in reality, all true Christians **have an anointing from the Holy One.**

Because believers have received that anointing, they have the true understanding of God that comes exclusively through Jesus Christ (2 Cor. 4:6), "in whom are hidden all the treasures of wisdom and knowledge" (Col. 2:3). They do not need any secret, special, or transcendent understanding or esoteric insight. **Anointing** (*chrisma*) literally means "ointment" or "oil" (cf. Heb. 1:9). In this text it refers figuratively to the Holy Spirit (cf. 2 Cor. 1:21–22), who has taken up residency in believers at the behest of Jesus Christ, **the Holy One** (cf. Luke 4:34; Acts 3:14), and reveals through Scripture all they need to know (John 14:26; 16:13; 1 Cor. 2:9–10).

In verse 21, John reiterates that believers have true knowledge of God by saying he had not **written to** them **because** they did **not know the truth, but because** they did **know it.** He then closes the verse with the axiomatic statement that **no lie is of the truth**—something cannot be simultaneously true and false. Because Christians are taught by the Spirit to know the truth, they can recognize doctrinal error for what it really is (cf. 1 Cor. 2:10–16). The apostle wrote as he did because his readers already knew the gospel and its attendant truths and would understand his appeal to the exclusivity of biblical truth. (For a basic discussion of truth's incompatibility with error, see John MacArthur, *Why One Way?* [Nashville: W Publishing, 2002], 59–65; cf. John 14:6; Acts 4:12; 2 Cor. 6:14–18; Gal. 1:6–9; 2 John 9–11.)

Verse 27 reiterates the truth that **the anointing** [Spirit-given knowledge of the truth] **which** John's readers **received from Him abides in** them. They possessed the truth; it resided in them permanently

(John 14:16–17; Rom. 8:9; Eph. 1:13); they had **no need for anyone to teach** them. And because God's truth is all-sufficient (Ps. 19:7–14; 2 Tim. 3:16–17) and incompatible with error, His anointing **teaches . . . about all things, and is true and is not a lie.**

When the apostle asserted that believers do not need other teachers, he was not advocating a mystical anti-intellectualism that spurns all human teachers. On the contrary, the Lord has given the church godly pastors, elders, and teachers "for the equipping of the saints for the work of service, to the building up of the body of Christ" (Eph. 4:12; cf. v. 11; 1 Cor. 12:28). John's point is that believers must not rely on human wisdom or man-centered philosophy (cf. 1 Cor. 1:18–2:9; Col. 2:8) but on the teaching of God's Word by Spirit-gifted human teachers and the illuminating work of the Holy Spirit.

CHRISTIANS REMAIN FAITHFUL

As for you, let that abide in you which you heard from the beginning. If what you heard from the beginning abides in you, you also will abide in the Son and in the Father. This is the promise which He Himself made to us: eternal life. (2:24–25)

Although John knew that the true sheep could never lose their salvation (John 10:27–29; cf. 1 Peter 1:5), he exhorted his audience to persevere, to **let that** [truth] **abide in** them **which** they **heard from the beginning.** Believers are commanded to actively persevere in the truth because it is the gracious means by which they are sanctified (John 8:31; 1 Cor. 15:1–2; Phil. 2:12–13; Col. 1:22–23; 2 Tim. 3:14) even as faith is the means by which they are graciously justified (Rom. 3:24–26). The word twice rendered **abide** and once **abides** is from *menō*, which refers to a continual action of remaining (cf. its use in John 6:56; 8:31; 14:17; 15:4, 9–10; 1 Cor. 13:13; 2 Tim. 3:14). Those who continue in what they have heard show that what they have **heard from the beginning abides in** them, and they **also will abide in the Son and in the Father** (1 John 3:17; 4:13).

The ultimate prize for those who remain faithful is, of course, **eternal life.** Concerning Himself, the true Bread of Life, and those who are spiritually united to Him, Jesus promised,

> Truly, truly, I say to you, unless you eat the flesh of the Son of Man and drink His blood, you have no life in yourselves. He who eats My flesh and drinks My blood has eternal life, and I will raise him up on the last day. For My flesh is true food, and My blood is true drink. He who eats My flesh and drinks My blood abides in Me, and I in him. As the living

Father sent Me, and I live because of the Father, so he who eats Me, he also will live because of Me. This is the bread which came down out of heaven; not as the fathers ate and died; he who eats this bread will live forever. (John 6:53–58; cf. 14:1–6; 2 Tim. 1:1; Titus 1:2; 3:7; 1 Peter 1:3–5; Jude 21)

The contrast between antichrists and Christians is absolutely clear. Antichrists deny the faith, depart from the faith, and seek to deceive the faithful. Christians, on the other hand, affirm the faith and remain faithful to the end—they cannot be permanently deceived. The Westminster Confession of Faith sets forth the following regarding the understanding of truth and perseverance:

> All things in Scripture are not alike plain in themselves, nor alike clear unto all: yet those things which are necessary to be known, believed, and observed for salvation, are so clearly propounded, and opened in some place of Scripture or other, that not only the learned, but the unlearned, in a due use of the ordinary means, may attain unto a sufficient understanding of them. (I:VII)

> They, whom God hath accepted in His Beloved, effectually called, and sanctified by His Spirit, can neither totally nor finally fall away from the state of grace, but shall certainly persevere therein to the end, and be eternally saved. (XVII:I)

All Christians can have lasting comfort in the truth of those words.

The Purifying Hope (1 John 2:28–3:3)

10

Now, little children, abide in Him, so that when He appears, we may have confidence and not shrink away from Him in shame at His coming. If you know that He is righteous, you know that everyone also who practices righteousness is born of Him. See how great a love the Father has bestowed on us, that we would be called children of God; and such we are. For this reason the world does not know us, because it did not know Him. Beloved, now we are children of God, and it has not appeared as yet what we will be. We know that when He appears, we will be like Him, because we will see Him just as He is. And everyone who has this hope fixed on Him purifies himself, just as He is pure. (2:28–3:3)

First Corinthians 13:13 expresses the three benchmark virtues of biblical Christianity: "Now faith, hope, love, abide these three; but the greatest of these is love." Of those three frequently discussed subjects, "faith" and "love" have engendered the most discussion among believers; while "hope," at least by comparison, has often been overlooked or neglected. Yet, like faith and love, hope is not only a fundamental biblical concept, but the ultimate reality to which all others point—one that all Christians need to understand in its profound richness and full significance if they are to maintain a right and true perspective regarding both this life and the next.

The concept of spiritual hope is analogous to turning on a blazing light in a dark place. It immediately illuminates one's outlook, uplifts the soul, and produces joy in the heart. Hope introduces life and happiness into this sin-stained and death-filled world (cf. Ps. 146:5; Prov. 10:28; Rom. 5:1–2; 12:12; 15:13; Gal. 5:5; 2 Thess. 2:16; Heb. 3:6). Yet, sadly, most people in this world know nothing of the advantages and privileges that true hope brings. Unbelievers simply do not have "an anchor of the soul, a hope both sure and steadfast" (Heb. 6:19). In fact, all they have are superficial sources of security—things like narcotics, alcohol, sex, entertainment, materialism, surface-level relationships, and a man-centered desire for a better future. But all of these false hopes are only spiritual mirages that instantly vanish when this life ends (Job 8:13; 27:8; 31:24–28; Prov. 10:28; cf. Eph. 2:12). For the world, "hope" is a mere wish based on a desire or plan, but not grounded in the promises of God who always speaks the truth and is faithful to all His Word. Biblical hope is not a wish but an absolute future reality guaranteed by the Lord.

The world's hopelessness stands in stark contrast to the genuine and lasting hope that God offers. As Paul instructed the Romans,

> For we know that the whole creation groans and suffers the pains of childbirth together until now. And not only this, but also we ourselves, having the first fruits of the Spirit, even we ourselves groan within ourselves, waiting eagerly for our adoption as sons, the redemption of our body. For in hope we have been saved, but hope that is seen is not hope; for who hopes for what he already sees? But if we hope for what we do not see, with perseverance we wait eagerly for it. (Rom. 8:22–25)

To be sure, the present joys of salvation cannot compare with the ultimate, surpassing joys that divine hope guarantees for the future, when salvation is fully realized. For instance, the continuing battle against sin that Christians experience here (Rom. 6:6, 12, 19; 7:24–25; 8:4–6, 12–13; 2 Cor. 7:1; Gal. 3:3; 5:24; Phil. 3:3) will terminate forever when they reach heaven (Rom. 8:30; 13:11; 2 Tim. 2:10; cf. Ps. 73:24). In addition to being made sinless, believers will also receive perfect, glorified bodies that God has prepared for them (Rom. 8:23; 1 Cor. 15:43; Phil. 3:20–21; cf. 2 Cor. 3:18), bodies that will complement their already redeemed souls.

In this life, it is good to experience the joy that comes with the forgiveness of sin (Ps. 32:1–2; Matt. 9:2; Luke 5:20; Col. 2:13), to know the power of the indwelling Spirit, to see His fruit in one's life (Gal. 5:22–23), to experience answered prayer (1 John 5:14–15), and to engage in spiritual fellowship (Ps. 133:1; Heb. 10:25), worship (Ps. 34:3), and service (cf.

2 Cor. 8:1–7); but all that satisfaction falls far short of the ultimate joy the saints will enjoy when God forever fulfills the promises that form their hope.

Since eternal glory—the goal of hope—is the reason for God's saving plan and purpose, Scripture sets forth a complete theology of hope that, first of all, finds its beginning in the unchanging God, who cannot speak anything but the truth. The psalmist wrote, "Why are you in despair, O my soul? And why are you disturbed within me? Hope in God, for I shall again praise Him, the help of my countenance and my God" (Ps. 43:5; cf. 78:7). God's promises of care (1 Peter 5:6–7), protection (Ps. 121:8; Jude 24), guidance (Ps. 23:3), and sustenance (Phil. 4:19) mean believers can confidently trust Him regarding His promises for the future.

Hope founded in the immutable and eternal Deity is sure and absolutely fixed. In the salutation of his letter to Titus, the apostle Paul refers to "those chosen of God . . . in the hope of eternal life, which God, who cannot lie, promised long ages ago" (1:1–2). God, who is always truthful (Num. 23:19; Deut. 32:4; Ps. 89:14; Isa. 65:16), recorded in His Book of Life before the foundation of the world the names of all those who would believe and receive the hope of eternal life (Rev. 13:8; 17:8; 20:12; cf. Matt. 25:34; Eph. 1:4; Phil. 4:3). So certain is their hope that the author of Hebrews could write, "This hope we have as an anchor of the soul, a hope both sure and steadfast and one which enters within the veil, where Jesus has entered as a forerunner for us, having become a high priest forever according to the order of Melchizedek" (Heb. 6:19–20). There is no certain or reliable anchor of hope other than one that rests in Christ and His finished work (cf. Col. 1:23, 27; 2 Thess. 2:16; Titus 1:2).

Second, hope is a gift of divine grace; it is not something anyone can earn. Paul offered these words of benediction to the Thessalonians, "Now may our Lord Jesus Christ Himself and God our Father, who has loved us and given us eternal comfort *and good hope by grace,* comfort and strengthen your hearts in every good work and word" (2 Thess. 2:16–17, emphasis added).

Third, genuine hope is revealed in Scripture. Romans 15:4 says, "Whatever was written in earlier times was written for our instruction, so that through perseverance and the encouragement of the Scriptures we might have hope." As the inspired (2 Tim. 3:16; 2 Peter 1:21) and inerrant (Ps. 119:160; John 17:17; cf. Dan. 10:21*a;* James 1:18*a*) Word of God, the Bible is full of God-given promises—divine guarantees in which believers can confidently trust. The psalmist, despite trials and difficulties, learned to live in that expectation: "My soul languishes for Your salvation; I wait for Your word" (Ps. 119:81; cf. v. 49).

Fourth, hope is reasonable and defensible. The believer's hope to reach holy perfection, receive a redeemed body, and eternally worship and rejoice in Christ in heaven is not an unrealistic, pie-in-the-sky yearning. It is a defensible hope because it comes from a trustworthy, truthful God who revealed it in His Word (Col. 1:5). Hence Peter urged his readers to "sanctify Christ as Lord in your hearts, always being ready to make a defense to everyone who asks you to give an account for the hope that is in you, yet with gentleness and reverence" (1 Peter 3:15).

Fifth, the bodily rising of Jesus Christ from the grave secures the Christian's hope. Earlier in his first epistle, the apostle Peter also attested to this truth: "Blessed be the God and Father of our Lord Jesus Christ, who according to His great mercy has caused us to be born again to a living hope through the resurrection of Jesus Christ from the dead" (1 Peter 1:3; cf. v. 21). The monumental, historical fact of the resurrection secured genuine hope for everyone who ever believed (1 Cor. 15:1–4; cf. vv. 20–28, 50–54). As Jesus told Martha, "I am the resurrection and the life; he who believes in Me will live even if he dies, and everyone who lives and believes in Me will never die" (John 11:25–26; cf. Job 19:25–26; Ps. 16:10).

Sixth, hope is confirmed and energized in believers by the Holy Spirit. To the Romans Paul wrote, "Now may the God of hope fill you with all joy and peace in believing, so that you will abound in hope by the power of the Holy Spirit" (Rom. 15:13). The Spirit supernaturally places into believers a hopeful attitude in anticipation of their heavenly righteousness (Gal. 5:5). Moreover, the Spirit serves as a divine seal and pledge of the believer's hope, guaranteeing that what God has started in the present, He will bring to full, glorious fruition in the future (Eph. 1:13–14).

Seventh, hope defends the saints against Satan's attacks. Paul included hope as an important part of the spiritual armor that believers must wear in the inevitable war against the enemy. In 1 Thessalonians 5:8, he wrote, "Since we are of the day, let us be sober, having put on the breastplate of faith and love, and as a helmet, the hope of salvation" (cf. Eph. 6:17). Satan and his forces seek to deal crushing blows of doubt and discouragement to believers. But when God's people wear the helmet of salvation, hope, they have protection from those satanic attacks.

Eighth, hope is also confirmed through trials. Because believers have hope, even the most severe adversity and suffering will not separate them from safekeeping in God's hands. Paul's encouragement to the Roman Christians illustrates this point:

> What then shall we say to these things? If God is for us, who is against us? He who did not spare His own Son, but delivered Him over for us all, how will He not also with Him freely give us all things? Who will bring a charge against God's elect? God is the one who justifies; who is

the one who condemns? Christ Jesus is He who died, yes, rather who was raised, who is at the right hand of God, who also intercedes for us. Who will separate us from the love of Christ? Will tribulation, or distress, or persecution, or famine, or nakedness, or peril, or sword? Just as it is written, "For Your sake we are being put to death all day long; we were considered as sheep to be slaughtered." But in all these things we overwhelmingly conquer through Him who loved us. For I am convinced that neither death, nor life, nor angels, nor principalities, nor things present, nor things to come, nor powers, nor height, nor depth, nor any other created thing, will be able to separate us from the love of God, which is in Christ Jesus our Lord. (Rom. 8:31–39; cf. 1 Thess. 5:9)

In actuality, trials not only confirm true hope; they serve to strengthen and sharpen that sense of hope and heavenly expectation (cf. James 1:2–12; 1 Peter 1:6–7).

Ninth, hope is the source of the believer's greatest joy and blessing. The psalmist exulted, "How blessed is he whose help is the God of Jacob, whose hope is in the Lord his God" (Ps. 146:5; cf. Jer. 17:7). Because of who the sovereign God is and what He does for His own, nothing can supersede hope in Him as a source of lasting joy. Those who hope in Him are able to endure the most difficult circumstances of this life without losing their joy. After all, no matter how uncertain this life seems, God always remains the same—the all-powerful King of the universe and the loving Father of His children, who will bring them all to glory. Consistent with the Father's purpose, the Son will keep all the Father gives Him and raise them "on the last day" (see John 6:39–40) to eternal glory.

A tenth feature of hope is that it removes the fear of death. Those who are genuinely saved are acutely aware of their sinful violations of God's holy law (Pss. 25:11; 38:3–4; 51:3–4; 69:5; Rom. 7:17–24; 1 Tim. 1:15; cf. Isa. 6:5) and the severity and earthly permanence of its consequences (cf. Gen. 3:7–24; Rom. 5:12; 1 Cor. 6:9–11; Gal. 6:7–8). But at the moment of salvation their sins are forgiven, they receive eternal life, and though gaining a stronger sense of sin, they lose the fear of death as divine judgment. Believers may still not relish the pain and suffering that can accompany death (hence the Bible's commands to trust God and not be anxious; cf. Ps. 55:22; Jonah 2:7; Phil. 4:6). However, they possess a hope that removes the ultimate sting of death, which is part of the penalty for those who reject God's law. Like Paul, they can look forward to death with joy, because the Savior has fulfilled the death penalty for all who believe:

When this perishable will have put on the imperishable, and this mortal will have put on immortality, then will come about the saying that is written, "Death is swallowed up in victory. O death, where is your victory? O death, where is your sting?" The sting of death is sin, and the

power of sin is the law; but thanks be to God, who gives us the victory
through our Lord Jesus Christ. (1 Cor. 15:54–57; cf. Col. 1:5, 22–23, 27)

Finally, all the glorious facets of Christian hope will be consum-
mated when Jesus Christ returns (1 Cor. 1:8; Col. 3:4; 1 Thess. 3:13; 5:23;
Heb. 9:28). His return (referring broadly to both the rapture and the second coming) will encompass all that believers hope for, including glorified resurrection bodies (1 Cor. 15:50–52; 1 Thess. 4:13–18), the privilege
of reigning with Christ in His earthly kingdom (2 Tim. 2:12; Rev. 20:4), and
the receiving of eternal reward (2 Tim. 4:8; Rev. 22:12). The believer's
hope will not be entirely complete until that time of resurrection; then it
will be fully realized at His coming—and it will continue in its full splendor for all eternity. Hence Paul could write that the saints are continually
"looking for the blessed hope and the appearing of the glory of [their]
great God and Savior, Christ Jesus" (Titus 2:13; cf. 1 Thess. 4:16–18; 1 Peter
1:3–5).

As should be clear by now, hope is not only foundational to
Christian doctrine and the believer's confidence, but it also has immense
ethical implications. Genuine hope will purify the lives of those who possess it (3:3), and thereby verify that they are Christians. This is one of the
primary themes of the apostle John's writings, especially in this passage.

In this letter John has already presented doctrinal and moral
tests that can determine one's true spiritual condition, and in this section
he further elaborates on the moral (ethical) test. Orthodox beliefs about
the nature of sin and the person of Christ, the practical presence of sincere love and obedience, and now a personal pursuit of purity and holiness are all evidences that a person has true, eternal hope.

This passage contains five perspectives that further define and
clarify the essence of biblical hope: it is secured by abiding, it is manifested
by righteousness, it is established by love, it is fulfilled by Christlikeness,
and it is characterized by purity.

Hope Is Secured by Abiding

**Now, little children, abide in Him, so that when He appears, we
may have confidence and not shrink away from Him in shame at
His coming.** (2:28)

The emphatic particle *nun* (**now**) introduces a new section and
plainly indicates a paragraph break. (It also strongly implies that, despite
the modern chapter divisions in the text, chapter 3 should begin at this
point.) The aged apostle John again chose a favorite pastoral term, **little**

children, to address his readers. That phrase encompasses believers at all levels of maturity (2:12; 3:7, 18; 4:4; 5:21; John 13:33; cf. Rom. 8:16–17; 1 Cor. 4:14; Gal. 4:19; Eph. 5:1; Phil. 2:15; 1 Peter 1:14; 1 John 3:1–2) and expresses John's continuing fatherly care and concern for the recipients of this letter (cf. 2:12).

Abide translates a form of the verb *menō,* which means "to stay" or "to remain." It is a term the apostle John used frequently in his New Testament writings; for instance, it appears nearly a dozen times in John 15 alone. There Jesus instructed the eleven apostles (Judas having already left; John 13:27–31), "Abide in Me, and I in you. As the branch cannot bear fruit of itself unless it abides in the vine, so neither can you unless you abide in Me" (John 15:4; cf. vv. 6, 7, 16). Earlier in this second chapter, John again focused on the importance of abiding in Christ and the general significance of aspects of abiding: "The one who says he abides in Him ought himself to walk in the same manner as He walked" (v. 6; cf. vv. 10, 14, 19, 24, 27). Neither Christ nor John referred to some mystical, elitist spiritual experience. They commanded believers to persevere daily and sustain their faith in the gospel and in the Christ of the gospel (1 Cor. 16:13; Gal. 6:9; Phil. 1:27; Col. 1:10, 22–23; 2 Tim. 3:14; Heb. 10:23; 2 Peter 3:18; cf. Pss. 73:24; 138:8; Prov. 4:18). In order to do that, believers must continue to love and obey the Scripture, submit to the direction of the Holy Spirit, and remain committed to the truth they first received (cf. 4:12–13, 15–16; 2 John 2, 9). Such abiding precludes clinging to a habitual pattern of sin (see the commentary on 3:6, 9, 14–15, and 17 in the next two chapters of this volume).

The apostle's teaching that true Christians **abide in Him** reinforces Jesus' statement, "The one who endures to the end, he will be saved" (Matt. 24:13). John's words are also consistent with Paul's exhortation to the Colossians to continue in the faith:

> Although you were formerly alienated and hostile in mind, engaged in evil deeds, yet He has now reconciled you in His fleshly body through death, in order to present you before Him holy and blameless and beyond reproach—if indeed you continue in the faith firmly established and steadfast, and not moved away from the hope of the gospel that you have heard, which was proclaimed in all creation under heaven, and of which I, Paul, was made a minister. (Col. 1:21–23)

No one who professes to believe the gospel but then permanently abandons the faith possesses eternal life. Earlier in this letter John wrote: "They went out from us, but they were not really of us; for if they had been of us, they would have remained with us; but they went out, so that it would be shown that they all are not of us" (2:19). Only those who remain faithful to the Lord and His Word, and give evidence of the fruits of righteousness (5:1–5, 10; Matt. 7:17–18; 12:33, 35; John 3:21, 36; 13:35; 2 Cor. 5:17; Gal. 5:22–23; 6:7–8; Eph. 5:9; James 2:14–26; cf. Isa. 3:10; Jer. 17:9–10) by the indwelling power and presence of the Spirit (cf. Rom. 8:9; 1 Cor. 3:16; 6:19; Gal. 4:6) are truly saved. As John penned earlier in this chapter:

> Whoever denies the Son does not have the Father; the one who confesses the Son has the Father also. As for you, let that abide in you which you heard from the beginning. If what you heard from the beginning abides in you, you also will abide in the Son and in the Father. This is the promise which He Himself made to us: eternal life. (2:23–25)

The Bible teaches the complementary truths that true Christians will persevere in their faith, and that God will keep them eternally secure. Without question, the Lord securely holds on to His own. As Jesus declared,

> My sheep hear My voice, and I know them, and they follow Me; and I give eternal life to them, and they will never perish; and no one will snatch them out of My hand. My Father, who has given them to Me, is greater than all; and no one is able to snatch them out of the Father's hand. (John 10:27–29; cf. Rom. 8:38–39; 1 Cor. 1:8–9; Jude 24–25)

But that wonderful reality does not absolve believers from the responsibility to persevere in their faith and abide in Christ (cf. Phil. 2:12–13; Jude 20–21).

The seemingly opposite truths of eternal security and perseverance actually work together in perfect harmony. It is not unlike salvation, when God sovereignly saves sinners, but not apart from their personal faith; or sanctification, when God supernaturally conforms believers to His Son, yet not apart from their obedience. In the Christian life, God always provides the power and means for believers to win the spiritual battle. Thus Jesus told Peter, "Simon, Simon, behold Satan has demanded permission to sift you like wheat; but I have prayed for you, that your faith may not fail" (Luke 22:31–32a). And Paul encouraged the Corinthians with this divine promise: "No temptation has overtaken you but such as is common to man; and God is faithful, who will not allow you to be tempted beyond what you are able, but with the temptation will provide the way of escape also, so that you will be able to endure it" (1 Cor. 10:13; cf. John 17:15; Heb. 2:18). But believers must also actively persevere; they must "fight the good fight of faith" (1 Tim. 6:12), knowing that, "Blessed is a man who perseveres under trial; for once he has been approved, he will under trial; for once he has been approved, he will receive the crown of life which the Lord has promised to those who love Him" (James 1:12). Perhaps nowhere in Scripture is the balance between God's work and the believer's work more clearly expressed than in Paul's words to the Philippians: "So then, my beloved, just as you have always obeyed, not as in my presence only, but now much more in my absence, work out your salvation with fear and trembling; for it is God who is at work in you, both to will and to work for His good pleasure" (2:12–13; cf. Col. 1:29).

As noted earlier, a crucial aspect of Christian hope is that it will culminate when Jesus Christ comes again, which gives believers strong incentive for godly living (3:3; cf. Col. 3:4; 1 Tim. 6:14; 2 Tim. 4:8; 2 Peter 3:14). **When He appears,** faithful saints will **have confidence and not shrink away from Him.** The appearance of Christ refers especially to the gathering of the church at the rapture (cf. John 14:1–6; 1 Cor. 15:51–54; 1 Thess. 4:13–18) and the activities that will follow at Christ's judgment seat (cf. 1 Cor. 4:5; 2 Cor. 5:9–10). **Confidence** translates a Greek word (*parrēsian*) that means "outspokenness" or "freedom of speech." Elsewhere in the New Testament it refers to believers' boldness in approaching God (Heb. 4:16; 10:19; 1 John 3:21; 5:14). In this verse it indicates an assurance derived from a holy life of abiding in Christ (cf. Eph. 5:27; Col. 1:22; 1 Thess. 3:13; 5:23). In contrast, nominal Christians, who are actually unbelievers, will **shrink away from Him in shame** because they are not genuine children of God (Matt. 13:20–22; cf. John 8:31; 15:6; Heb. 3:6, 12; 6:4–6; 10:39)—their hypocrisy having been evidenced by the fact that they did not persevere in the faith they initially professed.

By God's sovereign grace believers are saved and sanctified, and that same powerful grace will in the resurrection bring them to their full eternal reward **at His coming** (Titus 2:11–14; Rev. 22:12).

HOPE IS MANIFESTED BY RIGHTEOUSNESS

If you know that He is righteous, you know that everyone also who practices righteousness is born of Him. (2:29)

The new birth is inevitably and necessarily accompanied by righteousness (cf. Rom. 6:4; 2 Cor. 5:17; Eph. 2:10; 4:24). By the same token, all who profess to be saved but do not demonstrate any tangible fruit of righteousness prove that they are actually unforgiven and have an empty hope (cf. Luke 6:43–44; James 2:26). Such individuals can make no legitimate claim to eternal promises, since their lives betray a heart that is still unregenerate.

It is important to understand the different meanings of the words rendered **know** in this verse. The first occurrence is from *oida* and has the sense of perceiving an absolute truth, whereas the second occurrence (from *ginoskō*) conveys "to know by experience," "recognize," or "come to perceive." The apostle John asserts first that if believers **know that** God is **righteous,** they can recognize **that everyone also who practices righteousness** is reflecting His life (cf. 1 Peter 1:13–16); that is, they are **born of Him** (1 Peter 1:3; cf. John 3:7, where the same verb translated **born** is used). Thus John reiterates the point that real believers are not verified so much by what they claim as by how they live (Rom. 6:18; cf. Luke 1:6).

Of course, John's call to personal holiness was not a new concept. The book of Leviticus repeatedly sets forth God's standard of purity and righteousness (e.g., 18:4–5, 30; 19:2, 37; 20:7, 26; 22:32). In the New Testament, Paul's letters continually exhort believers to pursue holiness. Romans 12:1–2 is a notable and familiar example:

> Therefore I urge you, brethren, by the mercies of God, to present your bodies a living and holy sacrifice, acceptable to God, which is your spiritual service of worship. And do not be conformed to this world, but be transformed by the renewing of your mind, so that you may prove what the will of God is, that which is good and acceptable and perfect. (cf. 2 Cor. 7:1; Eph. 5:27; 1 Thess. 4:7; 1 Peter 1:14–16; 2:11)

In this verse, the apostle John looks from the effect (righteous behavior) to the cause (the new birth) and shows that righteous living—not mere outward profession—evidences the fact that regeneration has truly taken place (James 2:20, 26; 2 Peter 3:11; cf. Rom. 14:17).

Hope Is Established by Love

See how great a love the Father has bestowed on us, that we would be called children of God; and such we are. For this reason the world does not know us, because it did not know Him. (3:1)

John was overcome with wonder by the fact that sinners by divine grace became God's children. The opening phrase of this verse, **see how great a love,** reflects the apostle's amazement. The word translated **see** (*idete*) is both a command and an exclamation that exhorts readers to give close attention to the rest of the statement. **How great** (*potapēn*) is a seldom-used term that has no precise parallel in English. Concerning this word, D. Edmond Hiebert wrote,

The adjective rendered "what manner" ["how great"] (*potapēn*) occurs only seven times in the New Testament and implies a reaction of astonishment, and usually of admiration, upon viewing some person or thing. The expression conveys both a qualitative and quantitative force, "what glorious, measureless love!" (*The Epistles of John* [Greenville, S.C.: Bob Jones University Press, 1991], 133; cf. Matt. 8:27; 2 Peter 3:11)

God loves believers with a **love** that is impossible to articulate in any human language and that is utterly foreign to normal human understanding and experience. This is *agapē* love, God's volitional love that He, of His own free and uninfluenced choice, **has bestowed on** all whom He has called to savingly believe in Jesus Christ. The Lord summarized it this way: "Greater love has no one than this, that one lay down his life for his friends" (John 15:13). And later in this letter, John notes,

By this the love of God was manifested in us, that God has sent His only begotten Son into the world so that we might live through Him. In this is love, not that we loved God, but that He loved us and sent His Son to be the propitiation for our sins. (4:9–10; cf. vv. 16, 19; John 3:16; Rom. 5:8; 8:39; Eph. 2:4; Titus 3:4)

Such love seeks, at a great cost to itself, but only to give freely and spontaneously for the benefit of another, even if that person is not worthy of such an expression (cf. Deut. 7:7–8).

Since all of God's attributes work in perfect harmony, His love necessarily operates in conjunction with each of His other attributes. He is lovingly holy (Rev. 4:8; 15:4), just (Isa. 30:18; Rom. 3:26; 1 Peter 3:18), merciful (Ps. 86:15; Luke 6:36; 2 Cor. 1:3), gracious (Ps. 103:8; 1 Peter 5:10), patient (2 Peter 3:9, 15), omniscient (Ps. 147:5; Rom. 11:33–34), omnipotent (Rom. 1:20; Rev. 19:6), omnipresent (Ps. 139:7–10; Jer. 23:23–24), and even wrathful (Ps. 7:11; Rev. 19:15). With regard to mankind, God's love has a twofold expression: it is general toward unsaved humanity (common grace; Ps. 145:9; Matt. 5:45; cf. Mark 10:21*a*) and specific toward believers (special grace; cf. John 13:1; Rom. 5:8; 8:38–39; 9:13–15; Eph. 5:25). It is this specific and unique love of God for His own that stands as one of the unshakeable foundations of eternal hope.

In other words, believers can live in hope because they have experienced God's love in an eternal, saving way—having been adopted into His family (Rom. 8:16) and **called children of God** (John 1:12; cf. 2 Peter 1:4). They became His children solely because He lavishly bestowed on them a gracious, unmerited, sovereign love apart from any that has human merit. Such love is inexplicable in human terms. It is not surprising, then, that **the world does not know** the nature of the relationship between

God and His children (cf. Heb. 11:38*a*), **because it did not know Him.** Those outside of Christ cannot fathom (1 Cor. 2:15–16; 1 Peter 4:3–4) the true essence and character of believers, which shines forth in their likeness to the heavenly Father and His Son Jesus Christ, their Savior and Lord (Matt. 5:16; Phil. 2:15; 1 Peter 2:12; cf. 1 Cor. 14:24–25). Even for believers it is a challenge "to comprehend with all the saints what is the breadth and length and height and depth, and to know the love of Christ which surpasses knowledge" (Eph. 3:18–19*a*). Because Christians are so intrinsically different from the world around them, having been transformed by the Father who adopted them, the New Testament appropriately describes them as "strangers and exiles" (Heb. 11:13), "aliens" (1 Peter 1:1), and "aliens and strangers" (1 Peter 2:11). They are those who, in hope, "desire a better country, that is, a heavenly one. Therefore God is not ashamed to be called their God; for He has prepared a city for them" (Heb. 11:16). And having declared them righteous in justification, He is making them righteous in sanctification and will perfect that righteousness in glorification when hope is realized.

HOPE IS FULFILLED BY CHRISTLIKENESS

Beloved, now we are children of God, and it has not appeared as yet what we will be. We know that when He appears, we will be like Him, because we will see Him just as He is. (3:2)

Heaven is attractive for believers because there they will not only see the Lord Jesus Christ, but will become like Him. Concerning that dramatic and eternal change, the apostle Paul wrote:

> Just as we have borne the image of the earthy, we will also bear the image of the heavenly. Now I say this, brethren, that flesh and blood cannot inherit the kingdom of God; nor does the perishable inherit the imperishable. Behold, I tell you a mystery; we will not all sleep, but we will all be changed, in a moment, in the twinkling of an eye, at the last trumpet; for the trumpet will sound, and the dead will be raised imperishable, and we will be changed. For this perishable must put on the imperishable, and this mortal must put on immortality. (1 Cor. 15:49–53)

Even though all who exercise saving faith in the person and work of Christ **now . . . are children of God** (cf. Rom. 8:14–18), **it has not appeared as yet what** they **will be** when they experience what Paul called "the freedom of the glory of the children of God" (8:21). It is then that "the Lord Jesus Christ . . . will transform the body of our humble state into conformity with the body of His glory, by the exertion of the power that He has even to subject all things to Himself" (Phil. 3:20–21; cf. Ps. 73:24; Rom. 9:23; 1 Cor. 15:42–49; Col. 3:4; 1 Thess. 4:16; 2 Thess. 2:14; 2 Tim. 2:10). As a result, believers **will be like Him, because they will see Him just as He is.** God has promised to bring about such a climactic transformation because "those whom He foreknew, He also predestined to become conformed to the image of His Son, so that He would be the firstborn among many brethren" (Rom. 8:29). That transformation will make the redeemed perfectly holy and righteous, with a pure capacity to worship and glorify God in a totally satisfying, joyful, undiminished fashion forever (cf. Rev. 5:11–14).

It has been rightly said that imitation is the highest form of praise, and this transformation will be a supreme tribute to Jesus Christ—that He is the Chief One, the *prototokos,* among many who are made like Him. Those whom the Father has elected to salvation through the Son will be made like the Son, conformed to the image of Christ. He will be the first among His elect and redeemed humanity who will join with the holy angels to praise and glorify His name, reflect His goodness, and proclaim His greatness, as they worship Him endlessly.

HOPE IS CHARACTERIZED BY PURITY

And everyone who has this hope fixed on Him purifies himself, just as He is pure. (3:3)

The hope of Christ's return makes a practical difference in the lifestyle and behavior of believers. When **this hope** is **fixed on Him,** it produces a growing desire to become like Him now (Gal. 2:20; Eph. 4:17–32; Col. 3:1–17). Jesus Christ is the saints' Lord and Savior, who provides the ideal pattern for holy living. He is the goal of their lives, the One whom they must follow with increasing diligence and fervor, as the apostle Paul did (Phil. 3:12–14; cf. 1 Cor. 9:24–27; 1 Tim. 6:12; Heb. 12:1). Ultimately, it should be said of each believer that he **purifies himself, just as** Christ **is pure** (cf. Matt. 5:8; Phil. 4:8; 1 Tim. 1:5; 3:9; Heb. 9:14; 1 Peter 1:22). The idea of purifying oneself does not mean believers can generate their own sanctification. Rather, it emphasizes that the sanctifying work of the Holy Spirit does not take place apart from the believer's obedience and use of the means of sanctifying grace. This is a typical call to Christians to obey Scripture in all things.

In thinking about heaven, believers should not become overly preoccupied with speculations about what it might be like to float on clouds or walk down golden streets. Instead, their primary focus should be on the profound significance of being eternally conformed to the image of Christ. As they fix their hope on their absolutely holy Savior and Lord and yearn to be both with Him and fully like Him in the future, their lives will be positively affected toward righteousness in the present. Accordingly, Paul told the Corinthian believers, "We all, with unveiled face, beholding as in a mirror the glory of the Lord, are being transformed into the same image from glory to glory, just as from the Lord, the Spirit" (2 Cor. 3:18; cf. 4:6; 1 Cor. 13:12).

The gospel delivers to believers a message of hope. The apostle Peter eloquently articulated this hope in the opening of his first letter:

> Blessed be the God and Father of our Lord Jesus Christ, who according to His great mercy has caused us to be born again to a living hope through the resurrection of Jesus Christ from the dead, to obtain an inheritance which is imperishable and undefiled and will not fade away, reserved in heaven for you, who are protected by the power of God through faith for a salvation ready to be revealed in the last time. (1 Peter 1:3–5; cf. Phil. 3:20–21)

Paul reduced his spiritual objective to one thing: "one thing I do: forgetting what lies behind and reaching forward to what lies ahead, I press on toward the goal for the prize of the upward call of God in Christ Jesus" (Phil. 3:13b–14). The apostle's one consuming spiritual objective was to pursue in life ("I press on toward the goal") what was to be "the prize" when he received "the upward call." And that prize is Christlikeness, as John makes clear in this passage. The reward in the life to come —likeness to the Lord—is the pursuit of all believers in this life.

Those who are abiding in Christ, manifesting righteousness, gratefully recognizing God's love toward them, being increasingly conformed to Christ's image, and pursuing lives of purity can be confident that they have a hope that will not disappoint. Not even life's worst trials can diminish their eternal confidence in the promises of God. In fact, the more difficulties believers encounter in this life, the stronger and brighter their hope becomes. Such hope is foundational to every redeemed sinner's standing before God:

> Therefore, having been justified by faith, we have peace with God through our Lord Jesus Christ, through whom also we have obtained our introduction by faith into this grace in which we stand; and we exult in hope of the glory of God. And not only this, but we also exult in our tribulations, knowing that tribulation brings about perseverance; and perseverance, proven character; *and proven character, hope; and hope does not disappoint,* because the love of God has been poured out within our hearts through the Holy Spirit who was given to us. (Rom. 5:1–5, emphasis added)

The Christian's Incompatibility with Sin (1 John 3:4–10)

11

Everyone who practices sin also practices lawlessness; and sin is lawlessness. You know that He appeared in order to take away sins; and in Him there is no sin. No one who abides in Him sins; no one who sins has seen Him or knows Him. Little children, make sure no one deceives you; the one who practices righteousness is righteous, just as He is righteous; the one who practices sin is of the devil; for the devil has sinned from the beginning. The Son of God appeared for this purpose, to destroy the works of the devil. No one who is born of God practices sin, because His seed abides in him; and he cannot sin, because he is born of God. By this the children of God and the children of the devil are obvious: anyone who does not practice righteousness is not of God, nor the one who does not love his brother. (3:4–10)

Throughout its history the true church has always maintained that Scripture clearly sets forth certain basic standards of belief and behavior as necessary marks of genuine saving faith. An affirmation and acceptance of the biblical gospel, and a life that is characterized by a worthy walk, have rightly been seen as accurate indicators of the work of the Trinity on a person's heart. And when such fruit is absent in an individual's life, the church has appropriately called into question his or her profession of faith.

In recent decades, however, that has begun to change. More and more so-called evangelicals have downplayed the significance of biblical doctrine—even such crucial doctrines as the person of Christ and justification by faith alone. Incredibly, some have even asserted that the lost can be saved apart from any knowledge of the gospel at all, arguing that if pagan people merely live up to whatever standards of religion, morality, and ethics they have, God will accept them. (See the critique of this view in chapter 20 of this volume.) Since they claim there are scarcely any doctrinal necessities, there can hardly be any behavioral ones.

The apostle John would have been appalled by such contemporary evangelical equivocation. He wrote clearly and unmistakably that saving faith involves accepting certain essential doctrines—such as the Trinity and the substitutionary work of Christ on the cross—and results in certain essential actions—including repentance from sin, obedience to the Word, a desire to walk as Christ walked (live righteously), love for the brethren, and a hatred for the evils of the world and the flesh. John and all the writers of the New Testament taught that unless a person believes and practices such truths, he or she is not saved, no matter what he or she might claim. Bad theology damns, and bad behavior reveals bad theology. Yet, in spite of the unmistakable clarity with which this is presented in both this epistle (**No one who is born of God practices sin** [3:9a]) and the rest of the New Testament, a significant cross section of contemporary Christendom remains unpersuaded and confused concerning the truth.

For example, some commentators say the apostle was exhorting lawless, misbehaving Christians to rededicate their lives to the Lord and move from immature, carnal behavior to spirituality. In this way, they attempt to tone down the letter and make it less definitive or harsh. But their arguments cannot account for John's clear purpose for writing the letter (in 5:13), which was to enable his readers to examine themselves so that they might know whether or not their faith was saving. The dichotomy John presents is not deeper faith versus shallower faith, but rather a saving faith versus a non-saving one.

Others have missed the meaning and application of the passage due to an incorrect understanding of the nature of saving faith. Some, for example, believe that repentance is nothing more than a synonym for faith, thus does not refer to turning from sin, and is therefore not necessary for salvation. Saving faith, according to this view, is nothing more than mere intellectual assent to the facts of the gospel. (To ask sinners to repent would be asking them to contribute a work toward their salvation.) Hence, salvation may make no change in a person's doctrine or behavior. Even a lifelong state of carnality (living the same way as those who are unsaved) should not be sufficient reason to doubt someone's salvation. (For a complete discussion of these issues and an explication of the biblical gospel and its practical ramifications, see John MacArthur, *The Gospel According to Jesus* [Grand Rapids: Zondervan, 1988, 1994], and MacArthur, *The Gospel According to the Apostles* [Nashville: Thomas Nelson, 1993, 2000].)

Of course, none of the preceding positions can account for the New Testament's continual emphasis on repentance and the fruit that should be expected in a heart that has been changed (1:6; cf. Matt. 4:17; 11:20–21; Mark 6:12; Luke 5:32; 13:3, 5; 15:7, 10; 18:13–14; 24:47; Acts 2:38; 3:19; 11:18; 17:30; 20:21; 2 Cor. 7:9–10; 2 Tim. 2:25).

Even those who have wrestled more seriously with the text have sometimes misinterpreted what John says about the believer's relationship to sin. Perfectionists (usually Arminians who believe Christians can lose their salvation) assert that believers can gradually overcome sin until they become completely sinless. Having arrived at that point, they can no longer lose their salvation. But this directly conflicts with what John himself says in 1:8, "If we say that we have no sin, we are deceiving ourselves and the truth is not in us."

In a similar error, others say John means only that the believer's regenerated nature cannot sin. But that makes too great and artificial a separation between a believer's regenerated new nature and his unredeemed humanness (flesh, or old nature) and can lead to antinomianism, since one may become comfortable with the unredeemed flesh's being unable to do anything but sin. Every saint is a unified person, with both righteous aspirations as well as sinful tendencies. Sin comes from the flesh (Rom. 7:18, 25; cf. Matt. 26:41; Rom. 6:12; 8:3), but each believer must take personal responsibility for his or her sinful actions.

Some have attempted to explain John's instruction here by asserting that he is just describing an ideal but unrealized goal in sanctification—though Christians cannot become perfect in this life, they at least can strive for sinlessness. The primary problem with this idealistic interpretation is that it does not fit with the down-to-earth, realistic character of John's letter.

Another view sees the apostle's statement applying only to willful, deliberate sin by believers. As someone commented, "A Christian doesn't do sin; he suffers it." But nowhere in the text does John portray Christians as helpless victims of iniquity. Believers sin because they willfully choose to yield to temptation (James 1:14–15).

The historic Roman Catholic position is similar to this view, in that it also arbitrarily divides sin into two categories. Catholicism differentiates between venial sins (less serious ones) and mortal sins (those that result in eternal damnation). According to Rome, those who commit mortal sins forfeit the grace of justification and are no longer abiding in Christ. Such a classification for sins, however, is completely foreign to the New Testament.

In spite of the numerous interpretations of this passage, a true understanding of John's meaning is not difficult to apprehend. The correct view of John's references here to believers' not sinning derives from an accurate understanding of the Greek tenses. In this passage the verbs related to sin are all in the present tense, indicating continuous, habitual action. In other words, John is not referring to occasional acts of sin, but to established and continual patterns of sinful behavior. Believers will sometimes sin (Rom. 7:14–25)—even willfully—but they will not and cannot sin habitually, persistently, and as a way of life (cf. Rom. 6:4–14; Gal. 5:24; Eph. 2:10).

When the Holy Spirit draws sinners to God, regenerates them, and grants them eternal life through faith in Jesus Christ, they are recreated (2 Cor. 5:17) to obey the Word, follow Christ, reject the temptations of the world, and display the fruits of righteousness in their lives (Rom. 8:6; Phil. 3:9; Col. 3:2). That is nothing more than foundational new covenant truth (Jer. 31:33; Ezek. 36:25–27; Heb. 8:10; 10:16; cf. Ps. 119:1–5, 9–11, 97–105, 137–140).

The continuing aim of this epistle is to set forth tests by which a person's claim to salvation can be verified or rejected. In chapter one, John refutes the claim of the false teachers to have advanced beyond any struggle with sin (1:8–10). He goes on in chapter two to make it clear that no matter what anyone might claim to believe, if he does not obey Christ's commands (2:3) and live righteously (e.g., demonstrate love [2:9–10]), he is not a believer. In this passage, the apostle John reinforces the tests of faith he has already established. In so doing he further refutes the false teachers who minimized or denied the significance of sin. He gives three reasons that trinitarian Christians do not habitually practice sin: sin is incompatible with the law of God, it is incompatible with the work of Christ, and it is incompatible with the ministry of the Holy Spirit.

Sin Is Incompatible with the Law of God

Everyone who practices sin also practices lawlessness; and sin is lawlessness. (3:4)

The two primary biblical definitions of **sin** are "missing the mark" (*hamartia*), and "without righteousness" (*adikia*). Integral to both definitions is that sin is a transgression of God's law. In this verse John explicitly equates sin with an attitude of lawlessness and rebelliousness against God (Rom. 8:7; cf. John 3:20; 2 Cor. 4:4; Eph. 4:18; Col. 1:21). John no doubt learned this principle years earlier, during the Lord's earthly ministry, when Christ condemned the self-righteous theology of the Pharisees:

> Not everyone who says to Me, "Lord, Lord," will enter the kingdom of heaven, but he who does the will of My Father who is in heaven will enter. Many will say to Me on that day, "Lord, Lord, did we not prophesy in Your name, and in Your name cast out demons, and in Your name perform many miracles?" And then I will declare to them, "I never knew you; depart from Me, you who practice lawlessness." (Matt. 7:21–23)

John's description allows for no exceptions or dual standards. **Everyone who** habitually **practices sin** is living in an ongoing condition of **lawlessness** (James 2:10–11; cf. Rom. 4:15), which marks all who are outside the kingdom of God (cf. Rom. 1:32; Gal. 5:19–21; Rev. 21:8).

Believers, however, are not any longer marked by lawlessness. They have obeyed Jesus' command that "if anyone wishes to come after Me, he must deny himself, and take up his cross daily and follow Me" (Luke 9:23). The truly penitent heart resolves to obey God's law (1 Thess. 2:13), deny fleshly lusts (Rom. 13:14; 2 Tim. 2:22; 1 Peter 1:14), resist the world's allurements (Titus 2:12), and willingly submit to the sovereign lordship of Jesus Christ in all things (cf. Luke 6:46). Those whom God has savingly transformed have traded slavery to sin for slavery to God, as Paul wrote,

> Do you not know that when you present yourselves to someone as slaves for obedience, you are slaves of the one whom you obey, either of sin resulting in death, or of obedience resulting in righteousness? But thanks be to God that though you were slaves of sin, you became obedient from the heart to that form of teaching to which you were committed, and having been freed from sin, you became slaves of righteousness. (Rom. 6:16–18; cf. 8:12–14)

It is clear, then, that believers will not habitually violate the law of God. Whereas they formerly allowed lawlessness to dominate their lives, they now love God and desire to submit to Him. Obedience to the Word becomes precious to them, as it was to David:

> The law of the Lord is perfect, restoring the soul; the testimony of the Lord is sure, making wise the simple. The precepts of the Lord are right, rejoicing the heart; the commandment of the Lord is pure, enlightening the eyes. The fear of the Lord is clean, enduring forever; the judgments of the Lord are true; they are righteous altogether. They are more desir-

able than gold, yes, than much fine gold; sweeter also than honey and the drippings of the honeycomb. Moreover, by them Your servant is warned; in keeping them there is great reward. (Ps. 19:7–11; cf. 1:2; 40:7–8; 119:97)

SIN IS INCOMPATIBLE WITH THE WORK OF CHRIST

You know that He appeared in order to take away sins; and in Him there is no sin. No one who abides in Him sins; no one who sins has seen Him or knows Him. Little children, make sure no one deceives you; the one who practices righteousness is righteous, just as He is righteous; the one who practices sin is of the devil; for the devil has sinned from the beginning. The Son of God appeared for this purpose, to destroy the works of the devil. (3:5–8)

The primary reason for Jesus' coming to earth was **in order to take away sins.** Therefore, it is absolutely inconsistent with Jesus Christ's redeeming work on the cross for anyone who claims to be a Christian (one who shares the very life of Christ) to continue in sin. To do so utterly ignores the reality of the sanctifying element of salvation, whereby believers are set apart from sin to righteousness (1 Cor. 6:11; Eph. 5:7–9; cf. 1 Thess. 1:5–9).

John reminds his readers that they **know** (a form of the verb *oida*), not by mere information but by the confidence of personal perception, **that He appeared.** John used a form of the verb *phaneroō*, which in the New Testament often indicates either Christ's first or second coming (e.g., Col. 3:4; Heb. 9:26; 1 Peter 5:4), to refer to the indisputable fact that the Lord had come. He came not only to pay the penalty for sin and provide forgiveness (the doctrines of propitiation and justification [Rom. 3:25; 4:25; 5:9, 18; Heb. 2:17; 1 John 4:10]), but also to **take** sins **away** altogether. (**Away** is an aorist active form of the verb *airō*, which means to remove by lifting away [cf. John 1:29; Col. 2:14]). As a result of Christ's substitutionary atonement on the cross, believers have been set apart from sin unto holiness (cf. Eph. 1:3–4). The lawlessness that once characterized their lives has been removed. Because Christ died to sanctify (i.e., make holy) the believer (2 Cor. 5:21; Eph. 5:25–27), to live sinfully is contrary to His work of breaking the dominion of sin in the believer's life (Rom. 6:1–15).

The truth that Christ came to destroy sin is not just a future hope but also a present reality. John is not saying merely that believers will be delivered from sin when they die, and in the meantime will be as sinful as they were before their conversion. At salvation believers experience a real cleansing of and separation from their sins (cf. Eph. 5:26; Titus 3:5; Heb. 10:22), which on a practical level continues to occur as they become more and more conformed to the image of Christ (cf. 2 Cor. 3:18; 1 Thess. 4:1; 2 Peter 1:5–11). Titus 2:11–14 summarizes well the present and eschatological aspects of sanctification:

> For the grace of God has appeared, bringing salvation to all men, instructing us to deny ungodliness and worldly desires and to live sensibly, righteously and godly in the present age, looking for the blessed hope and the appearing of the glory of our great God and Savior, Christ Jesus, who gave Himself for us to redeem us from every lawless deed, and to purify for Himself a people for His own possession, zealous for good deeds. (cf. Eph. 2:10; 1 Peter 2:24)

John concludes verse 5 with the phrase **in Him there is no sin.** Jesus Christ is the absolutely sinless One (2 Cor. 5:21; Heb. 4:15; 7:26; 1 Peter 1:19), a truth that has immense practical ramifications. "If you know that He is righteous," John wrote earlier in this epistle, "you know that everyone also who practices righteousness is born of Him" (2:29). In 3:6 the apostle reiterates the principle that no one savingly connected to Jesus Christ can continue to live in sin: **No one who abides in Him sins; no one who sins has seen Him or knows Him.** Years earlier Paul taught the same truth to the Roman believers,

> Therefore we have been buried with Him through baptism into death, so that as Christ was raised from the dead through the glory of the Father, so we too might walk in newness of life. For if we have become united with Him in the likeness of His death, certainly we shall also be in the likeness of His resurrection, knowing this, that our old self was crucified with Him, in order that our body of sin might be done away with, so that we would no longer be slaves to sin; for he who has died is freed from sin. (Rom. 6:4–7; cf. vv. 20–22)

Again, that outlines key provisions of the new covenant, which Paul further elaborates: "But thanks be to God that though you were slaves of sin, you became obedient from the heart to that form of teaching to which you were committed, and having been freed from sin, you became slaves of righteousness" (Rom. 6:17–18). The emphasis of the apostle's statements is on sanctification, with true Christians having the Holy Spirit (Rom. 8:12–17), receiving a new heart (Acts 16:14; cf. Ezek. 36:26; Heb. 10:16–17), complete forgiveness (Col. 1:14), and a transformed life (Col. 3:5–10)—all evidenced in their new ability to obey the law of God.

Thus John taught that **no one who sins** (the present tense of the verb again denotes the habitual action of defiance and rebellion by a fallen heart) can also abide in Christ. It is not that people who become Christians will never sin again (1:8), but they will not live as they did, because **no one who sins** consistently or habitually in the pattern of the unregenerate **has seen Him or knows Him.**

John further cautioned his readers that they should **make sure no one deceive**[d] them concerning a correct understanding of sanctification. Despite any deceptive teaching to the contrary, only the one **who practices righteousness** can have any assurance that he **is righteous, just as He is righteous.**

The Lord Jesus came to earth to take away the sins of all who trust in Him, thus placing them on the path of sanctification. In contrast, **the one who practices sin is of the devil.** *Diabolos* (**devil**) means "accuser" or "slanderer."

The expression **the devil has sinned from the beginning** likely refers to the moment of Satan's rebellion against God (cf. Luke 10:18), because God originally created him as a perfect angelic being (Isa. 14:12–14; Ezek. 28:12–17). Satan is the prototypical rebel, the leading antagonist against God, and the ruler of this sinful world system (Eph. 2:2). Because he opposed God and His plan (Gen. 3:1–14; cf. Zech. 3:1; Matt. 4:1–11; 13:19; 1 Thess. 2:18) and instigated the original rebellion against God's law, all unsaved sinners are in a sense the Devil's children (cf. John 8:44; 2 Cor. 4:3–4; Eph. 2:1–3).

John makes the obvious conclusion that because **the Son of God appeared . . . to destroy the works of the devil** (Gen. 3:15; cf. John 12:31; Heb. 2:14), it is impossible and unthinkable that true believers would continue in devil-like behavior. Today Satan is still opposing the plans and people of God (1 Peter 5:8), but believers are no longer his children or under his rule, nor are they bound to do his **works.**

The phrase **the works of the devil** encompasses various satanic activities such as instigating sin and rebellion, tempting believers, inspiring unbiblical ideologies and false religions, persecuting and accusing believers, instigating the work of false teachers, and wielding the power of death (e.g., Luke 8:12; John 8:44; Acts 5:3; 1 Cor. 7:5; 2 Cor. 4:4; 10:3–5; Eph. 6:11–12; 1 Thess. 2:18; Heb. 2:14; Rev. 12:10). None of those **works** can ultimately defeat the saints, who have been delivered from his Kingdom (Col. 1:13).

SIN IS INCOMPATIBLE WITH THE MINISTRY OF THE HOLY SPIRIT

No one who is born of God practices sin, because His seed abides in him; and he cannot sin, because he is born of God. By this the

children of God and the children of the devil are obvious: any-one who does not practice righteousness is not of God, nor the one who does not love his brother. (3:9–10)

The new birth (being **born of God**) epitomizes the work of the Holy Spirit:

> Jesus answered and said to him, "Truly, truly, I say to you, unless one is born again he cannot see the kingdom of God." Nicodemus said to Him, "How can a man be born when he is old? He cannot enter a second time into his mother's womb and be born, can he?" Jesus answered, "Truly, truly, I say to you, unless one is born of water and the Spirit he cannot enter into the kingdom of God. That which is born of the flesh is flesh, and that which is born of the Spirit is spirit. Do not be amazed that I said to you, 'You must be born again.' The wind blows where it wishes and you hear the sound of it, but do not know where it comes from and where it is going; so is everyone who is born of the Spirit." (John 3:3–8; cf. 1:12–13)

The Holy Spirit implants in those He regenerates the principle of **His** divine life, which John pictures as a **seed.** Just as a human birth results from an implanted seed that grows into new physical life, so also spiritual life begins when, at the moment of regeneration, the divine seed is implanted by the Spirit within the one who believes.

The instrument by which the Spirit gives new birth to sinners is the Word of God. The apostle Peter explained to the readers of his first letter,

> You have been born again not of seed which is perishable but imperishable, that is, through the living and enduring word of God. For, "All flesh is like grass, and all its glory like the flower of grass. The grass withers, and the flower falls off, but the word of the Lord endures forever." And this is the word which was preached to you. (1 Peter 1:23–25; cf. Ps. 19:7; 2 Peter 1:4)

The new birth is from imperishable seed, securing the believer's salvation for eternity. It enlightens the mind so one can discern spiritual realities (John 14:26; 1 Cor. 2:10, 13–14; cf. Isa. 40:13–14). It gives believers the mind of Christ (1 Cor. 2:16) so they can understand the thoughts of God. It liberates and energizes the enslaved will, previously unable to obey God but now freely able and willing to do so (John 6:44, 65; Col. 2:13; cf. John 5:21*b*). The new birth signals the end of the sinner's old life; those who were hopelessly corrupt become new creatures in Christ (2 Cor. 5:17), buried with Him and raised unto a new life of righteousness (Rom. 6:4;

Eph. 4:24). Therefore he states again that believers **cannot** practice **sin, because** they are **born of God.**

The new birth is also a monergistic operation, which means God's Spirit alone accomplishes it. (It is not synergistic, which means that human effort would also play some part in the process.) Paul's language in Ephesians 2:1–6 is unmistakably clear in this regard:

> And you were dead in your trespasses and sins, in which you formerly walked according to the course of this world, according to the prince of the power of the air, of the spirit that is now working in the sons of disobedience. Among them we too all formerly lived in the lusts of our flesh, indulging the desires of the flesh and of the mind, and were by nature children of wrath, even as the rest. But God, being rich in mercy, because of His great love with which He loved us, even when we were dead in our transgressions, made us alive together with Christ (by grace you have been saved), and raised us up with Him, and seated us with Him in the heavenly places in Christ Jesus. (cf. Titus 3:5; James 1:18)

Because unregenerate people are spiritually dead, they are unable to respond to divine truth. This doctrine of total depravity—better stated, total human inability—does not mean that the unredeemed are all as sinful as they possibly could be. Rather, it means that their fallen, sinful natures affect every area of life and render them incapable of saving themselves. Thus the spiritually dead person needs to be made alive by God alone, through His Spirit. That same power energizes every aspect of Christian living (cf. Rom. 6:11–13).

John concludes this section with the summary statement, **By this the children of God and the children of the devil are obvious: anyone who does not practice righteousness is not of God.** There are only two groups of people in the world (cf. Prov. 15:9): **the children of God and the children of the devil.** The first exhibits God's righteous character through obeying His law (cf. Luke 1:6); the second exhibits Satan's sinful character by disregarding the Word and habitually sinning (cf. Pss. 36:3; 119:150; Rom. 2:8). No matter what people may profess, or what past religious ritual or experience they may point to, **anyone who does not practice righteousness is not of God, nor the one who does not love his brother.**

The final phrase of this section, **nor the one who does not love his brother,** reaffirms to readers another aspect of John's moral test to identify true believers, namely the test of love (cf. John 13:34–35). For the apostle, it was also obvious that anyone claiming to be a Christian but not demonstrating brotherly love could not really be in Christ. He develops this argument in the remaining portion of chapter 3.

The Children of the Devil versus the Children of God (1 John 3:11–18)

12

For this is the message which you have heard from the beginning, that we should love one another; not as Cain, who was of the evil one and slew his brother. And for what reason did he slay him? Because his deeds were evil, and his brother's were righteous. Do not be surprised, brethren, if the world hates you. We know that we have passed out of death into life, because we love the brethren. He who does not love abides in death. Everyone who hates his brother is a murderer; and you know that no murderer has eternal life abiding in him. We know love by this, that He laid down His life for us; and we ought to lay down our lives for the brethren. But whoever has the world's goods, and sees his brother in need and closes his heart against him, how does the love of God abide in him? Little children, let us not love with word or with tongue, but in deed and truth. (3:11–18)

In 1970, noted Christian apologist, evangelist, and author Francis Schaeffer (1912–1984) introduced his book *The Mark of the Christian* with the following statements:

Through the centuries men have displayed many different symbols to show that they are Christians. They have worn marks in the lapels of their coats, hung chains about their necks, even had special haircuts.

Of course, there is nothing wrong with any of this, if one feels it is his calling. But there is a much better sign—a mark that has not been thought up just as a matter of expediency for use on some special occasion or in some specific era. It is a universal mark that is to last through all the ages of the church till Jesus comes back.

What is this mark?

At the close of his ministry, Jesus looks forward to his death on the cross, the open tomb and the ascension. Knowing that he is about to leave, Jesus prepares his disciples for what is to come. It is here that he makes clear what will be the distinguishing mark of the Christian:

> Little children, yet a little while I am with you. Ye shall seek me; and as I said unto the Jews, Whither I go, ye cannot come; so now I say to you. A new commandment I give unto you, That ye *love* one another; as I have *loved* you, that ye also *love* one another. By this shall all men know that ye are my disciples, if ye have *love* one to another. (John 13:33–35)

> This passage reveals the mark that Jesus gives to label a Christian not just in one era or in one locality but at all times and all places until Jesus returns. (Downers Grove, Ill.: InterVarsity, 1970, 7–8; emphases added to Scripture quotation)

Love, then, in contrast to those in Satan's realm, has always been an essential characteristic of every true Christian. The rest of the New Testament consistently bears out this truth.

> Hope does not disappoint, because the love of God has been poured out within our hearts through the Holy Spirit who was given to us. (Rom. 5:5)

> But the fruit of the Spirit is love, joy, peace, patience, kindness, goodness, faithfulness, gentleness, self-control; against such things there is no law. (Gal. 5:22–23)

> Now as to the love of the brethren, you have no need for anyone to write to you, for you yourselves are taught by God to love one another. (1 Thess. 4:9)

> Since you have in obedience to the truth purified your souls for a sincere love of the brethren, fervently love one another from the heart. (1 Peter 1:22)

> And this is love, that we walk according to His commandments. This is

the commandment, just as you have heard from the beginning, that you should walk in it. (2 John 6)

God not only commands those who are in Christ to show love (cf. John 15:12: Rom. 12:10; 1 Peter 4:8). He also enables them to obey that mandate, granting them the capacity to do what He requires (cf. Rom. 5:5).

There is nothing novel or unprecedented, then, about John's teaching that Christians are marked by love for one another. (His teaching about love in this epistle serves as the second aspect of the moral test —cf. 2:7–11). Because God loves them (Rom. 5:8; Eph. 1:3–14; 2:4–5), true believers will surely reflect that love in their relationships with other people (Matt. 22:37–39; Eph. 5:2; 1 John 4:19). Thus the apostle's instruction here is not new, but is "an old commandment which you have had from the beginning; the old commandment is the word which you have heard" (2:7; cf. v. 10; 4:7–8).

John's readers knew that truth, because apostolic preachers had faithfully delivered it to them (cf. 1:5; 2:24). However, false teachers had also come and taught, apparently, that brotherly love is not an essential mark of true salvation. Those apostates added to their erroneous view of Christ's nature and their disobedience to God's commands a lack of love for true believers. In response, John directed his readers back to **the message** they had **heard from the beginning,** referring to the beginning of gospel proclamation. That teaching included the truth about Jesus Christ, the gospel, mankind's sinful condition, and the need for righteous living, as well as the command to **love one another.** The apostle urged his readers to remember what they were first taught and not allow anyone to lead them astray (cf. Jude 3).

In one sense, the Lord's command in John 13:34–35 was very old (Lev. 19:18; Rom. 13:10). But in another sense, it was new. Love had never before been manifested as it was by Christ—culminating in His sacrificial death for those He loved. "This is My commandment," He declared, "that you love one another, just as I have loved you. Greater love has no one than this, that one lay down his life for his friends" (John 15:12–13; cf. Luke 19:10; Gal. 2:20; Rev. 1:5). The Lord Jesus Christ is the perfect model of the love God has always commanded. Though believers cannot love to the degree He loves, they can obey John's command to **love one another** (3:23; 4:7, 21; 2 John 5; cf. Rom. 12:10; 13:8–9; Gal. 5:13–14; Col. 3:14; Heb. 10:24; 13:1; 1 Peter 1:22; 4:8) the way Christ loved, by the power of the Spirit (Rom. 5:5), lovingly and selflessly sacrificing for others.

Having stressed the importance of love in 3:11, John contrasted the children of God, who obey that command, with the children of the Devil, who do not. Instead of being characterized by love, Satan's children are marked by murder, hatred, and indifference toward the children of God.

SATAN'S CHILDREN
MURDER GOD'S CHILDREN

not as Cain, who was of the evil one and slew his brother. And for what reason did he slay him? Because his deeds were evil, and his brother's were righteous. . . . We know that we have passed out of death into life, because we love the brethren. He who does not love abides in death. (3:12, 14)

Murder is the ultimate act of hate (cf. Num. 35:20–21; Matt. 5:21–22) and demonstrates the absence of love in the most extreme way. To illustrate that point, John inserted the only Old Testament reference in the entire epistle: to **Cain,** the first murderer.

Cain, as a worshiper of God, offered Him a sacrifice (Gen. 4:3–5). Unlike his brother Abel, however, Cain did not bring an acceptable sacrifice to God (cf. Heb. 11:4). Abel brought an animal sacrifice, which the narrative implies was in obedience to God's command. On the other hand Cain, in his self-styled religion, ignored the divine requirement and brought the fruit of the ground for his offering.

But far from being a true worshiper of God, both Cain's disobedience and the fact that he **slew his brother** revealed that he **was of the evil one.** Genesis 4:2*b*–8 describes the shocking story of history's first murder:

> Abel was a keeper of flocks, but Cain was a tiller of the ground. So it came about in the course of time that Cain brought an offering to the Lord of the fruit of the ground. Abel, on his part also brought of the firstlings of his flock and of their fat portions. And the Lord had regard for Abel and for his offering; but for Cain and for his offering He had no regard. So Cain became very angry and his countenance fell. Then the Lord said to Cain, "Why are you angry? And why has your countenance fallen? If you do well, will not your countenance be lifted up? And if you do not do well, sin is crouching at the door; and its desire is for you, but you must master it." Cain told Abel his brother. And it came about when they were in the field, that Cain rose up against Abel his brother and killed him.

That Cain **was of the evil one** means he belonged to the kingdom of darkness, as did the unbelieving Jews who, like Cain, hated true righteousness and sought to kill Jesus. He said to them, "You are of your father the devil, and you want to do the desires of your father. He was a murderer from the beginning, and does not stand in the truth because there is no truth in him" (John 8:44*a*).

The word translated **evil one** (*ponēros*) denotes determined, aggressive, and fervent evil that actively opposes what is good (cf. Matt. 4:3–10; 2 Cor. 2:11; 1 Peter 5:8). Its meaning extends beyond basic evil or corruption (*kakos*) to include a type of malignant sinfulness that pulls others down into ruin (cf. Matt. 13:19, 38–39*a*; 2 Cor. 4:4).

The verb in John's phrase that Cain **slew his brother** is a form of *sphazō*, which is a vivid term that means to butcher or slaughter. It was used of animals killed in sacrifice (cf. Lev. 1:5, LXX) and implies a violent death. (In the only other reference to killing prior to Cain's action, God put to death an animal and used parts of its skin to cover Adam and Eve [Gen. 3:21].) It is as if Cain, intensely resentful and jealous because his inferior sacrifice was rejected by God while Abel's was accepted, violently slit his brother's throat, thus defiantly making him his "replacement sacrifice."

John's rhetorical question, **And for what reason did he slay him?** is easily answered in a general characterization of Cain: **Because his deeds were evil, and his brother's were righteous.** It is as simple as that. Cain was evil and hated righteousness so greatly that he even killed his own brother, whose righteous deeds had rebuked him.

Like Cain, the ungodly resent the righteous because, through their righteous actions, they expose the false beliefs and wicked practices of those who are evil (cf. Matt. 14:3–5; Acts 6:8–14; 7:51–60).

On the other hand, those who **have passed out of death into life** (cf. John 5:24) are assured of that reality **because** they **love the brethren** (cf. 1 John 4:7, 12). The new birth (John 3:8; Titus 3:5; 1 Peter 1:23), which grants life to the spiritually dead (cf. 2 Cor. 5:17; Gal. 6:15; Eph. 4:24), turns hateful and even murderous attitudes into loving ones (cf. Col. 2:11). John therefore reminded his readers that anyone who **does not** so **love** has not received spiritual life but **abides in** the condition of spiritual **death.**

SATAN'S CHILDREN
HATE GOD'S CHILDREN

Do not be surprised, brethren, if the world hates you. . . . Everyone who hates his brother is a murderer; and you know that no murderer has eternal life abiding in him. (3:13, 15)

In God's eyes, hatred is the moral equivalent of murder; thus **everyone who hates his brother is a murderer.** It is true, of course, that only a small percentage of people actually murder someone. Many more have been angry enough to have done so, had the circumstances been favorable and were they not afraid of the severe consequences they would have suffered (cf. Gen. 9:6; Matt. 26:52; Rom. 13:4). But the only outward difference between murder and hate is the deed itself—the attitudes are the same. In the Sermon on the Mount, Jesus made this clear:

> You have heard that the ancients were told, "You shall not commit murder" and "Whoever commits murder shall be liable to the court." But I say to you that everyone who is angry with his brother shall be guilty before the court; and whoever says to his brother, "You good-for-nothing," shall be guilty before the supreme court; and whoever says, "You fool," shall be guilty enough to go into the fiery hell. (Matt. 5:21–22)

Impenitent and unconverted sinners will be eternally condemned for their habitual attitudes of hate, even if those attitudes never translate into physical actions.

John warned his readers that even though they were transformed to love other believers and even unbelievers (cf. Matt. 5:44; Rom. 12:14, 20; 1 Peter 3:9), they should **not be surprised . . . if the world hates** them. The expression **do not be surprised** translates the present active imperative form of the verb *thaumazō*, a term that has the connotation of wonder, astonishment, or amazement. Rather than being shocked by the world's opposition, believers should instead expect it (cf. Acts 14:22; 2 Tim. 3:12; 1 Peter 4:12), because the world has nothing in common with the kingdom of God (cf. 2 Cor. 6:14–15), and the lives of the righteous rebuke those of the unrighteous. In the upper room, Jesus promised the apostles that the world would hate them:

> If the world hates you, you know that it has hated Me before it hated you. If you were of the world, the world would love its own; but because you are not of the world, but I chose you out of the world, because of this the world hates you. . . . He who hates Me hates My Father also. If I had not done among them the works which no one else did, they would not have sin; but now they have both seen and hated Me and My Father as well. But they have done this to fulfill the word that is written in their Law, "They hated Me without a cause." (John 15:18–19, 23–25)

By their hatred, the children of the Devil have always revealed their true character. Redemptive history contains many instances of the world persecuting God's people (cf. Heb. 11:36–40). The people of His own town hated Jesus and attempted to kill Him after hearing just one message from Him (Luke 4:28–29). The leaders of the nation later plotted to kill Him (cf. Matt. 12:14; Mark 3:6; 14:1–2, 11; John 10:39; 11:45–57; Acts 7:52). The world hated the apostles (Luke 21:12–13; John 16:2–3;

Acts 4:1–31; 5:17–41; cf. John 17:15–16) and martyred all but the apostle John, whom it exiled to the island of Patmos (Rev. 1:9). Enemies of the gospel have always persecuted those who love the truth. Even today believers around the world die under the hateful, murderous hands of the children of the Devil.

In his customary absolute, black-and-white style, John reminds readers that **no murderer has eternal life abiding in him.** That does not mean that a believer could never commit an act of murder, or that someone who has committed murder can never be saved. But it does mean that those who are characterized by hateful attitudes and who regularly harbor murderous thoughts evidence an unregenerate heart and will perish eternally (cf. Rev. 21:7–8; 22:14–15) unless they repent.

SATAN'S CHILDREN ARE
INDIFFERENT TOWARD GOD'S CHILDREN

We know love by this, that He laid down His life for us; and we ought to lay down our lives for the brethren. But whoever has the world's goods, and sees his brother in need and closes his heart against him, how does the love of God abide in him? Little children, let us not love with word or with tongue, but in deed and truth. (3:16–18)

The phrase **we know love by this** again affirms genuine love as the outstanding mark of the Christian (cf. the discussion of v. 11 above). By God's grace, a loving willingness to give up everything to help others (cf. 2 Cor. 9:6–12; 1 Tim. 6:17–19; Heb. 13:16, 21) permeates the attitudes of believers and shines forth in their lives. The New Testament contains several notable examples of such sacrificial love. One such example was Epaphroditus, whom the apostle Paul commended to the Philippians:

> I thought it necessary to send to you Epaphroditus, my brother and fellow worker and fellow soldier, who is also your messenger and minister to my need; because he was longing for you all and was distressed because you had heard that he was sick. For indeed he was sick to the point of death, but God had mercy on him, and not on him only but also on me, so that I would not have sorrow upon sorrow. Therefore I have sent him all the more eagerly so that when you see him again you may rejoice and I may be less concerned about you. Receive him then in the Lord with all joy, and hold men like him in high regard; because he came close to death for the work of Christ, risking his life to complete what was deficient in your service to me. (Phil. 2:25–30)

Paul also was willing to surrender his life for the cause of Christ, "For to me, to live is Christ and to die is gain" (Phil. 1:21; cf. Rom. 9:3–5; 2 Cor. 1:9–10). Of course, the Lord Jesus was Paul's role model, because at the cross He laid down His life for all who believe (cf. John 10:11, 14–18; 15:13; Rom. 8:32–34; Gal. 3:13; 1 Peter 2:24).

The expression **laid down His life for us** is unique to the apostle John (John 10:11, 15, 17, 18; 13:37–38; 15:13), and in addition to **life** itself it refers to divesting oneself of anything important. Obviously, Christ's atoning death is the supreme example of selfless love (John 15:12–13; Phil. 2:5–8; 1 Peter 2:19–23; cf. 2 Cor. 8:9). Thus John exhorts his readers, as followers of Christ, that they **ought to lay down their lives for the brethren,** should such sacrifice be necessary. That this expression refers to something far more extensive than only sacrificial death for a fellow believer is clear from the subsequent statement about having **goods** that someone needs.

The selfish indifference of unbelievers stands in sharp contrast to the generous, compassionate love that believers exhibit (Acts 2:45; 4:36–37; 9:36; 11:29–30; 2 Cor. 8:1–5; 9:2, 11–13; Phil. 4:14–16). John illustrates the difference in attitude in practical, specific terms: **But whoever has the world's goods, and sees his brother in need and closes his heart against him, how does the love of God abide in him?** The children of the Devil often have **the world's goods** (material wealth) at their disposal. When they do give sacrificially to anyone else (cf. Mark 12:43–44), they are motivated by selfishness. Unbelievers' philanthropic efforts are usually merely to pacify their consciences, satisfy their emotions, or bring honor to themselves (cf. Matt. 6:1–2) rather than glory to God.

But that is not to be the case with believers, as John's closing injunction to his readers indicates: **Little children, let us not love with word or with tongue, but in deed and truth.** It is not enough for an individual merely to profess love for others (which is also true regarding faith; cf. Luke 6:46; James 2:18–26). The proof that one has genuine love and is a child of God rests not in sentiments but in deeds (cf. Matt. 25:34–40).

For John, therefore, the differences between Satan's children and God's children could not be more distinct. Those who murder, habitually hate, or are chronically self-centered and indifferent to the needs of others do not have eternal life. But those who, as part of their repentance from sin and trust in Christ, have renounced murderous, hateful attitudes and all cold, selfish indifference to the needs of others give evidence that they have been born again. In place of those sinful traits, Christians manifest genuine love to others, especially fellow believers (Rom. 12:10–13; Gal. 6:10), because of the love of God shed abroad in their hearts. They sincerely obey James's injunction: "Pure and undefiled religion in the sight of our God and Father is this: to visit orphans and widows in their distress, and to keep oneself unstained by the world" (James 1:27; cf. 2:8, 15–17).

Holy Affections
(1 John 3:19–24)

13

We will know by this that we are of the truth, and will assure our heart before Him in whatever our heart condemns us; for God is greater than our heart and knows all things. Beloved, if our heart does not condemn us, we have confidence before God; and whatever we ask we receive from Him, because we keep His commandments and do the things that are pleasing in His sight. This is His commandment, that we believe in the name of His Son Jesus Christ, and love one another, just as He commanded us. The one who keeps His commandments abides in Him, and He in him. We know by this that He abides in us, by the Spirit whom He has given us. (3:19–24)

Jonathan Edwards (1703–1758) may rank as the greatest theologian America has ever known. He ministered during the First Great Awakening, in the early eighteenth century, being used by God to help spark one of the most notable revivals in American history (a Second Great Awakening occurred in the early nineteenth century, and the Layman's Prayer Revival took place in 1857–1858). Along with George Whitefield and others, the Holy Spirit used Edwards to draw countless numbers of sinners to genuine repentance and saving faith in the gospel.

The sermons he preached and the works he wrote powerfully called people to obey the gospel of Jesus Christ, turn from sin, and embrace the authority of Scripture and personal holiness, all of which led them to find their fulfillment in glorifying God.

The impact of the Holy Spirit through Jonathan Edwards and his colleagues, in igniting a widespread response to the gospel, meant that the assurance of salvation quickly became a major issue. The call to embrace the gospel, obey the Word of God, and persevere in holiness overwhelmed many of the new converts. People questioned whether or not they were doing all they should and whether or not they were truly saved. In response to those concerns, Edwards, in 1746, wrote his classic book *A Treatise Concerning Religious Affections*. This monumental work argues that the most accurate proof of salvation is the presence in one's life of holy, religious affections—a zealous and biblical inclination toward righteousness, evidenced by practical good works. Because Edwards saw the danger that Satan would counterfeit conversions, he was careful to warn his readers that it is possible to have an initial, positive interest in the gospel (like the seeds on shallow soil and weedy ground in Jesus' parable; Matt. 13:1–23) and yet not possess true saving faith. However, when the grace of God is truly planted in a person's heart, it will always result in a changed nature (cf. 2 Cor. 5:17), marked by an abiding desire to live a holy life.

Of course, Edwards's teaching did not originate with him. He drew it from the New Testament, as summarized in the book of James: "Even so faith, if it has no works, is dead, being by itself" (2:17). His understanding also represented the historic Reformed view that true salvation is a permanent gift from God that inevitably results in righteous living.

In contrast, the historic Arminian position teaches that salvation is conditional, guaranteeing nothing beyond an initial experience of desiring holiness. Thus Arminians believe Christians can and do lose their salvation (through unrepentant sin, disbelief, or denial), and along with it their ability to perform good works. Believers are left with a very fragile kind of assurance according to this view, because salvation itself can be forfeited, eternal life ended, and the Holy Spirit withdrawn due to the Christian's failures.

The twentieth century saw the emergence of a third position on assurance, one that combines certain elements of the other two. This view (often called the no-lordship or Free Grace view) denies that there is any necessary connection between justification and sanctification. Thus, it teaches that justified people are saved forever, even if they have only a temporary manifestation of and interest in obedience and holiness. In other words, once a decision is made to follow Christ, the individual is deemed saved no matter whether he or she overtly denies the faith or merely lives the rest of his or her life uninterested in matters honoring to the Lord. (For a critique of this teaching, see my book *The Gospel According to the Apostles* [Nashville: Thomas Nelson, 1993, 2000], 5–20, 193–216. And for extensive, additional exposition on the nature of the biblical gospel, see my prior book, *The Gospel According to Jesus* [Grand Rapids: Zondervan, 1988, 1994].) This view wrongly bases assurance on the past fact of a one-time profession, not on the present, consistent fruit of a holy life.

In contrast to the erroneous views of Arminianism and Free Grace, which either make assurance impossible to keep or provide the wrong criteria for sustaining it, John wrote this epistle so that those "who believe in the name of the Son of God, . . . may know that [they] have eternal life" (5:13). He wanted his readers to be certain of their salvation, possessing an assurance that was both legitimate and lasting. With that in mind, John concisely offers five familiar attitudes in verses 19–24 that true believers will consistently manifest in their lives. By examining themselves (cf. 2 Cor. 13:5), they can know for certain that they are saved, because their lives will be characterized by: gratitude for God's grace, boldness in prayer, submission to God's commands, faith in Jesus Christ, and appreciation for the indwelling Holy Spirit.

Each of these elements derives from the theme of love, most recently mentioned in verse 18 of this chapter: "Little children, let us not love with word or with tongue, but in deed and truth." Thus John maintains his emphasis on the noblest of virtues (1 Cor. 13:13) as he spells out these perspectives.

GRATITUDE FOR GOD'S GRACE

We will know by this that we are of the truth, and will assure our heart before Him in whatever our heart condemns us; for God is greater than our heart and knows all things. (3:19–20)

Every human being is born with the law of God written in the heart and with a conscience to accuse or excuse, depending on how the person acts in regard to that law:

> For when Gentiles who do not have the Law do instinctively the things of the Law, these, not having the Law, are a law to themselves, in that they show the work of the Law written in their hearts, their conscience bearing witness and their thoughts alternately accusing or else defending them. (Rom. 2:14–15)

This means every person has some degree of self-knowledge and some innate ability to recognize right and wrong.

Those who are Christians have embraced the truth of Scripture, by which they were regenerated (1 Peter 1:23) and are being sanctified (John 17:17). They desire to know and obey the Word (cf. 1 John 2:3–6; 3:6–10). And when believers obey the Word of God, their consciences inform them that they did the right thing (Rom. 9:1), giving them joy and godly confidence (2 Cor. 1:12). Similarly, if they sin, their consciences indict them on account of their wrong thoughts, words, or actions (John 8:9). If believers persist in sin, implicitly the conscience will make them fearful, depressed, and insecure (cf. Pss. 32:3–4; 38:1–8; 40:11–12). They will then begin to question the genuineness of their profession of faith, on account of their prolonged disobedience. While they cannot lose their salvation (if they are truly saved), they can begin to lose the assurance of that salvation due to a plaguing conscience that accuses them. Until they properly deal with their sin, their conscience, empowered by true, Spirit-aided knowledge of the scriptural standards for holiness, will continue to painfully remind them of the blatant discrepancy between what they profess and what they practice.

The conscience then is God's guilt-producing warning device, given to every person to confront sin. In the same way that pain is a physical warning mechanism that tells people they have a bodily injury or illness, the conscience is a spiritual warning mechanism that alerts of conduct dangerous to the soul. Of course, to function effectively, the conscience must be informed by the right standards, because it is only a reactor to the person's convictions about right and wrong. If ill-informed by falsehoods and lies, the conscience will still react to those untruths that govern an individual's beliefs (e.g., Muslim suicide bombers).

Conscience is thus not in itself an independent system of morality. Rather, it operates based on whatever knowledge and belief system that informs it, and in response to the cultural conditions surrounding it. If the level of moral and spiritual knowledge is drawn from any other source than Scripture, the conscience (like that of the Islamic suicide bomber who is convinced he is doing God's work) will function in response to those false ideas. It can be silenced not only by being misinformed, but by being constantly ignored or overridden, until it is scarred and unresponsive (1 Tim. 4:2).

That is why it is crucial to know God's law accurately (Pss. 19:7–9; 119:1–8; Luke 11:28; John 8:31–32; James 1:21–25) and allow it to properly inform the conscience. It is the law of God empowered by the Spirit that awakens people to their sinful condition and need of salvation (cf. John 16:8–11; Rom. 7:9–10). The sinner, seeing his true wretchedness as one guilty before God, is then faced with the reality of divine wrath and judgment against him, offset by the offer of mercy and deliverance through faith in the Lord Jesus Christ (cf. Luke 18:13).

In salvation, by the work of Christ on the cross, the wrath of God is propitiated and the guilt of sin removed from the forgiven sinner who then comes to enjoy the exhilarating, heartfelt deliverance of heavenly grace (cf. Eph. 2:1–9; Col. 2:11–14; 3:9–10). One of salvation's most gracious gifts is a cleansed conscience (cf. Heb. 10:19–22), meaning it ceases to accuse. Just before salvation it accuses most intensely, but afterward the accusation stops and the believer goes from fear to joy, dread to hope, and anxiety to peace. The writer of Hebrews refers to this work of God when he writes: "How much more will the blood of Christ, who through the eternal Spirit offered Himself without blemish to God, cleanse your conscience from dead works to serve the living God?" (Heb. 9:14). In Hebrews 10:22 he speaks of "having our hearts sprinkled clean from an evil conscience" in salvation.

Still the apostle John understood that at times true believers can struggle with their assurance. Some of his readers may have been so overwhelmed by the memory of their past sins and awareness of present ones that they found the thought of God's forgiveness nearly impossible to accept. Their overactive consciences, beleaguering them with their own shortcomings, perhaps made it difficult for them to have a settled confidence in their right standing before God. So John wrote to encourage those believers and enable them to accurately evaluate their own spiritual condition. In so doing, he sought to solidify their conviction, rightly inform their conscience, and strengthen their assurance with a true understanding of their transformation and its evidences. (For a fuller discussion of the human conscience, see my book *The Vanishing Conscience* [Dallas: Word, 1994], 35–75, 229–55.)

The phrase **we will know** translates a form of the common Greek verb *ginōskō,* which means "to know," "to learn," "to find out," or "to realize." John's use of the future tense indicates that what his readers would eventually grasp was not something intuitive or indefinite, but a promise based on an existing reality. This point is strengthened by the next short phrase **by this,** which most naturally refers back to verse 18's admonition for brotherly love. When believers **know** they have sincere love for one another, they can be certain **that** they **are of the truth** (the phrase literally reads, "out of the truth we exist"). Only those who have been genuinely converted through the supernatural work of God possess the sacrificial love that John describes in verses 14–18, which issues in the submissive obedience that John delineates in verses 4–12.

The **truth** in view here is the written truth of Scripture (Ps. 119:160; John 17:17), which encompasses the truth incarnate in the Lord

Jesus Christ (John 1:9, 14; 7:18; 14:6; 1 John 5:20). Belief in the truth marks all who repent and believe (2 Thess. 2:10, 12–13; 1 Tim. 3:15*b*).

Believers enjoy an assurance based not only on what Scripture promises to those who believe (Ps. 4:3; Phil. 1:6; 2 Tim. 1:12), but, on a practical level, based on the presence of a serving love for fellow believers (cf. vv. 13–18) and a desire to live in holiness (cf. vv. 4–12). These qualities, because they come from God, cannot exist in a person who is still unregenerate. **Assure** comes from the future active indicative of the verb *peithō* and means "will persuade." Some lexicographers give "to tranquilize" as a possible definition, which could have an interesting connotation in this context. Even though believers stand **before Him,** in the awesome, intimidating presence of the absolutely holy God (Ex. 15:11; 1 Sam. 2:2; Rev. 15:4), they can have a calm, tranquil, confident heart and an affirming conscience (Acts 23:1; 24:16; 2 Cor. 1:12; 1 Tim. 1:5; 3:9; 2 Tim. 1:3).

Being in the presence of God terrified even the noblest of saints. Moses "hid his face, for he was afraid to look at God" (Ex. 3:6). The prophets Isaiah (Isa. 6:1–5) and Ezekiel (Ezek. 1:26–28) also felt great fear as they stood in the presence of holiness. After witnessing one of His miracles, the apostle Peter "fell down at Jesus' feet, saying, 'Go away from me Lord, for I am a sinful man, O Lord!'" (Luke 5:8). He and fellow apostles James and John were traumatized on the Mount of Transfiguration (Matt. 17:1–8), as was John when he saw the glorified Christ (Rev. 1:12–18). Although believers are no longer slaves to sin but to righteousness (Rom. 6:16–18), the remaining sin within their unredeemed humanness (cf. Rom. 7:14–25) could make God's holy presence very frightening were it not for the gracious gift of assurance.

Those who have been justified by faith are at peace *with* God (Rom. 5:1) and enjoy the peace *of* God (Phil. 4:7). Nevertheless, a believer may experience unnecessary guilt as his heart condemns him. But there is a higher court than the human heart, for God **is greater than our heart and knows all things.** If He has declared believers righteous in Christ, then they are righteous. Thus Paul wrote, "Therefore there is now no condemnation for those who are in Christ Jesus" (Rom. 8:1). And no one can ever separate them from the saving love of God in Christ (8:31–39). He sees believers' greatest, most profound failures, and He knows far more about their weaknesses than even their consciences do (Pss. 1:6; 103:14; 139:1–6; Prov. 24:12; Heb. 4:13). Yet God has forgiven those who by faith in Christ have been adopted into His family (Rom. 8:14–17). Moreover, He is at work in their hearts, continuing to cleanse them from the sin that still lingers there (cf. Phil. 2:12–13). He looks beyond the remaining sin and sees the holy affections He has planted in them that demonstrate the transformed natures of His children. Therefore even when overwhelmed by their sinfulness believers can say with Peter, "Lord, You know all things; You know that I love You" (John 21:17b; cf. Rom. 7:14–25).

BOLDNESS IN PRAYER

Beloved, if our heart does not condemn us, we have confidence before God; and whatever we ask we receive from Him, (3:21–22a)

Doubt ceases when believers are walking in faithfulness and obedience, because the **heart does not condemn** so that insecurity and fear give way to **confidence before God.** Such assurance causes believers to enter God's presence with certainty (Eph. 3:12; Heb. 10:19; cf. 2 Cor. 3:4; 1 Tim. 3:13), so that whatever they ask in prayer they will receive from Him. The word rendered **confidence** (*parrēsia*) means "boldness" and "freedom of speech." It describes the privilege of coming before someone of importance, power, and authority and feeling free to express whatever is on one's mind. For believers it means coming into the presence of our loving heavenly Father without fear (cf. 2:28; 4:17) and with full assurance that **whatever** we **ask** we **receive from Him** (cf. 5:14; John 14:13–14; 15:7, 16; 16:23–24). The writer to the Hebrews used a form of *parrēsia* in 4:16: "Therefore let us draw near with confidence to the throne of grace, so that we may receive mercy and find grace to help in time of need."

Some might consider that approach presumptuous. But obviously, any requests believers make to God must be in accordance with His will (cf. Matt. 26:39, 42). John R. W. Stott provides helpful insight in this regard:

> John does not mean to imply that God hears and answers our prayers merely for the subjective reason that we have a clear conscience and an uncondemning heart. There is an objective, moral reason, namely *because we keep his commandments, and,* more generally, *do those things that are pleasing in his sight.* Obedience is the indispensable condition, not the meritorious cause, of answered prayer. *Whatsoever we ask, we receive* describes the Christian's habitual experience (the verbs are in the present tense), and Candlish is right to point to the incarnate Son as the supreme example of pleasing God and so being heard by God (Jn. viii. 29, xi. 41, 42). The statement echoes our Lord's promise, where the same two verbs occur: "Ask, and it shall be given you ... for every one that asketh receiveth" (Mt. vii. 7, 8). (*The Epistles of John,* The Tyndale New Testament Commentaries [Grand Rapids: Eerdmans, 1964], 149; emphases in original)

Boldness in prayer is therefore clear evidence of a changed heart. Because they know God as "Abba! Father!" (Rom. 8:15; Gal. 4:6), believers realize that anything they ask within His will (cf. John 14:13–14) He is going to hear because He has promised to meet all their needs (Phil. 4:19; cf. Ps. 23:1; 2 Cor. 9:8).

SUBMISSION TO GOD'S COMMANDS

because we keep His commandments and do the things that are pleasing in His sight. (3:22b)

Having emphasized boldness in prayer, John continues to focus on assurance by again highlighting that believers willingly submit to God's commands because they desire to bring Him pleasure. John's purpose here, however, in tying the concepts of answered prayer and active obedience together is not to give believers a selfish, ulterior motive for obeying. As one commentator explains,

> Is John stating two prerequisites to answered prayer? Really not. Obeying God's commands must never be done under compulsion or for the purpose of [selfishly] receiving [earthly] rewards. The Christian fulfills God's command with a cheerful heart that expresses gratitude. John is saying that when we obey his commands, we are doing what is pleasing to God. By adding the clause *and do what pleases him*, John rules out any notion of merit; pleasing God flows forth from love and loyalty. Implicitly John reminds his readers of Jesus. During his earthly ministry, Jesus always sought to please the Father by doing his will (John 8:29).
>
> The basis for answered prayer is not blind obedience but a desire to please God with dedicated love. And God fulfills our requests because of the bond of love and fellowship between Father and child. (Simon J. Kistemaker, *1 John*, New Testament Commentary [Grand Rapids: Baker, 2004], 317)

John's emphasis then is on true, heartfelt obedience (motivated by love), as opposed to a false, external legalism (motivated by selfish ambition and pride). Jesus declared this truth to His apostles in the upper room:

> If you abide in Me, and My words abide in you, ask whatever you wish, and it will be done for you. My Father is glorified by this, that you bear much fruit, and so prove to be My disciples. Just as the Father has loved Me, I have also loved you; abide in My love. If you keep My commandments, you will abide in My love; just as I have kept My Father's commandments and abide in His love. (John 15:7–10)

Throughout the New Testament, the necessity that believers **keep His commandments** is explicitly or implicitly indicated by every command given to them (e.g., Matt. 7:21; 16:24; John 14:15; James 1:22). Doing **the things that are pleasing in His sight** should motivate everything Christians do; as the rich benediction of the epistle to the Hebrews says:

> Now the God of peace, who brought up from the dead the great Shepherd of the sheep through the blood of the eternal covenant, even Jesus our Lord, equip you in every good thing to do His will, working in us that which is pleasing in His sight, through Jesus Christ, to whom be the glory forever and ever. Amen. (13:20–21)

FAITH IN JESUS CHRIST

This is His commandment, that we believe in the name of His Son Jesus Christ, and love one another, just as He commanded us. (3:23)

Having entered the Christian life through the God-given gift of faith that endures (Eph. 2:8–9), Christians can draw assurance from the reality that they never stop believing **in the name of His Son Jesus Christ;** the faith that saves can never die. This foundational faith is in response to **His** [God's] **commandment** and results in continued obedience to His mandate to **love one another** (Eph. 2:8–10; Heb. 12:1–2).

Saving faith contains three inseparable and essential elements, which John has reiterated throughout the epistle: faith, love, and an eagerness to obey. In this verse, **believe** translates an aorist form of the verb *pisteuō* and refers to a point in time when one believed. But that act produces continuing results that last for the remainder of a believer's life. The object of faith is **the name of . . . Jesus Christ;** His **name** denotes all that He is (including the fact that He is both Savior and Lord, cf. Phil. 2:9–11). Believing in the name of Christ is an important, oft-repeated New Testament theme (John 3:15–16; 20:31; Acts 16:31; cf. Mark 1:15; Luke 24:47), especially in this letter (2:12; 4:2, 15). It was the reason John wrote both his gospel (20:31) and his first epistle (5:13).

While this command to believe certainly is directed at those who have yet to trust in the saving work of Christ on the cross, it also has direct bearing on the lives of the redeemed. To those who already believe, R. S. Candlish exhorts,

> Keep on believing. Continue to believe more and more, simply because you see and feel it more and more to be "his commandment that you should believe on the name of his Son Jesus Christ." Unbelief, in

you who have believed, is aggravated disobedience. And, as such, it is and must be especially displeasing to God. It is his pleasure that his Son should be known, trusted, worshipped, loved; honoured as he himself would be honoured. You cannot displease the Father more than by dishonouring the Son; refusing to receive him, and rest upon him, and embrace him, and hold him fast, and place full reliance upon him as redeemer, brother, friend. Do not deceive yourselves by imagining that there may be something rather gracious in your doubts and fears; your unsettled and unassured frame of mind; as if it betokened humility, and a low esteem of yourselves. Beware lest God see in it only a low esteem of his Son Jesus Christ. (R. S. Candlish, *1 John* [Carlisle, Pa.: Banner of Truth, 1993], 339)

A mark of genuine saving faith is that its level of confident trust in Christ only grows deeper and stronger over time.

Love translates a present, active form of the familiar New Testament verb *agapaō;* the sacrificial love not of feeling, but of will and choice. The present tense of the verb signifies that love is to continually and habitually characterize a believer's attitudes and actions, as the apostle John has repeatedly made clear (cf. Luke 6:31–35; Gal. 5:13, 22; Phil. 1:9; 1 Thess. 4:9; Heb. 10:24; James 2:8). That love will express itself to all men (Gal. 6:10), but especially to fellow believers, just as Jesus commanded (John 13:34–35; 15:12, 17). This is another reminder from John to his readers that faith in Christ and love for the brethren are inseparable, and that they are both realities and imperatives for all Christians.

APPRECIATION FOR THE INDWELLING HOLY SPIRIT

The one who keeps His commandments abides in Him, and He in him. We know by this that He abides in us, by the Spirit whom He has given us. (3:24)

The blessing promised to **the one who keeps His commandments** is that he **abides in** Christ **and He in him.** The term translated **abides** (from the verb *menō,* "to stay, remain") is one of John's favorite words for salvation (see John 15:4–10) and is a repeated reference in this letter (cf. 2:6, 10, 24, 28; 3:6; 4:13, 16). (For more on the theme of abiding, see the earlier discussions of 2:6 and 2:28 in chapters 5 and 10, respectively, of this volume.) That shared life is possible only **by the Spirit whom He has given** (cf. Luke 11:13; 12:12; John 14:16–17, 26; 15:26; Acts 1:4–8; Rom. 5:5; 8:11, 16; Gal. 4:6; 5:16, 22; Eph. 1:13–14; 1 John 2:20, 27; 4:1–2, 13).

To be sure, the workings of the Holy Spirit include an element of the mysterious; they cannot be controlled or fully understood by frail, sinful human beings. Nevertheless, the results of those workings are readily apparent, as Jesus told Nicodemus by means of a familiar illustration: "The wind blows where it wishes and you hear the sound of it, but do not know where it comes from and where it is going; so is everyone who is born of the Spirit" (John 3:8). As the effects of the wind can be seen, felt, and heard, so the Spirit's working in lives is manifest and those who see that work will **know by this that He** [Christ] **abides in them.**

It was the Spirit of Christ (Rom. 8:9) who made saints' spiritually dead souls alive (John 3:5–8; Titus 3:5), gave sight to their blind eyes, caused their sinful hearts to repent (cf. Acts 16:14), and drew them in faith to Jesus (1 Peter 1:2). It was the Spirit who placed them into the body of Christ (1 Cor. 12:13) and gifted them for ministry in the church (1 Cor. 12:7; cf. Rom. 12:3–8; 1 Peter 4:10–11). It is through His illuminating instruction that Scripture comes alive for believers as they read and meditate on it (1 Cor. 2:10–14; cf. Eph. 6:17). The Spirit also energizes the saints' prayers (Eph. 6:18; Jude 20) and intercedes for them (Rom. 8:26–27). He leads and guides Christians (8:14) and assures them that they are children of God (vv. 15–16; Eph. 1:13–14).

Salvation is not a one-time event but a way of life and entails a willingness to follow Jesus no matter the cost (cf. Luke 9:23, 57–62). The presence of genuine holy affections—gratitude toward God, boldness in prayer, submission to His commandments, faith in the Lord Jesus Christ, and an appreciation of the Holy Spirit's power in their lives—all characterized and undergirded by a continual love for other believers—marks those who persevere in this true faith (cf. Rom. 2:7; Col. 1:21–23). The presence of those godly virtues gives those who manifest them true assurance (2 Peter 1:8–10; cf. Phil. 1:6; 2 Tim. 1:12*b*) and confidence that they have been born from above by the power of God.

Testing the Spirits
(1 John 4:1–6)

14

Beloved, do not believe every spirit, but test the spirits to see whether they are from God, because many false prophets have gone out into the world. By this you know the Spirit of God: every spirit that confesses that Jesus Christ has come in the flesh is from God; and every spirit that does not confess Jesus is not from God; this is the spirit of the antichrist, of which you have heard that it is coming, and now it is already in the world. You are from God, little children, and have overcome them; because greater is He who is in you than he who is in the world. They are from the world; therefore they speak as from the world, and the world listens to them. We are from God; he who knows God listens to us; he who is not from God does not listen to us. By this we know the spirit of truth and the spirit of error. (4:1–6)

Eureka!

This simple Greek word—meaning "I have found it!"—became a life slogan for thousands of California gold prospectors in the mid-1800s. It summed up every treasure hunter's dream and expressed the thrill of striking pay dirt. For James Marshall (the first to discover the precious metal in 1848) and the "forty-niners" who followed him, the term *eureka* meant instant riches, early retirement, and a life of carefree ease.

But would-be prospectors quickly learned that not everything that appeared to be gold actually was. Riverbeds and rock quarries could be full of golden specks that were nevertheless entirely worthless. This "fool's gold" was iron pyrite, and miners had to be careful to distinguish it from the real thing. Their very livelihood depended on it.

Experienced miners could usually distinguish pyrite from gold simply by looking at it. But, in some cases, the distinction was not quite so clear. So, they developed tests to discern what was genuine from what was not. One test involved biting the rock in question. Real gold is softer than the human tooth, whereas fool's gold is harder. A second test involved scraping the rock on a piece of white stone, such as ceramic. True gold leaves a yellow streak, whereas the residue left by fool's gold is greenish black. In either case, a miner relied on tests to authenticate his finds—both his fortune and his future depended on the results.

Spiritually speaking, Christians often find themselves in a similar position to the California gold rushers of the mid-1800s. When confronted with various doctrines and religious teachings, all of which claim to be true, believers must be able to tell those that are biblically sound from those that are not.

As was true in the gold rush, just because something glitters doesn't mean it's good. Christians need to be equally wary of spiritual "fool's gold." They must not accept something as true without first testing it to see if it meets with God's approval. If it fails the test, Christians should discard it as false and warn others also. But if it passes the test, in keeping with the truth of God's Word, believers can embrace and endorse it wholeheartedly.

California gold prospectors would cry "Eureka!" only when they found true gold. When it comes to spiritual things, Christians should be careful to do the same.

LEARNING TO LIVE DISCERNINGLY

Spiritual "fool's gold" is nothing new. In fact, the Old and New Testaments are filled with warnings about false teachers (Deut. 13:1–3; Isa. 8:19–20; Matt. 7:15; 24:4–5, 11, 24; Acts 20:29; Rom. 16:17–19; 2 Cor. 11:4, 13–15; Jude 4) and their counterfeit doctrines (Acts 20:30; 1 Tim. 1:4–7, 19; 6:20–21; 2 Tim. 2:17–18; 2 Peter 2:1; cf. Isa. 30:10). Christians must be discerning lest they be "children, tossed here and there by waves and carried about by every wind of doctrine, by the trickery of men, by craftiness in deceitful scheming" (Eph. 4:14). It is crucial that they "examine everything carefully" in order to "hold fast to that which is good [and] abstain from every form of evil" (1 Thess. 5:21–22). Otherwise, they increase their vulnerability to satanic deception (Matt. 13:19; 2 Cor. 2:11; 4:4; 11:3, 14; 2 Thess. 2:9; cf. Gen. 3:1; Matt. 4:3–10; Luke 22:31; Eph. 6:10).

Satan's basic strategy for attacking the truth first became evident in the Garden of Eden, where he mounted a three-pronged assault on God's Word. First, he cast doubt on what God had said about eating the fruit of the tree of life ("Indeed, has God said, 'You shall not eat . . . ?'", Gen. 3:1). Second, he denied outright what God had said to Adam ("You surely will not die!", v. 4). Finally, he added a distortion to what God had specifically told Adam ("you will be like God, knowing good and evil," v. 5). Ever since, Satan and his demonic forces have waged a relentless, non-stop campaign (cf. Rev. 16:14*a*) against the truth—still using their original tactics of doubt, denial, and distortion (cf. 2 Cor. 4:4).

Scripture contains many references to the long struggle for knowing, upholding, and obeying the truth. In the Old Testament, Moses (e.g., Deut. 4:1–31; 6:1–25; 8:1–20; 12:29–13:18; 30:1–20), Joshua (Josh. 23:1–24:28), Samuel (1 Sam. 12:1–25), Elijah (1 Kings 18:20–40), and the prophets (Isa. 31:6; 42:17; Jer. 8:5; 17:5; Ezek. 18:26; Hos. 14:1) continually called God's people back to the truth from falsehood and idolatry. And in the New Testament, Jesus Himself warned of false prophets (Matt. 7:15; 24:4–5, 11, 24), as did Paul (Acts 20:29; Rom. 16:17–18), Peter (2 Peter 2:1–3), John (1 John 2:18–24), and Jude (Jude 4–19).

As in the Garden of Eden, the source of error can always be traced to satanic roots (John 8:44). Thus Paul told Timothy: "But the Spirit explicitly says that in later times some will fall away from the faith, paying attention to deceitful spirits and doctrines of demons, by means of the hypocrisy of liars seared in their own conscience as with a branding iron" (1 Tim. 4:1–2; cf. Lev. 17:7; Deut. 32:17; Ps. 106:34–39; James 3:14–16; Rev. 16:13–14). Any ideology, philosophy, opinion, or religion other than God's truth fits Satan's agenda—which is why it is so crucial for believers to recognize the difference between the Spirit of truth and the spirit of error.

If they fail to be discerning, Christians will not only be confused and unable to discern for themselves, but they will also be unable to accurately convey the truth to others. Thus, they must guard the truth (1 Tim. 6:20–21; 2 Tim. 1:13–14; Jude 3; cf. Acts 20:28; Prov. 23:23) by knowing it, firmly holding to it as a conviction (cf. Luke 1:4; John 8:32; 19:35; 1 Tim. 2:4; 2 Tim. 2:15), and distinguishing it from that which is false (cf. Phil. 3:2; Col. 2:8). By being faithful to sound doctrine, they will be able to teach others also (cf. 2 Tim. 2:2).

The apostle John knew that his readers were under attack from false teachers. As a safeguard, he commanded them to test those who claim to teach the truth. He gave them reasons that such testing is crucial, and guidelines for how it should be conducted. In so doing, he laid out a strategy all Christians can use for distinguishing between true spiritual riches and doctrinal "fool's gold."

A COMMAND TO TEST

Beloved, do not believe every spirit, (4:1*a*)

Having just discussed the abiding work of the Holy Spirit in true believers (3:24), John makes the transition to the work of unholy **spirits** in false teachers and their false teachings. Because these ancient, supernatural spirits are experts in deception, Christians must be careful to closely examine every spiritual message they encounter (cf. Matt. 10:16; 1 Thess. 5:21–22).

The imperative form of the verb **believe,** with the negative particle **not,** could literally be translated "stop believing." John's phrase indicates the forbidding of an action already under way. If any of his readers were uncritically accepting the message of false teachers, they were to stop doing so immediately. They needed to exercise biblical discernment, like the Bereans of whom Luke wrote, "Now these were more noble-minded than those in Thessalonica, for they received the word with great eagerness, examining the Scriptures daily to see whether these things were so" (Acts 17:11).

Unbelievers, "being darkened in their understanding" (Eph. 4:18), have no basis on which to evaluate various teachings that claim divine origin (1 Cor. 2:14). Consequently they are highly susceptible to aberrant doctrine and can easily be led astray into error. But believers, who have the Word of truth and the Spirit of truth, must test what they hear with what they know to be true, as revealed in the Scriptures (1 Thess. 5:21–22).

A REASON TO TEST

but test the spirits to see whether they are from God, because many false prophets have gone out into the world. (4:1*b*)

The term translated **test** is a present imperative form of the verb *dokimazō*. The term was used to refer to a metallurgist's assaying of metals to test their purity and value. John's use of the present tense indicates that believers are to continually test the spirits **to see whether they are**

from God. Contrary to the view of some, this command has nothing to do with personally confronting demons or performing exorcisms. Instead, Christians are to continually evaluate what they see, hear (cf. 1 Cor. 14:29; 1 Thess. 5:20–21), and read to determine if it originated from the Spirit of God or, alternatively, from demons.

The only reliable way to test any teaching is to measure it against what God has revealed in His infallible, written Word (Isa. 8:20; cf. Prov. 6:23; 2 Tim. 3:16–17). As the perfect standard of truth (John 17:17) and the sword of the Spirit (Eph. 6:17), the Word of God provides believers with their primary defense against error (cf. 2 Cor. 10:3–5; Heb. 4:12).

The urgency of John's command resides in the fact that not a few but **many false prophets have gone out into the world.** Satan does not merely want to oppose the church (cf. Acts 5:3; 13:8–10; 16:16–23; 1 Thess. 2:18); he wants to deceive her (cf. 2 Cor. 11:14). In keeping with his fraudulent schemes, his minions have infiltrated denominations, churches, and other Christian schools, institutions, and organizations, resulting in compromise and error (cf. Jude 4).

Satan not only develops lies that directly deny biblical truth, but is also subtle, often sabotaging the truth by mixing it with error. Truth mixed with error is usually far more effective and far more destructive than a straightforward contradiction of the truth. Those who trust everything they read from the Christian bookstore or hear on Christian radio and television are prime targets for doctrinal deception. After all, as Paul wrote, "Satan disguises himself as an angel of light. Therefore it is not surprising if his servants also disguise themselves as servants of righteousness" (2 Cor. 11:14b–15a).

So Satan masquerades his lies as truth. He does not always wage war openly against the gospel. He is much more likely to attack the church by infiltrating her walls with subtle error. He uses the Trojan horse stratagem by placing his false teachers in the church, where they can "secretly introduce destructive heresies" (2 Peter 2:1). He puts his lies in the mouth of someone who claims to speak for Jesus Christ (Matt. 4:6; Acts 20:30). In this way, the Devil disguises falsehood as truth, making that which is evil look like that which is good.

For this reason, Jesus Himself warned of false prophets:

> Beware of the false prophets, who come to you in sheep's clothing, but inwardly are ravenous wolves. You will know them by their fruits. Grapes are not gathered from thorn bushes nor figs from thistles, are they? So every good tree bears good fruit, but the bad tree bears bad fruit. (Matt. 7:15–17; cf. Mark 13:21–23; 2 Peter 2:1–2)

Christians who ignore the Lord's warning do so to their own harm. There are many powerful voices clamoring for attention within the church. Thus it is imperative that believers practice biblical discernment (cf. 1 Cor. 2:12–13; Eph. 6:17; 2 Tim. 1:13; 3:15–17). It is especially mandated for pastors, who

> as God's steward[s], not self-willed, not quick-tempered, not addicted to wine, not pugnacious, not fond of sordid gain, but hospitable, loving what is good, sensible, just, devout, self-controlled, holding fast the faithful word which is in accordance with the teaching, so that they will be able both to exhort in sound doctrine and to refute those who contradict. For there are many rebellious men, empty talkers and deceivers, especially those of the circumcision, who must be silenced because they are upsetting whole families, teaching things they should not teach for the sake of sordid gain. (Titus 1:7–11)

GUIDELINES FOR HOW TO TEST

By this you know the Spirit of God: every spirit that confesses that Jesus Christ has come in the flesh is from God; and every spirit that does not confess Jesus is not from God; this is the spirit of the antichrist, of which you have heard that it is coming, and now it is already in the world. You are from God, little children, and have overcome them; because greater is He who is in you than he who is in the world. They are from the world; therefore they speak as from the world, and the world listens to them. We are from God; he who knows God listens to us; he who is not from God does not listen to us. By this we know the spirit of truth and the spirit of error. (4:2–6)

John sets forth three familiar tests for determining whether a teacher and his message reflect the Spirit of God or the spirit of Satan. These tests are theological (Does the person confess Jesus Christ?), behavioral (Does the person manifest evidence of the fruit of righteousness?), and presuppositional (Is the person committed to the Word of God?). True teachers are thus characterized by a confession of the divine Lord, a possession of the divine life, and a profession of the divine law. Those who fail to exhibit these traits prove that they are not from God.

THE CONFESSION OF THE DIVINE LORD

By this you know the Spirit of God: every spirit that confesses that Jesus Christ has come in the flesh is from God; and every spirit that does not confess Jesus is not from God; this is the spirit of the antichrist, of which you have heard that it is coming, and now it is already in the world. (4:2–3)

The first test is theological, or more specifically, christological. It asks the question: What does this person teach about Jesus Christ? The verb rendered **confesses** is a present tense form of the verb *homologeō*, which means "to say the same thing." **Every spirit** (human teacher) who agrees with Scripture **that Jesus Christ has come in the flesh** is therefore **from God,** confessing a truth taught by the Holy Spirit—that **Jesus Christ** is God incarnate.

The apostle does not explore all the nuances of Christology here; he simply echoes the definitive christological statement with which he opened this epistle:

> What was from the beginning, what we have heard, what we have seen with our eyes, what we have looked at and touched with our hands, concerning the Word of Life—and the life was manifested, and we have seen and testify and proclaim to you the eternal life, which was with the Father and was manifested to us—what we have seen and heard we proclaim to you also, so that you too may have fellowship with us; and indeed our fellowship is with the Father, and with His Son Jesus Christ. (1:1–3)

Jesus Christ proceeded from God the Father as the living Word of God (John 1:1–2) who became flesh (Luke 1:31; John 1:14; cf. Col. 2:9). He is one with the Father (John 10:30, 38; 14:7–10), manifested to humanity as the second person of the Trinity (a correct understanding of Christology will inevitably be Trinitarian), the Son of God (Isa. 9:6; John 3:16; cf. John 1:18; Heb. 1:5, 8). According to the plan of God, Jesus came in the flesh so that He might die a substitutionary death as a man for the sins of other men. That is the only way He could redeem all who would believe (Gal. 4:4–5; Heb. 2:17; cf. 1 Tim. 2:5; 1 John 2:1–2).

John repeatedly emphasizes the deity of Christ and teaches the massive truth with vast implications—that no one can honor the Father without honoring the Son (2:22–23; John 5:23; 2 John 3, 7, 9) because they share the same divine, perfect nature (3:21–23; 5:6, 20). To be saved, one must believe that Jesus is eternal deity, the second person of the Godhead who became a man. He is not merely a created being (contrary to what ancient false teachers taught and the modern-day sects, such as the Mormons and Jehovah's Witnesses, teach). But mere intellectual assent to that truth saves no one (cf. James 2:19); to be saved one must also acknowledge Jesus as Lord (Rom. 10:9–10).

A person's understanding and acceptance of Jesus' identity is the ultimate litmus test of the legitimacy of his professed faith. In today's evangelical world it is increasingly politically correct to affirm that all monotheistic religions worship the same God. But the fact is they do not. Jesus Himself made that crystal clear: "The one who listens to you [the disciples] listens to Me, and the one who rejects you rejects Me; and he who rejects Me rejects the One who sent Me" (Luke 10:16); "I am the way, and the truth, and the life; no one comes to the Father but through Me" (John 14:6; cf. Acts 4:12; 1 John 2:23). **Every spirit** propagating any religion or philosophy **that does not confess Jesus is not from God.** Such teaching is erroneous, heretical, and a rejection of Christ (2 Peter 2:1; cf. Gal. 1:8–9). John calls it **the spirit of the antichrist** (cf. 2:18, 22; for a more complete discussion of this topic, see chapter 9 of this volume). Believers **have heard** that the final Antichrist **is coming** (2 Thess. 2:3–4, 8–9), but **the spirit of the antichrist,** which evidences itself in false religion and aberrant doctrine, **is already in the world.** The true nature of Jesus Christ is inevitably denied by false teachers and the systems they promote (Jude 4; cf. Acts 3:14). However, those who rightly understand Jesus Christ and portray Him and His work accurately prove they possess the Spirit of truth.

THE POSSESSION OF THE DIVINE LIFE

You are from God, little children, and have overcome them; because greater is He who is in you than he who is in the world. They are from the world; therefore they speak as from the world, and the world listens to them. (4:4–5)

In the incarnation, God became a partaker of human nature (Phil. 2:7–8; Heb. 2:14, 17; 4:15). Through regeneration, on the other hand, human beings become partakers of the divine nature (2 Peter 1:4; cf. 2 Cor. 3:18). John's statement, **You are from God, little children, and have overcome them; because greater is He who is in you than he who is in the world,** is primarily an affirmation of the believer's security against the false teachers (cf. 2:20, 24, 27). All true Christians possess an incorruptible seed of eternal life (1 Peter 1:23–25), meaning that no satanic deception can take them out of God's saving hand (John 10:28–29). Those truly born again have been given not only a supernatural insight into the truth (Luke 10:21) but a love for it as well (Pss. 1:2;

119:97, 113, 159, 167; cf. 2 Thess. 2:10; 1 Peter 1:22) and a discernment that protects them from apostasy (cf. Mark 13:22; Heb. 10:39). As Paul wrote:

> Now we have received, not the spirit of the world, but the Spirit who is from God, so that we may know the things freely given to us by God, which things we also speak, not in words taught by human wisdom, but in those taught by the Spirit, combining spiritual thoughts with spiritual words. But a natural man does not accept the things of the Spirit of God, for they are foolishness to him; and he cannot understand them, because they are spiritually appraised. But he who is spiritual appraises all things, yet he himself is appraised by no one. For who has known the mind of the Lord, that he will instruct Him? But we have the mind of Christ. (1 Cor. 2:12–16)

Believers may be unsure about secondary, peripheral matters, but not about the foundational truths of the gospel, such as the person and work of Christ (cf. John 3:14–16; Rom. 1:16–17; 3:24–26; 5:1; Gal. 2:16; Eph. 2:8–9; 2 Tim. 1:9). They will not be fooled when false teachers invariably devalue the work of Christ by championing some form of salvation by works (cf. Gal. 4:9–11; Col. 2:20–23).

On the other hand, false teachers and their followers cling to worldly ideas (see 2:15–17 and 1 Cor. 2:14) because **they are from the world; they speak as from the world, and the world listens to them.** Through what they say and how they live, false teachers demonstrate that they are anything but genuine servants of Christ. True believers, however, resist worldly ideas because they **have overcome** the world (cf. John 16:33).

THE PROFESSION OF THE DIVINE LAW

We are from God; he who knows God listens to us; he who is not from God does not listen to us. By this we know the spirit of truth and the spirit of error. (4:6)

In contrast to the demonic purveyors of falsehood (Acts 13:10; Gal. 1:7; cf. John 8:44), teachers who **are from God** proclaim His revealed Word as the source of truth (cf. 2 Cor. 6:7; 1 Tim. 2:7; Titus 1:3). The pronoun **we** primarily refers to John and the other writers of Scripture. Like them, all true teachers accurately proclaim the Word of God, and the person **who knows God listens to** them (cf. John 8:47; 10:4–5, 16, 26–27; 14:26; 18:37). By contrast, anyone **who is not from God does not listen to** their teachings.

The completed, written revelation of the Old and New Testaments is therefore the sole authority by which Christians must test all spiritual ideologies. As Paul told Timothy, "All Scripture is given by inspiration of God, and is profitable for doctrine, for reproof, for correction, for instruction in righteousness, that the man of God may be complete, thoroughly equipped for every good work" (2 Tim. 3:16–17, NKJV). It is "more sure" than human experiences or senses (2 Peter 1:19, KJV). It endures forever (1 Peter 1:25). It is trustworthy in every jot and tittle (Matt. 5:18). It is unchanging and eternal (Isa. 40:8); Jesus Himself said, "Heaven and earth will pass away, but My words will by no means pass away" (Matt. 24:35, NKJV). It is the standard of truth (John 17:17). And it is by that standard, with the help of the Holy Spirit (cf. John 14:17; 15:26; 16:13), that believers **know the spirit of truth and the spirit of error.**

In a world rife with demonic false teaching, believers must constantly test the spirits to discern what is from God and what is not. Using the tests that John has outlined here, they can discern true spiritual gems from doctrinal "fool's gold." Like the noble Bereans, today's saints are called to compare every spiritual message they encounter to the revealed standard of Scripture (Acts 17:11). Only then can they obey Jude's admonition to "contend earnestly for the faith which was once for all handed down to the saints" (Jude 3). By faithfully guarding the truth in the present, believers will preserve it in purity both for themselves and for future generations.

Manifesting Perfect Love
(1 John 4:7–21)

15

Beloved, let us love one another, for love is from God; and everyone who loves is born of God and knows God. The one who does not love does not know God, for God is love. By this the love of God was manifested in us, that God has sent His only begotten Son into the world so that we might live through Him. In this is love, not that we loved God, but that He loved us and sent His Son to be the propitiation for our sins. Beloved, if God so loved us, we also ought to love one another. No one has seen God at any time; if we love one another, God abides in us, and His love is perfected in us. By this we know that we abide in Him and He in us, because He has given us of His Spirit. We have seen and testify that the Father has sent the Son to be the Savior of the world. Whoever confesses that Jesus is the Son of God, God abides in him, and he in God. We have come to know and have believed the love which God has for us. God is love, and the one who abides in love abides in God, and God abides in him. By this, love is perfected with us, so that we may have confidence in the day of judgment; because as He is, so also are we in this world. There is no fear in love; but perfect love casts out fear, because fear involves punishment, and the one who fears is not perfected in

love. We love, because He first loved us. If someone says, "I love God," and hates his brother, he is a liar; for the one who does not love his brother whom he has seen, cannot love God whom he has not seen. And this commandment we have from Him, that the one who loves God should love his brother also. (4:7–21)

The Trinity is an unfathomable and yet unmistakable doctrine in Scripture. As Jonathan Edwards noted, after studying the topic extensively, "I think [the doctrine of the Trinity] to be the highest and deepest of all Divine mysteries still, notwithstanding anything that I have said or conceived about it" (*An Unpublished Treatise on the Trinity*). Yet, though the fullness of the Trinity is far beyond human comprehension, it is unquestionably how God has revealed Himself in Scripture—as one God eternally existing in three persons.

This is not to suggest, of course, that the Bible presents three different gods (cf. Deut. 6:4). Rather, God is three persons in one essence; the Divine essence subsists wholly and indivisibly, simultaneously and eternally, in the three members of the one Godhead—the Father, Son, and Holy Spirit.

The Scriptures are clear that these three persons together are one and only one God (Deut. 6:4). John 10:30 and 33 explain that the Father and the Son are one. First Corinthians 3:16 shows that the Father and the Spirit are one. Romans 8:9 makes clear that the Son and the Spirit are one. And John 14:16, 18, and 23 demonstrate that the Father, Son, and Spirit are one.

Yet, in exhibiting the unity between the members of the Trinity, the Word of God in no way denies the simultaneous existence and distinctiveness of each of the three persons of the Godhead. In other words, the Bible makes it clear that God is one God (not three), but that the one God is a Trinity of persons.

In the Old Testament, the Bible implies the idea of the Trinity in several ways. The title *Elohim* ("God"), for instance, is a plural noun, which can suggest multiplicity (cf. Gen. 1:26). This corresponds to the fact that the plural pronoun ("us") is sometimes used of God (Gen. 1:26; Isa. 6:8). More directly, there are places in which God's name is applied to more than one person in the same text (Ps. 110:1; cf. Gen. 19:24). And there are also passages where all three divine persons are seen at work (Isa. 48:16; 61:1).

The New Testament builds significantly on these truths, revealing them more explicitly. The baptismal formula of Matthew 28:19 designates all three persons of the Trinity: "Go therefore and make disciples of all the nations, baptizing them in the name of the Father and the Son and the Holy Spirit." In his apostolic benediction to the Corinthians, Paul underscored this same reality. He wrote, "The grace of the Lord Jesus Christ, and the love of God [the Father], and the fellowship of the Holy Spirit, be with you all" (2 Cor. 13:14). Other New Testament passages also spell out the glorious truth of the triune God (Rom. 15:16, 30; 2 Cor. 1:21–22; Eph. 2:18).

In describing the Trinity, the New Testament clearly distinguishes three persons who are all simultaneously active. They are not merely modes or manifestations of the same person (as the heresies of Modalism or Sabellianism and the more modern Oneness theology incorrectly assert) who sometimes act as Father, sometimes as Son, and sometimes as Spirit. At Christ's baptism, all three persons were simultaneously active (Matt. 3:16–17), with the Son being baptized, the Spirit descending, and the Father speaking from heaven. Jesus Himself prayed to the Father (cf. Matt. 6:9), taught that His will was distinct from His Father's (Matt. 26:39), promised that He would ask the Father to send the Spirit (John 14:26), and asked the Father to glorify Him (John 17:5). These actions would not make sense unless the Father and the Son were two distinct persons. Elsewhere in the New Testament, the Holy Spirit intercedes before the Father on behalf of believers (Rom. 8:26–27), as does the Son, who is our Advocate (1 John 2:1). In the gospel of John, the apostle reports that Jesus said the Holy Spirit would abide in believers (14:16), that He Himself would abide in them (vv. 18, 20–21), and that the Father would abide in them (v. 23). Again, the distinctness of each person is in view.

The Bible is clear. There is only one God, yet He exists, and always has existed, as a Trinity of persons—the Father, the Son, and the Holy Spirit (cf. John 1:1, 2). To deny or misunderstand the Trinity is to deny or misunderstand the very nature of God Himself.

The doctrine of the Trinity is crucial on an infinite number of levels, since it is at the very heart of the doctrine of God. As one writer explains:

> The Trinity is the highest revelation God has made of Himself to His people. It is the capstone, the summit, the brightest star in the firmament of divine truths. . . . We must know, understand, and love the Trinity to be fully and completely Christian. This is why we say the Trinity is the greatest of God's revealed truths. (James White, *The Forgotten Trinity* [Minneapolis: Bethany House, 1998], 14–15)

It is very significant that the Trinity has implications not only for what believers think about God, but also for how they relate to Him and to one another. After all, it is the truth of the Trinity that explains God as a relational being. From eternity past, the Father, Son, and Holy Spirit have enjoyed the fullness of interpersonal relationships. They have always gloried in the infinite closeness that they share. To put it simply, God has never been lonely, but has always been satisfied in the perfect fellowship of inter-Trinitarian bliss. As John Piper explains:

> From all eternity, before creation, the one reality that has always existed is God. This is a great mystery, because it is so hard for us to think of God having absolutely no beginning, and just being there forever and ever and ever, without anything or anyone making him be there—just absolute reality that everyone of us has to reckon with whether we like it or not. But this ever-living God has not been "alone." He has not been a solitary center of consciousness. There has always been another, who has been one with God in essence and glory, and yet distinct in personhood so that they have had a personal relationship for all eternity. (*The Pleasures of God* [Sisters, Ore.: Multnomah, 2000], 41)

Based on that flawless relational model and His perfect desire and purpose to have fellowship with His creatures, the triune God designed man as a relational being. Man's creation in the image of God gave him self-awareness and the ability to think rationally, appreciate beauty, acquire wisdom, feel emotion, and understand morality. But the most significant aspect of the image of God is seen in man's capacity to love others—as demonstrated through his relational fellowship with God and with other human beings. Though only a shadow, human love (both for God and for others) is a reflection of the perfect inter-Trinitarian love that has characterized God from before time began.

The Trinitarian origin of perfect love brings the apostle's theme in 1 John 4:7–21 into sharp focus. Four times in the passage (once in verse 12, once in verse 17, and twice in verse 18) John refers to perfect or perfected love. The New Testament mentions many kinds of love (Matt. 5:44; 22:37–38; John 13:34; 14:15, 21; 15:12; Rom. 12:9–10; 13:8–10; 1 Cor. 8:3; 13:4–8, 13; 2 Cor. 5:14; Gal. 5:22; Eph. 5:25, 28, 33; Phil. 1:9; Col. 3:14; 1 Thess. 4:9; 2 Thess. 3:5; Heb. 13:1; James 2:8; 1 Peter 1:22; 4:8; Jude 21), but the supreme love is the perfected and completed love that comes from God at salvation. In Romans 5:5 Paul wrote, "The love of God has been poured out within our hearts through the Holy Spirit who was given to us." It is a love that does not derive from mystical experience or attach to emotional sentimentality, but that originates in salvation (cf. Rom. 8:28–30) and demonstrates itself in the good works of sanctification (cf. Eph. 2:10; Heb. 10:24). The fullest expression of it occurs when believers obey the Lord: "Whoever keeps His word, in him the love of God has truly been perfected" (1 John 2:5*a*; cf. 5:3).

This passage is actually the third time John discusses love in this letter. First in 2:7–11 he presented love as a proof of true fellowship. Then in 3:10–17 John discussed love as evidence of believers' sonship. This third discussion of love is an example of John's cycling back through the letter's moral and doctrinal proofs of salvation, each time providing his readers with greater depth and breadth.

In this passage, John discusses the nature of perfect Trinitarian love as it relates to the character of God, the coming of Christ, the Christian's claim of faith, and the Christian's confidence in judgment.

PERFECT LOVE AND THE CHARACTER OF GOD

Beloved, let us love one another, for love is from God; and everyone who loves is born of God and knows God. The one who does not love does not know God, for God is love. (4:7–8)

John addressed his audience as **beloved** (*agapētoi,* "[divinely] loved ones") (cf. 2:7; 3:2, 21; 4:1, 11) whom he urged to **love one another.** Again, unlike emotional, physical, or friendship love, *agapē* (**love**) is the love of self-sacrificing service (Phil. 2:2–5; Col. 3:12–14; cf. Rom. 14:19; 1 Cor. 10:23–24; 13:4–7), the love granted to someone who needs to be loved (Heb. 6:10; 1 Peter 2:17; cf. Rom. 12:15), not necessarily to someone who is attractive or lovable.

The first reason believers are to extend such sacrificial love to one another is that **love is from God.** Just as God is life (Ps. 36:9) and the source of eternal life (1:1–2; 3:1–2, 9; 5:12; 2 Tim. 1:1; Titus 1:2), and just as He is light (1:5–7; 2:8–11; cf. Isa. 60:19), He is also love (cf. 4:16). Therefore, if believers possess His life and walk in His light (righteousness and truth), they will also both possess and manifest His love, since **everyone who loves is born of God and knows God.** Because they are God's children, manifesting His nature, they will reflect His love to others.

As alluded to earlier, the love John refers to is the divine, perfect love that God gives only to His own. The verb rendered **is born** is a perfect passive form of *gennaō* and could be literally translated "has been begotten." Everyone God has saved in the past continues to give evidence of that fact in the present. Those who possess the life of God have the capacity and the experience of loving. In contrast, **the one who does not love does not know God.** Those whose lives are not characterized by love for others are not Christians, no matter what they claim. The Jewish religionists (scribes, Pharisees, and other leaders) of Jesus' day, as well as the false teachers in the church of John's day, knew a lot *about* God, but they did not really *know* Him (cf. 1 Tim. 6:20; 2 Tim. 3:7). The absence of God's love in their lives revealed their unregenerate condition as conclusively as did their aberrant theology.

God by nature **is love,** and therefore He defines love; it does not define Him. People constantly impose on God a human view of love, but He transcends any such human limitations. That God is love explains a number of things in the biblical worldview. First, it explains the reason He created. In eternity past, within the perfect fellowship of the Trinity, God the Father purposed, as a love gift to His Son, to redeem a people who would honor and glorify the Son (cf. John 6:39; 17:9–15). Thus, though God existed in perfect Trinitarian solitude, He created a race of beings out of which He would love and redeem those who would in turn love Him forever.

Second, the truth that God is love explains human choice. He designed sinners to know and love Him by an act of their wills (cf. John 7:17–18), though not apart from the work of His Spirit (cf. John 1:12–13; Eph. 2:5; Titus 3:5). God's greatest commandment is that people love Him with all their heart, soul, mind, and strength (Mark 12:29–30).

Third, the reality that God is love also explains His providence. He orchestrates all the circumstances of life, in all their wonder, beauty, and even difficulty, to reveal many evidences of His love (Pss. 36:6; 145:9; Rom. 8:28).

Fourth, that He is love explains the divine plan of redemption. If God operated only on the basis of His law, He would convict people of their sin, and justly consign everyone to spend forever in hell (cf. Ps. 130:3). But His love provided a remedy for sin through the atoning work of Jesus Christ (Matt. 1:21; Gal. 4:4–5) on behalf of all who repent of their sin and trust in His mercy (John 3:14–15). In the most well-known statement of His earthly ministry, Jesus said, "For God so loved the world, that He gave His only begotten Son, that whoever believes in Him shall not perish, but have eternal life" (John 3:16; cf. 2 Cor. 5:19–20; 1 Tim. 4:10; Titus 3:4–5).

God's general love for mankind manifests itself in several ways. First, He expresses His love and goodness to all through common grace. The psalmist wrote, "The Lord is good to all, and His mercies are over all His works" (Ps. 145:9; cf. Matt. 5:45). As part of this, God reveals His love through His compassion, primarily in that He delays His final judgment against unrepentant sinners (Gen. 15:16; Acts 17:30–31; Rom. 3:25; cf. Gen. 18:20–33). That compassion is further expressed in His myriad of warnings to sinners (Jer. 7:13–15, 23–25; 25:4–6; Ezek. 33:7–8; Zeph. 2:1–3; Luke 3:7–9; 1 Cor. 10:6–11; Rev. 3:1–3). He finds no pleasure in the damnation of anyone (Ezek. 18:23, 32; 2 Peter 3:9). Accompanied with His warnings, God extends His love to every part of the world through His general offer of the gospel (Matt. 11:28; John 7:37; 1 Tim. 2:4; Titus 2:11). As Jesus told the apostles, "Go into all the world and preach the gospel to all creation" (Mark 16:15; cf. Matt. 28:19).

That general love, however, is limited to this life. After death, unrepentant sinners will experience God's final wrath and judgment for all eternity (Dan. 12:2; Matt. 25:41; 2 Thess. 1:9; Rev. 20:12–15). But God has a special, perfect, eternal love that He lavishes on everyone who believes. The apostle John aptly characterized that love Jesus displayed to the apostles when he wrote at the beginning of the upper room narrative: "Having loved his own who were in the world, he now showed them the full extent of his love" (John 13:1*b*, NIV). Paul later celebrated that special love in his letter to the Ephesians:

> God, being rich in mercy, because of His great love with which He loved us, even when we were dead in our transgressions, made us alive together with Christ (by grace you have been saved), and raised us up with Him, and seated us with Him in the heavenly places in Christ Jesus, so that in the ages to come He might show the surpassing riches of His grace in kindness toward us in Christ Jesus. (Eph. 2:4–7)

(For a complete discussion of the love of God, see John MacArthur, *The God Who Loves* [Nashville: Word], 1996, 2001.)

PERFECT LOVE AND THE COMING OF CHRIST

By this the love of God was manifested in us, that God has sent His only begotten Son into the world so that we might live through Him. In this is love, not that we loved God, but that He loved us and sent His Son to be the propitiation for our sins. Beloved, if God so loved us, we also ought to love one another. (4:9–11)

Jesus Christ is the preeminent manifestation of God's love (John 1:14; cf. Rom. 5:8); He is God's **only begotten** (unique) **Son** (Heb. 1:5), who came to earth in the flesh (Luke 2:7–14; John 1:14, 18; Heb. 5:5). The incarnation was the supreme demonstration of a divine love that was and is sovereign and seeking; it was **not that** [believers] **loved God, but that He loved** [them] **and sent His Son to be the propitiation for** [their] **sins.** The term **propitiation** refers to a covering for sin (Rom. 3:25; Heb. 2:17), and is a form of the same word (*hilasmos*) used in 2:2 (for a more detailed explanation of this important word and its background, see chapter 4 of this volume). Hundreds of years before Christ, the prophet Isaiah foresaw His propitiatory sacrifice:

Surely our griefs He Himself bore, and our sorrows He carried; yet we ourselves esteemed Him stricken, smitten of God, and afflicted. But He was pierced through for our transgressions, He was crushed for our iniquities; the chastening for our well-being fell upon Him, and by His scourging we are healed. All of us like sheep have gone astray, each of us has turned to his own way; but the Lord has caused the iniquity of us all to fall on Him. (Isa. 53:4–6; cf. 2 Cor. 5:21; Gal. 3:13; 1 Peter 3:18)

By this the perfect **love of God was manifested in** [believers], John wrote, **that God has sent His only begotten Son into the world so that** [believers] **might live through Him.** The apostle's point is that since God, in sovereign mercy, graciously displayed His love in sending Christ, the saints should surely follow His example and love others with sacrificial, Christlike love (Eph. 4:32). The Father not only gave His children a perfect love when He redeemed them (Rom. 5:5), but He also gave them the ultimate model in Christ of how that love functions in selfless sacrifice. The cross of Christ compels believers to such love. Thus John exhorted his readers: **Beloved, if God so loved us, we also ought to love one another** (cf. John 15:13). The apostle really just restated his admonition from 3:16, "We know love by this, that He laid down His life for us; and we ought to lay down our lives for the brethren." No one who has ever savingly believed in Christ's atoning sacrifice, and thus been granted eternal life, can return permanently to a self-centered lifestyle. Instead such persons will obey Paul's exhortation to the Ephesians to "be imitators of God, as beloved children; and walk in love, just as Christ also loved you and gave Himself up for us, an offering and a sacrifice to God as a fragrant aroma" (Eph. 5:1–2; cf. 1 Peter 1:15–16).

PERFECT LOVE AND THE CHRISTIAN'S CLAIM OF FAITH

No one has seen God at any time; if we love one another, God abides in us, and His love is perfected in us. By this we know that we abide in Him and He in us, because He has given us of His Spirit. We have seen and testify that the Father has sent the Son to be the Savior of the world. Whoever confesses that Jesus is the Son of God, God abides in him, and he in God. We have come to know and have believed the love which God has for us. God is love, and the one who abides in love abides in God, and God abides in him. (4:12–16)

In verse 12 John makes the simple point that if **no one has seen God** the Father **at any time** (cf. John 4:24; 1 Tim. 1:17; 6:16), and Jesus is no longer visibly present to manifest Him, people will not see God's love unless believers **love one another.** If they love one another, God will be on display, testifying that He **abides in** [them], **and His love is perfected in** [them] (cf. John 13:34–35; 1 John 3:24). The unseen God thus reveals Himself through the visible love of believers; the love that originated in God and was manifested in His Son is now demonstrated in His people.

In this section the apostle John also sets forth a key sequence of evidences to remind readers once again that they can know they are saved. Assurance begins with the work of the Holy Spirit (2:20, 27; Rom. 8:9, 14–16; 1 Cor. 6:19–20; Eph. 1:13–14). Bruce Milne summarizes it for believers this way:

> The heart of Christian experience of the Holy Spirit lies in his bringing us into a living relationship to Jesus Christ so that we share in his redemption and all its blessings. All Christian experience can be focused in this one gift of God to us through his Spirit, our union with Christ. (*Know the Truth* [Downers Grove, Ill.: InterVarsity, 1982], 182)

Therefore John assures his believing readers they can **know that** [they] **abide in** God and **He in** [them], **because He has given** [them] **of His Spirit.**

Having already focused on the Father and the Son within his discussion on perfect love, John now emphasizes the role of the Spirit. By noting the work of each member of the Trinity, the apostle underscores the Trinitarian origins of perfect love. Such love, which is accomplished through the work of each member of the Trinity and subsequently manifested in the lives of believers, finds its source in the triune God, who from eternity past enjoyed perfect fellowship as Father, Son, and Spirit. As those who **abide in** God, believers will reflect His love, because God abides in them and His Spirit is at work in their hearts.

Jesus compared the Holy Spirit to the wind (John 3:8) and said people can see only the Spirit's effects; there are no visible, physical signs that guarantee that someone is filled with the Spirit. But the reality of their faith enables believers to know they have the indwelling Spirit, as John reminds his readers: **We have seen and testify that the Father has sent the Son to be the Savior of the world. Whoever confesses that Jesus is the Son of God, God abides in him, and he in God.** Belief in the gospel (the doctrinal test) provides evidence of the Spirit's ministry and presence (cf. 1 Cor. 12:3). Because sinners are spiritually dead (Eph. 2:1, 5), they cannot come to God on their own (cf. Matt. 12:35; John 1:12–13). Saving faith is possible only because God grants it (Eph. 2:8). In John's case, his own experience of seeing and being with Jesus verified his faith (1 John 1:1–3). He bore witness **that the Father has sent the Son to be Savior of the world,** but he would not have believed had the Father not chosen him (John 6:44; 15:16, 19) and the Spirit opened his eyes to the truth.

Whoever confesses that Jesus is the Son of God, knows that **God abides in him, and he in God.** The true believer has discerned the presence of the Holy Spirit, and has **come to know and** [has] **believed the love which God has for us.** Such persons understand the eternal love of God, who **is love,** for all believers. They can rest confidently in the assurance that **the one who abides in love abides in God, and God abides in him.** They will further demonstrate the genuineness of their salvation by loving the Father and the Son, loving righteousness and fellow believers rather than the world's system, and even loving their enemies. In summary, they will increasingly love the way God loves (cf. Matt. 5:48; 22:37–40; 2 Cor. 3:18).

PERFECT LOVE AND THE
CHRISTIAN'S CONFIDENCE IN JUDGMENT

By this, love is perfected with us, so that we may have confidence in the day of judgment; because as He is, so also are we in this world. There is no fear in love; but perfect love casts out fear, because fear involves punishment, and the one who fears is not perfected in love. We love, because He first loved us. If someone says, "I love God," and hates his brother, he is a liar; for the one who does not love his brother whom he has seen, cannot love God whom he has not seen. And this commandment we have from Him, that the one who loves God should love his brother also. (4:17–21)

Confidence in the day of judgment is the experience of believers who not only know when they have an accurate grasp of the gospel and other biblical doctrines, but also when **love is perfected** within them (cf. 1 Cor. 13:10–13; Gal. 5:24–25; Eph. 5:15–21; Col. 3:12–17).

The **day of judgment** refers in the broadest sense to the final time of reckoning before God (cf. 2:28). John says believers can live their lives with **confidence** (literally, "boldness") as they look to the day when Christ returns and they stand before God (1 Cor. 3:9–15; 2 Cor. 5:10; cf. James 1:12; Rev. 2:10). In 3:21 John used the same word (*parrēsia*) to refer to the confidence believers can have that God will grant their prayer requests. In the present verse the apostle declares that boldness and lack of fear should characterize believers (cf. Rom. 5:2; Heb. 6:19) whenever they think ahead to God's time of judgment (cf. Titus 2:13).

Why can believers have such confidence? **Because as He is, so**

also are we in this world. This stunning statement means the Father treats the saints the same way He does His Son Jesus Christ. God clothes believers with the righteousness of Christ (Rom. 3:21–22; 2 Cor. 5:21; Phil. 3:9), and grants the Son's perfect love (Matt. 9:36; John 10:11, 14–16; 13:1; 14:21) and obedience (cf. John 4:34; 5:30; 18:37). Someday believers will stand before God's throne as confidently as their Lord and Savior does. When they reach that final accounting, they will see the fulfillment of 1 John 3:2*b*, "We [believers] know that when He appears, we will be like Him, because we will see Him just as He is."

Those whose perfect (complete, mature) love demonstrates the reality of their salvation need have no fear of the return of Christ or God's judgment, because **perfect love casts out fear.** That kind of love dispels fear **because fear involves punishment,** and believers perfected in love do not face final punishment (Rom. 5:9; 1 Thess. 1:10; 5:9; cf. Eph. 5:6). However, anyone **who fears** God's judgment **is not perfected in love.** Someone who professes Christ but fears His return evidences that something is seriously amiss, because all true saints love His appearing (2 Tim. 4:8; cf. James 1:12).

The motive for those who have such confident assurance regarding the future is obvious: **we** [Christians] **love, because He first loved us.** It was God's perfect and eternal love that first sovereignly drew believers to Him (4:10; John 15:9, 16, 19; Acts 13:48; Rom. 5:8; Eph. 1:4), thus enabling them to reflect His love to others.

The apostle repeats his warning (cf. 2:4, 9; 3:10, 17; 4:8) that anyone who claims to love God but does not love others is a deceiver: **If someone says, "I love God," and hates his brother, he is a liar; for the one who does not love his brother whom he has seen, cannot love God whom he has not seen.** It is absurd to claim to love the invisible God but at the same time not show love to His people. John counters that hypocritical notion with a closing command: **this commandment we have from Him, that the one who loves God should love his brother also.** Brotherly love seeks nothing in return; instead it unconditionally forgives (cf. Matt. 18:21–22), bears others' burdens (Gal. 6:2), and sacrifices to meet their needs (Acts 20:35; Phil. 2:3–4). Yet it is also a righteous love that tolerates neither false doctrine nor habitual sin (1 Tim. 5:20; cf. 2 Thess. 3:15).

God's perfect love is a blessing for believers to know and a joy for them to manifest to others. Although it enhances and enriches the emotional love they have for other people, perfect love far transcends any kind of feeling the world might experience. It is a complete, mature love that reflects the essence of God and the work of Christ and flows through believers to anybody with a need (3:17; Matt. 25:34–40; 2 Cor. 8:1–7; 9:7–15; James 1:27; cf. Matt. 5:16; Acts 9:36; Titus 3:8), especially others in the family of God (Gal. 6:2, 10; cf. 1 Tim. 5:8; Heb. 6:9–10). This love, which has characterized the triune God from eternity past, is also the mark of His children (John 13:35). Because this love so clearly comes from Him, those who love like Him can be assured that He is their Father. As the hymn "I Am His, and He Is Mine" so aptly expresses:

> Loved with everlasting love, Led by grace that love to know;
> Gracious Spirit from above, Thou hast taught me it is so!
> O, this full and perfect peace! O, this transport all divine!
> In a love which cannot cease, I am His, and He is mine.

How to Recognize an Overcomer (1 John 5:1–5)

16

Whoever believes that Jesus is the Christ is born of God, and whoever loves the Father loves the child born of Him. By this we know that we love the children of God, when we love God and observe His commandments. For this is the love of God, that we keep His commandments; and His commandments are not burdensome. For whatever is born of God overcomes the world; and this is the victory that has overcome the world—our faith. Who is the one who overcomes the world, but he who believes that Jesus is the Son of God? (5:1–5)

God's people are identified by many designations in Scripture, including *believers* (1 Thess. 1:7; 2:10; 1 Tim. 6:2), *Christians* (Acts 11:26; cf. 26:28; 1 Peter 4:16), *children* (Matt. 18:3; Eph. 5:1; 1 Peter 1:14), *children of God* (John 1:12; Rom. 8:16; Phil. 2:15; 1 John 3:1), *children of light* (Eph. 5:8; cf. Luke 16:8), *children of promise* (Gal. 4:28); *sons of the day* (1 Thess. 5:5), *sons of the kingdom* (Matt. 13:38), *friends of Jesus Christ* (John 15:15; cf. James 2:23), *brethren* (Matt. 28:10; Acts 1:15; 11:1; 14:2; 16:2; 28:14; Rom. 8:29; 1 Cor. 8:12; 15:6; Gal. 1:2; Phil. 4:21; Col. 1:2; 1 Thess. 4:9; 5:27; 1 Tim. 4:6; 6:2; Heb. 2:11; 13:1; 1 Peter 1:22; 1 John 3:14, 16; 3 John 3, 5; Rev. 12:10), *sheep* (John 10:1–16, 26–27; 21:16–17; Heb. 13:20), *saints* (or *holy ones*; Acts 9:13, 32, 41; 26:10; Rom. 1:7; 12:13; 1 Cor. 1:2; 2 Cor. 1:1; Eph. 1:1; 3:8; Phil. 1:1; 4:21, 22; Col. 1:2, 4; Philem. 5; Heb. 13:24; Jude 3), *soldiers* (Phil. 2:25; 2 Tim. 2:3; Philem. 2), *witnesses* (Heb. 12:1), *stewards* (1 Peter 4:10), *fellow citizens* (Eph. 2:19), *lights in the world* (Phil. 2:15), *the elect* (Matt. 24:22, 24; Luke 18:7; Rom. 8:33), *the chosen* (Matt. 22:14; Col. 3:12; 2 Thess. 2:13; 2 Tim. 2:10; Titus 1:1; 1 Peter 1:1; 2:9; 2 John 1, 13), *the called* (Rom. 1:6–7; 8:28, 30; 1 Cor. 1:9, 24), *ambassadors of Christ* (2 Cor. 5:20), *heirs* (Rom. 8:17; Gal. 3:29; Titus 3:7; James 2:5), *branches in the vine* (John 15:5; cf. Rom. 11:16–21), *members of the body of Christ* (Rom. 12:5; 1 Cor. 12:12, 27; Eph. 3:6; 4:12; 5:23; Col. 1:24; 3:15), *living stones* (1 Peter 2:5), *the beloved of God* (Rom. 1:7; Eph. 5:1; Col. 3:12; 1 Thess. 1:4; 2 Thess. 2:13; Jude 1), *followers of Christ* (Mark 9:41), *sons of Abraham* (Gal. 3:7), *disciples* (John 15:8; Acts 6:1, 2, 7; 9:1, 26; 11:26; 15:10), *letters of Christ* (2 Cor. 3:3), *servants of Christ* (1 Cor. 7:22; Eph. 6:6; Rev. 6:11), *the godly* (2 Peter 2:9), *the people of God* (Heb. 4:9; 1 Peter 2:10), *a royal priesthood* (1 Peter 2:9), *the salt of the earth* (Matt. 5:13), *vessels for honor* (2 Tim. 2:21), *the righteous* (Matt. 13:43), *aliens and strangers* (1 Peter 2:11), and *members of God's household* (Eph. 2:19).

Like a multifaceted diamond, each of those names reveals something of the character, blessings, and privileges of believers. But John reveals yet another title for Christians in this passage: *overcomers*. Believers are victors, winners, or conquerors. The verb form, *nikaō* ("overcomes"), appears twice in verse 4 and once in verse 5. It is one of John's favorite terms; twenty-four of its twenty-eight occurrences in the New Testament are in his writings. The word means "to conquer," "to gain the victory," or "to defeat." It was a popular term among the Greeks, who believed that ultimate victory could not be achieved by mortals, but only by the gods. They even had a goddess named Nike, the goddess of victory who aided Zeus in his battle against the Titans. Against that pagan backdrop, it was stunning for the New Testament to assign to Christians the invincibility associated only with the gods.

The Lord Jesus Christ used *nikaō* in John 16:33 to speak of His victory over the satanic world system. That victory forms the basis of believers' overcoming, which the apostle Paul described in Romans 8:37: "But in all these things we overwhelmingly conquer through Him who loved us" (cf. 1 Cor. 15:57). "Overwhelmingly conquer" translates an intensified, compound form of *nikaō* (*hupernikaō*), which refers to being absolutely, completely victorious. In Jesus Christ, believers are invincible and unconquerable, so that "neither death, nor life, nor angels, nor principalities, nor things present, nor things to come, nor powers, nor height, nor depth, nor any other created thing, will be able to separate [them] from the love of God, which is in Christ Jesus our Lord" (Romans 8:38–39).

Believers are overcomers of Satan. Earlier in this epistle, John wrote that spiritual young men overcome the Devil through the power of the Word (2:13–14). In John's vision of the future, the tribulation saints "overcame [Satan] because of the blood of the Lamb and because of the word of their testimony, and they did not love their life even when faced with death" (Rev. 12:11). Not only have believers overcome Satan, but also his servants (1 John 4:1–4).

Though still a dangerous foe (1 Peter 5:8), Satan's defeat is certain. In Romans 16:20 Paul wrote, "The God of peace will soon crush Satan under your feet." James added, "Resist the devil and he will flee from you" (James 4:7*b*). Satan will ultimately be cast into hell, where he will be punished forever in "the eternal fire which has been prepared for [him] and his angels" (Matt. 25:41; cf. Rev. 20:10). In the meantime, believers can triumph over Satan by being wary of his schemes (2 Cor. 2:11; Eph. 6:11), refusing to give him an opportunity to take advantage of them (2 Cor. 2:11; Eph. 4:27), and putting on the "full armor of God" (Eph. 6:11).

Believers have also overcome death. As he concluded his magnificent chapter on the resurrection, Paul wrote,

> But when this perishable will have put on the imperishable, and this mortal will have put on immortality, then will come about the saying that is written, "Death is swallowed up in victory. O death, where is your victory? O death, where is your sting?" The sting of death is sin, and the power of sin is the law; but thanks be to God, who gives us the victory through our Lord Jesus Christ. (1 Cor. 15:54–57)

The apostle taunts death, likening it to a bee whose stinger (sin and its deserved punishment) has been removed. God grants believers victory over death through Jesus Christ, who "redeemed us from the curse of the Law, having become a curse for us—for it is written, 'Cursed is everyone who hangs on a tree'" (Gal. 3:13).

Finally, as John notes three times in this passage (vv. 4, 5), Christians have overcome the world. The world is the invisible spiritual system of evil, which is hostile to God (John 1:10; 7:7; 15:18–19; 17:14, 25; James 4:4) and is ruled by Satan (John 12:31; 14:30; 16:11; 2 Cor. 4:4; Eph. 2:2; 1 John 5:19). Its citizens are dominated by carnal ambition, pride, greed, selfishness, and pleasure, all of which constitute "the lust of the flesh and the lust of the eyes and the boastful pride of life" (1 John 2:16).

But through their relationship with the Lord Jesus Christ, believers are no longer part of the world system, even as He is not (John 17:14, 16). According to Colossians 1:13, God "rescued us from the domain of darkness, and transferred us to the kingdom of His beloved Son." As a result, "our citizenship is in heaven, from which also we eagerly wait for a Savior, the Lord Jesus Christ" (Phil. 3:20). Although they still live in the world (John 17:11), Christians have no ongoing relationship to it (1 John 3:1); they are "aliens and strangers" (1 Peter 2:11; cf. Heb. 11:13) in it. Their new natures, along with the prompting of the Holy Spirit, drive them away from the world and toward God. The world's allurements no longer captivate their hearts, and they do not love what it has to offer (1 John 2:15–17; cf. Titus 2:11–12).

Far from being enamored with the world, believers struggle against it. The apostle Paul is a clear example of one who faced intense opposition from the world, some of which he described in 2 Corinthians 11:23–27:

> Are they servants of Christ?—I speak as if insane—I more so; in far more labors, in far more imprisonments, beaten times without number, often in danger of death. Five times I received from the Jews thirty-nine lashes. Three times I was beaten with rods, once I was stoned, three times I was shipwrecked, a night and a day I have spent in the deep. I have been on frequent journeys, in dangers from rivers, dangers from robbers, dangers from my countrymen, dangers from the Gentiles, dangers in the city, dangers in the wilderness, dangers on the sea, dangers among false brethren; I have been in labor and hardship, through many sleepless nights, in hunger and thirst, often without food, in cold and exposure.

But that hostility did not defeat him, because the world had no hold on him. "I do not consider my life of any account as dear to myself," he declared, "so that I may finish my course and the ministry which I received from the Lord Jesus, to testify solemnly of the gospel of the grace of God" (Acts 20:24). When those who loved Paul tearfully begged him not to go to Jerusalem, where he faced arrest, he replied, "What are you doing, weeping and breaking my heart? For I am ready not only to be bound, but even to die at Jerusalem for the name of the Lord Jesus" (Acts 21:13).

Paul knew that his ultimate triumph over the world was certain. To the Corinthians he wrote, "For momentary, light affliction is producing for us an eternal weight of glory far beyond all comparison, while we look not at the things which are seen, but at the things which are not seen; for the things which are seen are temporal, but the things which are not seen are eternal" (2 Cor. 4:17–18). Or, as he simply and directly put it in Philippians 1:21, "For to me, to live is Christ and to die is gain."

Believers, then, are invincible overcomers—not in themselves or by their own power, but in Jesus Christ and by His power. Although their ultimate victory is assured, Christians still lose some of the battles. They succumb to Satan's temptations, the world's allurements, and the corruption of their own hearts, and fall into sin. But if believers are not always victorious in the skirmishes of this life, how can they be sure that they are truly overcomers? Reiterating, recycling, and enriching familiar themes from earlier in this epistle, John gives three characteristics of an overcomer in verses 1–5: faith in the truth, love for God and others, and obedience to the Word.

FAITH IN THE TRUTH

Whoever believes that Jesus is the Christ is born of God . . . For whatever is born of God overcomes the world; and this is the victory that has overcome the world—our faith. Who is the one who overcomes the world, but he who believes that Jesus is the Son of God? (1a, 4–5)

The foundational mark of an overcomer is believing **that Jesus is the Christ** (Messiah). That abbreviated statement implies all that is true about Him; that **Jesus is the Son of God,** the second person of the Trinity, who came to earth to die and rise to accomplish salvation for sinners. Only the one who **believes** in the truth about Him **is born of God** (lit., "out of God has been begotten") and **overcomes the world.** All who are **born of God** are overcomers, and only those who believe in Jesus Christ are born of God.

In the prologue to his gospel, John wrote, "But as many as received Him, to them He gave the right to become children of God, even to those who believe in His name" (John 1:12). The Lord Himself declared, "I am the way, and the truth, and the life; no one comes to the Father but through Me" (John 14:6). In Acts 4:12 Peter boldly told the hostile Jewish authorities that "there is salvation in no one else [other than Jesus; v. 10]; for there is no other name under heaven that has been given among men by which we must be saved." Paul wrote, "For no man can lay a foundation other than the one which is laid, which is Jesus Christ" (1 Cor. 3:11), and, "There is one God, and one mediator also between God and men, the man Christ Jesus, who gave Himself as a ransom for all, the testimony given at the proper time" (1 Tim. 2:5–6). Any teaching that people can be saved apart from faith in Jesus Christ is biblically untenable (see the discussion of this point in chapter 20 of this volume).

The tenses of the verbs in verse 1 reveal a significant theological truth. **Believes** translates a present tense form of the verb *pisteuō,* whereas *gegennētai* (**is born**) is in the perfect tense. The opening phrase of verse 1 literally reads, "Whoever is believing that Jesus is the Christ has been begotten of God." The point is that, contrary to Arminian theology, continual faith is the result of the new birth, not its cause. Christians do not keep themselves born again by believing, and lose their salvation if they stop believing. On the contrary, it is their perseverance in the faith that gives evidence that they have been born again. The faith that God grants in regeneration (Eph. 2:8) is permanent, and cannot be lost. Nor, as some teach, can it die, for dead faith does not save (James 2:14–26). There is no such thing as an "unbelieving believer."

The question sometimes arises concerning those who profess faith in Christ, but then stop believing in Him. Our Lord described such people in the parable of the soils:

> Others [seeds] fell on the rocky places, where they did not have much soil; and immediately they sprang up, because they had no depth of soil. But when the sun had risen, they were scorched; and because they had no root, they withered away. Others fell among the thorns, and the thorns came up and choked them out. . . .

> The one on whom seed was sown on the rocky places, this is the man who hears the word and immediately receives it with joy; yet he has no firm root in himself, but is only temporary, and when affliction or persecution arises because of the word, immediately he falls away. And the one on whom seed was sown among the thorns, this is the man who hears the word, and the worry of the world and the deceitfulness of wealth choke the word, and it becomes unfruitful. (Matt. 13:5–7, 20–22)

Such false, temporary faith produces no fruit, in contrast to genuine saving faith, which alone produces the fruit that proves one's new birth:

> And others fell on the good soil and yielded a crop, some a hundredfold, some sixty, and some thirty. . . .

> And the one on whom seed was sown on the good soil, this is the man who hears the word and understands it; who indeed bears fruit and brings forth, some a hundredfold, some sixty, and some thirty. (Matt. 13:8, 23; cf. 3:8; Acts 26:20)

Earlier in this epistle, John explained that those who permanently fall away from the faith were never redeemed in the first place: "They went out from us, but they were not really of us; for if they had been of us, they would have remained with us; but they went out, so that it would be shown that they all are not of us" (2:19; cf. the exposition of this verse in chapter 9 of this volume). Their professed faith was never true saving faith. Saving faith is not mere intellectual knowledge of gospel facts, but involves a wholehearted, permanent commitment to Jesus as Lord, Savior, Messiah, and God incarnate.

The content of saving faith, as noted above, is **that Jesus is the Christ;** He is its object. People who are born of God believe the truth about Christ; those who do not are liars and antichrists. As John warned earlier in this letter, "Who is the liar but the one who denies that Jesus is the Christ? This is the antichrist, the one who denies the Father and the Son" (2:22). Then, making it unmistakably clear that no one can come to the Father apart from Jesus Christ, he added, "Whoever denies the Son does not have the Father; the one who confesses the Son has the Father also" (v. 23; cf. chapter 9 of this volume for an exposition of 2:22–23). No one who rejects Jesus Christ will ever see heaven, since anyone who "does not confess Jesus is not from God" (4:3), and only in the one who "confesses that Jesus is the Son of God [does God abide], and he in God" (v. 15).

John repeated for emphasis the truth from verse 1 that those who believe in Jesus Christ and have been **born of God . . . overcome the world,** gaining **the victory** over it through their **faith.** The phrase **our faith** literally reads, "the faith of us." It could refer to the subjective, personal faith of individual believers, or objectively to the Christian faith, "the faith which was once for all handed down to the saints" (Jude 3; cf. Acts 6:7; 13:8; 14:22; 16:5; 1 Cor. 16:13; 2 Cor. 13:5; Gal. 1:23; Phil. 1:27; 1 Tim. 4:1; 6:10, 21; 2 Tim. 4:7). It is safe to see in this context of believing that John is referring not to the objective content of the gospel as theology, but to the subjective trust by which God makes saints overcomers.

This interpretation is supported by the apostle's rhetorical question, **Who is the one who overcomes the world, but he who believes that Jesus is the Son of God?** (cf. 4:15). Christians are victorious overcomers from the moment of salvation, when they are granted a faith that will never fail to embrace the gospel. They may experience times of doubt; they may cry out with David, "How long, O Lord? Will You forget me forever? How long will You hide Your face from me? (Ps. 13:1; cf. 22:1; 27:9; 44:24; 69:17; 88:14; 102:2; 143:7; 2 Tim. 2:11–13). But true saving faith will never fail, because those who possess it have in Christ triumphed over every foe. The "great . . . cloud of witnesses" (Heb. 12:1; cf. Rom. 8:31–39)—the heroes of faith described in Hebrews 11—testify that true faith endures every trial and emerges victorious over them all. Job expressed the triumph of faith when he cried out in the midst of his trials, "Though He slay me, I will hope in Him" (Job 13:15*a*).

LOVE FOR GOD AND OTHERS

whoever loves the Father loves the child born of Him. (5:1*b*)

The primary mark of an overcomer involves the doctrinal test of believing the truth of the Christian faith. The second mark is again a moral characteristic: an overcomer **loves** both **the Father** and **the child born of Him.** The new birth brings people not only into a faith relationship with God, but also into a love relationship with Him and His children. John has emphasized that principle throughout this epistle:

> The one who loves his brother abides in the Light and there is no cause for stumbling in him. But the one who hates his brother is in the darkness and walks in the darkness, and does not know where he is going because the darkness has blinded his eyes. (2:10–11)

> By this the children of God and the children of the devil are obvious: anyone who does not practice righteousness is not of God, nor the one who does not love his brother. (3:10)

> We know that we have passed out of death into life, because we love the brethren. He who does not love abides in death. (3:14)

> But whoever has the world's goods, and sees his brother in need and closes his heart against him, how does the love of God abide in him? (3:17)

> This is His commandment, that we believe in the name of His Son Jesus Christ, and love one another, just as He commanded us. (3:23)

> Beloved, let us love one another, for love is from God; and everyone who loves is born of God and knows God. The one who does not love does not know God, for God is love. (4:7–8)

> No one has seen God at any time; if we love one another, God abides in us, and His love is perfected in us. (4:12)

> If someone says, "I love God," and hates his brother, he is a liar; for the one who does not love his brother whom he has seen, cannot love God whom he has not seen. And this commandment we have from Him, that the one who loves God should love his brother also. (4:20–21)

The love of which John writes is not mere emotion or sentimentality, but a desire to honor, please, and obey God. Directed toward people, it is the love of the will and choice, the love that sacrificially meets the needs of others. Paul described it in 1 Corinthians 13:4–7:

> Love is patient, love is kind and is not jealous; love does not brag and is not arrogant, does not act unbecomingly; it does not seek its own, is not provoked, does not take into account a wrong suffered, does not rejoice in unrighteousness, but rejoices with the truth; bears all things, believes all things, hopes all things, endures all things.

The New Testament repeatedly commands such love (e.g., John 13:34–35; 15:12, 17; Gal 5:13; 1 Thess. 4:9; Heb. 13:1; 1 Peter 1:22).

OBEDIENCE TO THE WORD

By this we know that we love the children of God, when we love God and observe His commandments. For this is the love of God, that we keep His commandments; and His commandments are not burdensome. (5:2–3)

The opening statement of verse 2, **by this we know that we love the children of God, when we love God,** is the corollary to the truth John expressed in verse 1. Just as it is impossible to love God without loving His children, so also is it impossible to truly love His children apart from loving Him. Those twin priorities of loving God and other Christians mark all who have been born again.

The proof of genuine faith is sustained and loving obedience; it is to **love God and observe His commandments.** Genuine saving faith produces love, which results in obedience. Those who believe God is who Scripture reveals Him to be will respond in **love,** praise, and adoration. Because He is the supreme object of their affections, they will long to obey Him. **Observe** translates a present tense form of the verb *poieō*, which has the connotation of "to accomplish," "to carry out," or "to practice." The present tense indicates that believers' obedience is to be continuous. It will always be the direction, though not the perfection, of their lives. A different word, a form of the verb *tēreō*, is translated **keep** in verse 3. It has the connotation of keeping watch over, guarding, or preserving. One who truly loves God will view His commandments as a precious treasure, to be guarded at all costs (2 Tim. 1:14). *Poieō* refers to action, *tēreō* to the heart attitude that prompts obedience.

The principle that those who truly love God will obey Him permeates Scripture. In Deuteronomy 13:4 Moses commanded Israel, "You shall follow the Lord your God and fear Him; and you shall keep His commandments, listen to His voice, serve Him, and cling to Him." Samuel rebuked Saul's disobedience by reminding him that "to obey is better than sacrifice, and to heed than the fat of rams" (1 Sam. 15:22*b*). Solomon, the wisest man who ever lived, wrote, "The conclusion, when all has been heard, is: fear God and keep His commandments, because this applies to every person" (Eccl. 12:13). God commanded Israel through the prophet Jeremiah, "Obey My voice, and I will be your God, and you will be My people; and you will walk in all the way which I command you, that it may be well with you" (Jer. 7:23).

Obedience was also a foundational theme in the teaching of the Lord Jesus Christ. In Matthew 12:50 He said, "Whoever does the will of My Father who is in heaven, he is My brother and sister and mother." He pronounced "blessed . . . those who hear the word of God and observe it" (Luke 11:28). In John 8:31 He challenged those who professed faith in Him, "If you continue in My word, then you are truly disciples of Mine." To His disciples in the upper room He stated plainly, "If you love Me, you will keep My commandments" (John 14:15), and He repeated that truth several times during that discourse:

> He who has My commandments and keeps them is the one who loves Me; and he who loves Me will be loved by My Father, and I will love him and will disclose Myself to him. (14:21)

> If anyone loves Me, he will keep My word. . . . He who does not love Me does not keep My words. (14:23–24)

> If you keep My commandments, you will abide in My love; just as I have kept My Father's commandments and abide in His love. (15:10)

> You are My friends if you do what I command you. (15:14)

The apostles also taught that obedience is an essential mark of the redeemed:

> And we are witnesses of these things; and so is the Holy Spirit, whom God has given to those who obey Him. (Acts 5:32)

> Through whom we have received grace and apostleship to bring about the obedience of faith among all the Gentiles for His name's sake. (Rom. 1:5)

> For I will not presume to speak of anything except what Christ has accomplished through me, resulting in the obedience of the Gentiles by word and deed. (Rom. 15:18)

> Now to Him who is able to establish you according to my gospel and the preaching of Jesus Christ, according to the revelation of the mystery which has been kept secret for long ages past, but now is manifested, and by the Scriptures of the prophets, according to the commandment of the eternal God, has been made known to all the nations, leading to obedience of faith. (Rom. 16:25–26)

> And having been made perfect, He became to all those who obey Him the source of eternal salvation. (Heb. 5:9)

> Peter, an apostle of Jesus Christ, to those who reside as aliens, scattered throughout Pontus, Galatia, Cappadocia, Asia, and Bithynia, who are chosen according to the foreknowledge of God the Father, by the sanctifying work of the Spirit, to obey Jesus Christ and be sprinkled with His blood: May grace and peace be yours in the fullest measure. (1 Peter 1:1–2)

> As obedient children, do not be conformed to the former lusts which were yours in your ignorance. (1 Peter 1:14)

> Since you have in obedience to the truth purified your souls for a sincere love of the brethren, fervently love one another from the heart. (1 Peter 1:22)

The obedience that characterizes a true child of God is not external, ritualistic, legalistic compliance. Nor is it unwilling, partial, inconsistent, or grudging. Loving obedience is from the heart (Deut. 11:13; 30:2, 10; Rom. 6:17), willing (Ex. 25:2; 1 Peter 5:2; cf. Lev. 26:21), total (Deut. 27:26; Gal. 3:10; James 2:10), constant (Phil. 2:12), and joyful (Ps. 119:54; cf. 2 Cor. 9:7).

Those who truly obey God do not find **His commandments . . . burdensome.** In Matthew 11:28–30 Jesus invited weary sinners, "Come to Me, all who are weary and heavy-laden, and I will give you rest. Take My yoke upon you and learn from Me, for I am gentle and humble in heart, and you will find rest for your souls. For My yoke is easy and My burden is light." In Psalm 119, the psalmist repeatedly expressed his delight in God's law:

> I have rejoiced in the way of Your testimonies, as much as in all riches. (v. 14)

> I shall delight in Your statutes; I shall not forget Your word. (v. 16)

> Your testimonies also are my delight; they are my counselors. (v. 24)

> O how I love Your law! It is my meditation all the day. (v. 97)

> How sweet are Your words to my taste! Yes, sweeter than honey to my mouth! (v. 103)

Those who love God will obey His law, because they want to honor His holy nature. They do so not out of dread, but out of loving adoration.

Because of His delight in overcomers, God will pour out rich blessings on them. The letters to the seven churches (Rev. 2, 3) contain those delightful, special gifts that God promises to all overcomers.

The first promise is found in the letter to the church at Ephesus. In Revelation 2:7 Jesus said, "To him who overcomes, I will grant to eat of the tree of life which is in the Paradise of God." After Adam and Eve sinned, God drove them from the Garden of Eden, in part so that they would not "take also from the tree of life, and eat, and live forever" in their sinful state (Gen. 3:22; cf. v. 24). The tree of life symbolizes eternal life; the "Paradise of God" is heaven (cf. Luke 23:43; 2 Cor. 12:2, 4). The promise to overcomers, then, is that they will live forever in heaven.

The second promise is the flip side of the first. In the letter to the church at Smyrna, Jesus promised, "He who overcomes will not be hurt by the second death" (Rev. 2:11). The fall resulted not only in physical death, but also in the second death—eternal punishment in hell (Rev. 20:14; 21:8). But while overcomers will experience the first death (physical death), they will not die spiritually and eternally. The second death has no power over them (Rev. 20:6), since God has granted them eternal life (John 3:16; 5:24; Acts 13:48; Rom. 6:23; 1 John 2:25; 5:11) and promised them heaven.

The letter to the church at Pergamum reveals two more promises from Christ to overcomers: "To him who overcomes, to him I will give some of the hidden manna, and I will give him a white stone, and a new name written on the stone which no one knows but he who receives it" (Rev. 2:17). The "hidden manna" pictures God's supplying His people's needs. For Israel, the manna was a visible, tangible manifestation of God's provision. For Christians, Jesus Christ, "the bread that came down out of heaven" (John 6:41; cf. vv. 31, 35), is God's provision for all their needs (cf. 2 Cor. 9:8; Phil. 4:19). The "white stone" was given to victorious athletes in the games, and served as an admission pass to a special celebration for the winners. God promises overcomers admittance to the eternal victory celebration in heaven.

The overcomers in the church at Thyatira (Rev. 2:26–28) also received two promises. First, Jesus assured them, "He who overcomes, and he who keeps My deeds until the end, to him I will give authority over the nations; and he shall rule them with a rod of iron, as the vessels of the potter are broken to pieces, as I also have received authority from My Father" (vv. 26–27). According to Psalm 2:8–9, Jesus Christ Himself will rule the nations with a rod of iron (cf. Rev. 12:5; 19:15). The Lord will delegate His authority to believers and, during His millennial kingdom, they will reign with Him (cf. 1 Cor. 6:2; 2 Tim. 2:12; Rev. 20:6) as under-shepherds (cf. John 21:16; Acts 20:28; 1 Peter 5:2) of the Chief Shepherd (1 Peter 5:4; cf. John 10:11, 14; Heb. 13:20; 1 Peter 2:25; Rev. 7:17). More than that, Christ promises them the "morning star" (Rev. 2:28). Since He is the morning star (Rev. 22:16), that is nothing less than a promise of Christ Himself in all His fullness (cf. 1 Cor. 13:12).

The church at Sardis was so filled with unregenerate people that the Lord declared it to be dead (Rev. 3:1). Yet there were some even there who were redeemed. To those overcomers, Christ addressed the three-part promise, "He who overcomes will thus be clothed in white garments; and I will not erase his name from the book of life, and I will confess his name before My Father and before His angels" (Rev. 3:5). White symbolizes purity (cf. Rev. 6:11; 7:9, 13, 14; 19:8, 14) and is fitting for those clothed with the righteousness of Christ (Gal. 3:27; cf. Isa. 61:10). Having had their sins washed in the blood of the Lamb (Rev. 7:14; cf. 1 Peter 1:18–19), they will one day be freed from the remainder of sin that still entangles them (Heb. 12:1) and given perfect holiness and purity.

Because He has purified them from their sins, Christ also promises not to erase overcomers' names from the Book of Life (cf. Phil. 4:3; Rev. 13:8; 17:8; 20:12, 15; 21:27). In ancient times, rulers kept a register of their city's citizens. Those who had committed particularly heinous crimes might have had their names expunged from that register, thus making them outcasts. But under no circumstances will Christ blot out a true Christian's name from the roll of those whose names were "written from the foundation of the world in the book of life of the Lamb who has been slain" (Rev. 13:8), because "He is able also to save forever those who draw near to God through Him, since He always lives to make intercession for them" (Heb. 7:25).

Far from blotting their names from the Book of Life, Jesus promised to "confess" every overcomer's "name before [His] Father and before His angels," thus affirming that they belong to Him (Rev. 3:5). He made that same promise in Matthew 10:32: "Everyone who confesses Me before men, I will also confess him before My Father who is in heaven."

To the overcomers in the faithful church at Philadelphia Christ promised, "He who overcomes, I will make him a pillar in the temple of My God, and he will not go out from it anymore; and I will write on him the name of My God, and the name of the city of My God, the new Jerusalem, which comes down out of heaven from My God, and My new name" (Rev. 3:12). A "pillar" suggests stability, permanence, and immovability. The New Testament pictures the church metaphorically as God's temple (1 Cor. 3:16–17; 2 Cor. 6:16; Eph. 2:21; cf. 1 Peter 2:5), of which each believer is an integral, permanent part.

The Lord's assurance that believers "will not go out" from heaven further reinforces the truth of their absolute, eternal security. His words were especially meaningful to the Philadelphians, since their city was in a region prone to earthquakes and they sometimes had to flee for their lives. But no one will ever be forced to leave heaven.

In still more imagery reflecting believers' eternal security, Jesus said, "I will write on [overcomers] the name of My God [a mark of His possession of them], and the name of the city of My God, the new Jerusalem, which comes down out of heaven from My God [a mark of their heavenly citizenship], and My new name [a mark of His love]" (Rev. 3:12).

The final promise was addressed to the faithful believers in the lukewarm church at Laodicea. As if all the previous ones were not enough, Jesus made the staggering promise, "He who overcomes, I will grant to him to sit down with Me on My throne [cf. Matt. 19:28; Luke 22:29–30], as I also overcame and sat down with My Father on His throne" (Rev. 3:21). As He shares His Father's throne, so will overcomers share His throne and reign victoriously with Him forever. (For a complete exposition of the letters to the seven churches, see *Revelation 1–11*, The MacArthur New Testament Commentary [Chicago: Moody, 1999], chapters 4–10.)

The Witness of God (1 John 5:6–12)

17

This is the One who came by water and blood, Jesus Christ; not with the water only, but with the water and with the blood. It is the Spirit who testifies, because the Spirit is the truth. For there are three that testify: the Spirit and the water and the blood; and the three are in agreement. If we receive the testimony of men, the testimony of God is greater; for the testimony of God is this, that He has testified concerning His Son. The one who believes in the Son of God has the testimony in himself; the one who does not believe God has made Him a liar, because he has not believed in the testimony that God has given concerning His Son. And the testimony is this, that God has given us eternal life, and this life is in His Son. He who has the Son has the life; he who does not have the Son of God does not have the life. (5:6–12)

The apostle John has relentlessly hammered home throughout this epistle the truth that a correct view of the Lord Jesus Christ is essential to salvation. That was the apostle's theme at the outset, and it is valuable to read the previous texts that support that emphasis:

What was from the beginning, what we have heard, what we have seen with our eyes, what we have looked at and touched with our hands, concerning the Word of Life—and the life was manifested, and we have seen and testify and proclaim to you the eternal life, which was with the Father and was manifested to us—what we have seen and heard we proclaim to you also, so that you too may have fellowship with us; and indeed our fellowship is with the Father, and with His Son Jesus Christ. These things we write, so that our joy may be made complete. (1:1–4)

In 2:22 he asked rhetorically, "Who is the liar but the one who denies that Jesus is the Christ? This is the antichrist, the one who denies the Father and the Son." "This is His commandment," he wrote, "that we believe in the name of His Son Jesus Christ, and love one another, just as He commanded us" (3:23). In 4:1–2 John warned his readers against false teachers who deny the truth about Jesus Christ:

Beloved, do not believe every spirit, but test the spirits to see whether they are from God, because many false prophets have gone out into the world. By this you know the Spirit of God: every spirit that confesses that Jesus Christ has come in the flesh is from God.

Verses 9 and 10 of that same chapter declare that

by this the love of God was manifested in us, that God has sent His only begotten Son into the world so that we might live through Him. In this is love, not that we loved God, but that He loved us and sent His Son to be the propitiation for our sins.

John began chapter 5 by reminding his readers that only the one who "believes that Jesus is the Christ is born of God" (v. 1), while again we note that verse 13 is the key to the entire letter: "These things I have written to you who believe in the name of the Son of God, so that you may know that you have eternal life" (v. 13). Finally, John wrote in verse 20, "And we know that the Son of God has come, and has given us understanding so that we may know Him who is true; and we are in Him who is true, in His Son Jesus Christ. This is the true God and eternal life."

Jesus Christ is the focal point of redemptive history, and the Father has repeatedly testified that He is the Messiah, Savior, Redeemer, and King. That testimony first came as a bright ray of hope in the bleak aftermath of Adam and Eve's sin. In the context of God's curse on mankind came the promise of a deliverer: "I will put enmity between you and the woman," God told the serpent (Satan), "and between your seed and her seed; He shall bruise you on the head, and you shall bruise him on the heel" (Gen. 3:15). Later in Genesis, God reiterated His promise to send His Son, who would rule as King: "The scepter shall not depart from Judah, nor the ruler's staff from between his feet, until Shiloh [Messiah] comes, and to him shall be the obedience of the peoples" (49:10; cf. Rev. 5:5). God sovereignly chose to reveal a messianic prophecy through the false prophet Balaam: "A star shall come forth from Jacob, a scepter shall rise from Israel" (Num. 24:17). In Hannah's inspired song, God again promised to send His messianic King (1 Sam. 2:10, 35; cf. 2 Sam. 22:51). Second Samuel 7:12–15 records God's promise to David of a Son greater than Solomon, who would establish an eternal kingdom (v. 13). In Psalm 2 the psalmist reiterates the great hope of the coming messianic King (vv. 2, 6), who will rule the nations (vv. 8, 9), and is the Son of God (v. 12).

The Old Testament also predicted the precise details of Jesus' life. Isaiah prophesied that He would be born of a virgin (7:14), Micah that He would be born in Bethlehem (5:2), Hosea that He would be called out of Egypt (11:1), Jeremiah the attempt to murder Him in the slaughter of the innocents by Herod at His birth (31:15; cf. Matt. 2:17–18), Malachi the forerunner (John the Baptist) who would prepare the way for Him (4:5–6), and Isaiah His ministry in Galilee (9:1–2; cf. Matt. 4:12–16). Psalm 41:9 predicts His betrayal by a close friend, Psalm 22 delineates the details of His crucifixion, Isaiah 53 explains the theological significance of His death, and Psalm 16 foresees His resurrection.

Since the Old Testament Scriptures point unambiguously and unmistakably to Jesus Christ and no other as the Messiah, there is no excuse for not recognizing Him as such. The Lord chided His followers for their obtuseness in the face of overwhelming evidence:

> "O foolish men and slow of heart to believe in all that the prophets have spoken! Was it not necessary for the Christ to suffer these things and to enter into His glory?" Then beginning with Moses and with all the prophets, He explained to them the things concerning Himself in all the Scriptures. . . . Now He said to them, "These are My words which I spoke to you while I was still with you, that all things which are written about Me in the Law of Moses and the Prophets and the Psalms must be fulfilled." Then He opened their minds to understand the Scriptures, and He said to them, "Thus it is written, that the Christ would suffer and rise again from the dead the third day, and that repentance for forgiveness of sins would be proclaimed in His name to all the nations, beginning from Jerusalem." (Luke 24:25–27, 44–47)

He also rebuked the hostile Jewish leaders for failing to heed the Old Testament's witness to Him: "You search the Scriptures," He told them, "because you think that in them you have eternal life; it is these that testify about Me" (John 5:39). The issue was not that the Old Testament's testimony to Jesus was unclear, but rather that they were "unwilling to come to [Him] so that [they might] have life" (v. 40).

In Acts 13:26–29 Paul elaborated on that theme:

> Brethren, sons of Abraham's family, and those among you who fear God, to us the message of this salvation has been sent. For those who live in Jerusalem, and their rulers, recognizing neither Him nor the utterances of the prophets which are read every Sabbath, fulfilled these by condemning Him. And though they found no ground for putting Him to death, they asked Pilate that He be executed. When they had carried out all that was written concerning Him, they took Him down from the cross and laid Him in a tomb. (Acts 13:26–29)

In this section of his epistle, John elaborates on the theme of his gospel, which was "written so that [people] may believe that Jesus is the Christ, the Son of God; and that believing [they] may have life in His name" (John 20:31). The gospel of John records that the Father witnessed to the deity of Christ from a variety of sources: Scripture (5:39–40), John the Baptist (1:6–8, 34), the disciples (15:27), Christ's words (8:14, 18; 18:37), His works (5:36; 10:25, 38), the Holy Spirit (15:26), and the Father Himself (5:37; 8:18).

The key to this section is the word *testify,* which in its noun and verb forms appears nine times in verses 6–12. The root word from which both derive is *martus,* a common word that appears nearly 175 times in its various forms in the New Testament. It has the basic meaning of remembering something and testifying concerning it. That testimony could be in a legal setting (as in Mark 14:63; Acts 6:13; 7:58; Heb. 10:28), or in the general sense of recounting firsthand knowledge (as in Luke 11:48; 1 Tim. 6:12; Heb. 12:1; 1 Peter 5:1). Perhaps because so many people who testified to the true gospel paid with their lives, *martus* became the root of the English word *martyr.*

In the Old Testament, God called the people of Israel to be witnesses that He alone is God (Isa. 43:10–13; 44:6–8). The New Testament is supremely God's witness to His Son. The Gospels record the story of Christ's life, death, and resurrection; the book of Acts describes the initial spread of the truth about Him into the world; the epistles unpack the rich theological meaning of His life, death, resurrection, ascension, and second coming; the book of Revelation reveals the consummation of God's redemptive purpose in Him.

In keeping with the biblical injunction that "every fact is to be confirmed by the testimony of two or three witnesses" (2 Cor. 13:1; cf. Deut. 19:15; Matt. 18:16; 1 Tim. 5:19; Heb. 10:28), John presents three aspects of God's witness to Jesus Christ. Then, after delineating the particulars of the

Father's testimony to the Son, the apostle reveals the purpose of that testimony, and, finally, closes this section by illustrating its power.

THE PARTICULARS OF GOD'S TESTIMONY

This is the One who came by water and blood, Jesus Christ; not with the water only, but with the water and with the blood. It is the Spirit who testifies, because the Spirit is the truth. For there are three that testify: the Spirit and the water and the blood; and the three are in agreement. If we receive the testimony of men, the testimony of God is greater; for the testimony of God is this, that He has testified concerning His Son. (5:6–9)

In the preceding section (vv. 1–5), John described the joys and blessings of overcomers, those who believe that Jesus Christ is the Son of God. But the apostle knew that many would ask why they should believe that Jesus is who John claimed Him to be. After all, Israel rejected Him; "He came to His own, and those who were His own did not receive Him" (John 1:11). The Jews contemptuously referred to Him as a lying deceiver (Matt. 27:63), guilty of leading the people astray (John 7:12, 47; Luke 23:2) and of fomenting insurrection against Rome (Luke 23:5; cf. John 11:47–48). They blasphemously accused Him of being a glutton and a drunkard (Matt. 11:19), of being insane (John 10:20; cf. Mark 3:21), and, most heinous of all, of being demon-possessed (John 8:48; cf. v. 52; 7:20; Matt. 9:34; 10:25; 12:24; cf. vv. 31–32). Ultimately, their murderous hatred of Jesus led them to call for His crucifixion (Matt. 27:22–23). Why then, in light of Israel's rejection, should anyone believe that Jesus Christ is the Messiah, God Incarnate, the only Savior of sinners? Because of the infallible, unassailable, incontrovertible testimony of God Himself.

Houtos (**the One**) points ahead to **Jesus Christ.** Its emphatic position in the Greek text stresses Christ's uniqueness. This **One** and no other is God the Son, **who came** into the world. Jesus Christ's life did not begin when He was born; He had existed from all eternity (John 1:1–2). Hence the New Testament speaks of Jesus coming into this world, not of His coming into existence. In the incarnation the eternally existing "Word became flesh, and dwelt among us" (John 1:14). In John 16:28 Jesus declared, "I came forth from the Father and have come into the world; I am leaving the world again and going to the Father" (cf. 8:14; 13:3; 18:37). Earlier in this epistle John wrote, "The Son of God appeared [not "was created"] for this purpose, to destroy the works of the devil" (3:8).

The incarnation of Jesus Christ is the glorious central truth of redemptive history and the foundation of the Christian faith. It is to the coming of the Son and to His deity that the Father testifies in this passage. John gives three elements of that confirming testimony: the **water,** the **blood,** and the **Spirit.**

Some connect the phrase **water and blood** with Jesus' death, when "one of the soldiers pierced His side with a spear, and immediately blood and water came out" (John 19:34). But there is no reason to assume that John had that incident in mind. It is also difficult to see how the piercing of Jesus' side was a divine witness to His deity; that act was not a divine statement of anything, but rather a very human affirmation that Jesus was dead (but Zech. 12:10 did prophesy it).

Others see in these terms a reference to baptism and the Lord's Supper. But again, there is no exegetical or contextual reason to associate John's reference to water and blood with those ordinances. Further, baptism and the Lord's Supper are the church's witness to Christ, not the Father's (cf. 1 Cor. 11:26).

It is best to see the **water** here as a reference to Christ's baptism and the **blood** as a reference to His death. Those two notable events bracketed the Lord's earthly ministry, and in both of them the Father testified concerning His Son.

The phrase **not with the water only, but with the water and with the blood** is not redundant, but addresses an important theological point. The Father did not, as the false teachers whom John was combating insisted, affirm Jesus at His baptism, but not at His death. Those heretics, purveyors of an incipient form of Gnosticism, taught that the "Christ spirit" descended on the man Jesus at His baptism, making Him the anointed One of God. According to this heresy, Jesus, under the control of the "Christ spirit," gave valuable ethical teachings during His ministry. But the Christ spirit left Him before the crucifixion and, the false teachers further claimed, He died as a mere man, not the God-man whose sacrificial death atoned for the sins of all who would ever be justified.

Like any teaching that denies the efficacy of Christ's substitutionary atonement, that teaching was a satanic lie, since "Jesus Christ the righteous . . . is the propitiation for our sins" (2:1–2; cf. 4:10; Rom. 3:25; Heb. 2:17). If He did not possess His divine nature on the cross, Jesus could not and did not conquer sin and death for believers. But the glorious truth is that "He . . . who knew no sin [became] sin on our behalf, so that we might become the righteousness of God in Him" (2 Cor. 5:21).

At the beginning of Christ's earthly ministry, the Father gave testimony to Him at the **water** when He was baptized. Matthew records that "Jesus arrived from Galilee at the Jordan coming to John, to be baptized by him" (3:13). As the forerunner of the Messiah, John the Baptist proclaimed a "baptism of repentance" (v. 11; Mark 1:4; Luke 3:3; Acts 13:24;

19:4). He called on the people of Israel to prepare their hearts for the coming of the Messiah by confessing and repenting of their sin, and asking God to cleanse them. Their baptism was a public affirmation of repentance from sin, an external act symbolizing an internal reality. Since only Gentile proselytes were baptized, the Jews were acknowledging that they were no better than Gentiles and needed to become in reality the people of God (cf. Rom. 2:28–29).

But John the Baptist knew that as the spotless "Lamb of God who takes away the sin of the world" (John 1:29), Jesus had no sin to repent of and hence no need to be baptized. Therefore "John tried to prevent Him, saying, 'I have need to be baptized by You, and do You come to me?'" (Matt. 3:14). John was shocked by the reversal of what he knew to be true. He was the sinner, Jesus the sinless one; he was the lesser, Jesus the greater (cf. John 1:27; 3:30).

Although He was without sin (2 Cor. 5:21; Heb. 4:15; 7:26; 1 Peter 2:22; cf. John 8:46), it was still necessary for Jesus to be baptized. By doing so, He publicly identified with sinners. Therefore He told John, "Permit it at this time; for in this way it is fitting for us to fulfill all righteousness" (Matt. 3:15*a*). Jesus always performed what God required of His people; He claimed no exemption here, just as He claimed no exemption from paying the temple tax (17:24–27). His perfect obedience (cf. John 4:34; 8:29; 14:31; 15:10) made Him the sinless sacrifice whose death made atonement for sin.

After John baptized Him, "Jesus came up immediately from the water; and behold, the heavens were opened, and he saw the Spirit of God descending as a dove and lighting on Him" (Matt. 3:16). The physical manifestation of the Holy Spirit's presence provided visible evidence of the Father's testimony to the Son, especially to John the Baptist. As he later declared,

> I have seen the Spirit descending as a dove out of heaven, and He remained upon Him. I did not recognize Him, but He who sent me to baptize in water said to me, "He upon whom you see the Spirit descending and remaining upon Him, this is the One who baptizes in the Holy Spirit." I myself have seen, and have testified that this is the Son of God. (John 1:32–34)

After the Father's visual testimony by the Spirit to Jesus came His explicit declaration, "This is My beloved Son, in whom I am well-pleased" (Matt. 3:17). Those words, reminiscent of Psalm 2:7 and Isaiah 42:1, expressed the Father's approval of the Son, and His attestation of Him as the Messiah.

John then introduces a second witness, the **blood,** representing Christ's death. As He had at His baptism, the Father gave striking testimony to Jesus in the miraculous events surrounding His crucifixion. Matthew 27:45 records that "from the sixth hour darkness fell upon all the land until the ninth hour." In the middle of the day came a supernatural darkness, symbolizing the Father's forsaking of the Son as the sin-bearing sacrifice. Sensing that, "Jesus cried out with a loud voice, saying, 'Eli, Eli, lama sabachthani?' that is, 'My God, my God, why have You forsaken Me?'" (v. 46; cf. Ps. 22:1).

At the moment of Jesus' death there was another astonishing miracle as "the veil of the temple was torn in two from top to bottom" (Matt. 27:51a). That curtain, separating the Most Holy Place from the Holy Place, was far too large and heavy for men to tear, especially from the top down. The Father's act symbolized His acceptance of Jesus' sacrifice, through which the way into His presence was opened (cf. Heb. 10:19–20).

In yet another amazing miracle, "the earth shook and the rocks were split. The tombs were opened, and many bodies of the saints who had fallen asleep were raised; and coming out of the tombs after His resurrection they entered the holy city and appeared to many" (Matt. 27:51b–53). Their appearance in bodily form testified to Christ's resurrection as the "first fruits of those who are asleep" (1 Cor. 15:20). So overwhelming was God's miraculous testimony to Jesus that a battle-hardened Roman centurion who witnessed it cried out in terror, "Truly this was the Son of God!" (Matt. 27:54; cf. Mark 15:39).

The Father's testimony to Jesus also appears in the Old Testament prophecies that His death fulfilled, most notably in Psalm 22:

> All who see me sneer at me; they separate with the lip, they wag the head, saying, "Commit yourself to the Lord; let Him deliver him; let Him rescue him, because He delights in him." (vv. 7–8; cf. Matt. 27:39–40)

> I am poured out like water, and all my bones are out of joint; my heart is like wax; it is melted within me. My strength is dried up like a potsherd, and my tongue cleaves to my jaws; and You lay me in the dust of death. For dogs have surrounded me; a band of evildoers has encompassed me; they pierced my hands and my feet. I can count all my bones. They look, they stare at me; they divide my garments among them, and for my clothing they cast lots. (vv. 14–18)

and Isaiah 53:

> For He grew up before Him like a tender shoot, and like a root out of parched ground; He has no stately form or majesty that we should look upon Him, nor appearance that we should be attracted to Him. He was despised and forsaken of men, a man of sorrows and acquainted with grief; and like one from whom men hide their face He was despised, and we did not esteem Him. Surely our griefs He Himself bore, and our

sorrows He carried; yet we ourselves esteemed Him stricken, smitten of God, and afflicted. But He was pierced through for our transgressions, He was crushed for our iniquities; the chastening for our well-being fell upon Him, and by His scourging we are healed. All of us like sheep have gone astray, each of us has turned to his own way; but the Lord has caused the iniquity of us all to fall on Him. He was oppressed and He was afflicted, yet He did not open His mouth; like a lamb that is led to slaughter, and like a sheep that is silent before its shearers, so He did not open His mouth. By oppression and judgment He was taken away; and as for His generation, who considered that He was cut off out of the land of the living for the transgression of my people, to whom the stroke was due? His grave was assigned with wicked men, yet He was with a rich man in His death, because He had done no violence, nor was there any deceit in His mouth. (vv. 2–9)

The Father also testified to the Son through the ministry of **the Spirit,** who **is the truth** (cf. John 14:17; 15:26; 16:13). The Holy Spirit is the Spirit of truth in that He is true and, therefore, the source and revealer of divine truth (1 Peter 1:12; cf. Acts 1:16; 28:25; Heb. 3:7; 10:15–17), particularly about Jesus Christ (John 15:26). The Spirit was involved at Jesus' conception (Matt. 1:18, 20; Luke 1:35), baptism (Matt. 3:16), temptation (Mark 1:12; Luke 4:1), and throughout His ministry. Peter said to those gathered in Cornelius's house, "You know of Jesus of Nazareth, how God anointed Him with the Holy Spirit and with power, and how He went about doing good and healing all who were oppressed by the devil, for God was with Him" (Acts 10:38; cf. Matt. 12:28; Luke 4:14; John 3:34). Because the Holy Spirit empowered Jesus for ministry, to attribute Christ's miraculous works to Satan was to blaspheme the Holy Spirit (Mark 3:28–30). Jesus always did the will of the Father in the power of the Spirit.

The witness of the **three that testify: the Spirit and the water and the blood** is in perfect **agreement** and convincingly demonstrates that Jesus is the Christ, the Son of God. How foolish to **receive the testimony of men** about matters of far less significance while rejecting **the** infinitely **greater . . . testimony of God . . . that He has testified concerning His Son.**

Some English versions (e.g., the KJV and NKJV) add between vv. 7 and 8 the so-called *comma Johanneum,* which reads, "in heaven, the Father, the Word, and the Holy Spirit, and these three are one. And there are three that bear witness on earth." Though what it teaches is true, the added passage itself is spurious. Noted textual scholar Bruce M. Metzger summarizes the overwhelming evidence against its authenticity:

> The passage is absent from every known Greek manuscript except eight [all of which date from the Middle Ages], and these contain the passage in what appears to be a translation from a late recension of the

Latin Vulgate. Four of the eight manuscripts contain the passage as a variant reading written in the margin as a later addition to the manuscript.

The passage is quoted by none of the Greek Fathers, who, had they known it, would most certainly have employed it in the Trinitarian controversies (Sabellian and Arian). Its first appearance in Greek is in a Greek version of the (Latin) Acts of the Lateran Council in 1215.

The passage is absent from the manuscripts of all ancient versions . . . except the Latin; and it is not found (*a*) in the Old Latin in its early form . . . or in the Vulgate (*b*) as issued by Jerome . . . or (*c*) as revised by Alcuin [in the ninth century].

The earliest instance of the passage being quoted as a part of the actual text of the Epistle is in a fourth century Latin treatise entitled *Liber Apologeticus* . . . attributed either to the Spanish heretic Priscillian (died about 385) or to his follower Bishop Instantius. . . . In the fifth century the gloss was quoted by Latin Fathers in North Africa and Italy as part of the text of the Epistle, and from the sixth century onwards it is found more and more frequently in manuscripts of the Old Latin and of the Vulgate. (*A Textual Commentary on the Greek New Testament,* second edition [Stuttgart: Deutsche Bibelgesellschaft, 2002], 647–48)

F. F. Bruce relates how this passage found its way into English Bibles:

When [the Dutch Christian humanist scholar and contemporary of Luther Desiderius] Erasmus prepared his printed edition of the Greek Testament, he rightly left those words out, but was attacked for this by people who felt that the passage was a valuable proof-text for the doctrine of the Trinity. He replied (rather incautiously) that if he could be shown any Greek manuscript which contained the words, he would include them in his next edition. Unfortunately, a Greek manuscript not more than some twenty years old was produced in which the words appeared: they had been translated into Greek from Latin. Of course, the fact that the only Greek manuscript exhibiting the words belonged to the sixteenth century was in itself an argument against their authenticity, but Erasmus had given his promise, and so in his 1522 edition he included the passage. (*History of the Bible in English* [New York: Oxford University Press, 1978], 141–42)

From Erasmus's Greek New Testament the passage found its way into the Textus Receptus, the Greek text used by the King James Version translators. That this passage is not part of the inspired text does not affect the biblical doctrine of the Trinity, which does not rest on this spurious insertion.

THE PURPOSE OF GOD'S TESTIMONY

And the testimony is this, that God has given us eternal life, and this life is in His Son. (5:11)

The purpose of God's **testimony** through the water, the blood, and the Spirit is that sinners might receive **eternal life.** Eternal life involves far more than merely living forever in a chronological sense. The essence of **eternal life** is the believer's participation in the blessed everlasting life of Christ (cf. John 1:4) through his or her union with Him (Rom. 5:21; 6:4, 11, 23; 1 Cor. 15:22; 2 Cor. 5:17; Gal. 2:20; Col. 3:3–4; 2 Tim. 1:1, 10; Jude 21). Jesus defined it in His High Priestly Prayer to the Father: "This is eternal life, that they may know You, the only true God, and Jesus Christ whom You have sent" (John 17:3). It is the life of the age to come (Eph. 2:6–7), which believers will most fully experience in the perfect, unending glory, holiness, and joy of heaven (Rom. 8:19–23, 29; 1 Cor. 15:49; Phil. 3:20–21; 1 John 3:2).

The eternal life promised by God in the Old Testament (e.g., 2 Sam. 12:23; Pss. 16:8–11; 133:3; Dan. 12:2) and sought by the Jews of Jesus' day (Luke 10:25; John 5:39) comes only to those who believe God's testimony and place their faith **in His Son.** The gospel is exclusive; there are not many ways to God, but only one. In John 14:6 Jesus declared, "I am the way, and the truth, and the life; no one comes to the Father but through Me." "And there is salvation in no one else," Peter added, "for there is no other name under heaven that has been given among men by which we must be saved" (Acts 4:12; cf. John 6:68; 17:2; Rom. 6:23; 1 Tim. 1:16; Jude 21).

THE RESPONSE TO GOD'S TESTIMONY

The one who believes in the Son of God has the testimony in himself; the one who does not believe God has made Him a liar, because he has not believed in the testimony that God has given concerning His Son. . . . He who has the Son has the life; he who does not have the Son of God does not have the life. (5:10, 12)

What people do with God's testimony to Jesus Christ determines their eternal destiny. There are only two possible responses: to believe God's testimony, or to reject it. No one can remain neutral, for as Jesus said, "He who is not with Me is against Me" (Matt. 12:30). **The one who believes in the Son of God has the testimony in himself.** Saving faith in Jesus Christ results in a lifelong hold on eternal life (cf. 3:23; 4:2, 15; 5:1, 4–5). Since true faith perseveres, those who turn away from the gospel reveal that they were never saved in the first place (see the exposition of 1 John 2:19 in chapter 9 of this volume).

On the other hand, **the one who does not believe God has made Him a liar.** To deny that Jesus Christ is who God said He is, to refuse to believe **in the testimony that God has given concerning His Son,** renders God a **liar**—which is the severest of all blasphemies since God is perfect truth and cannot lie (cf. Num. 23:19; 1 Sam. 15:29; Titus 1:2; Heb. 6:18). Rejecting God's witness concerning His Son is not a misfortune to be pitied, or overlooked in the name of tolerance. It is a heinous, damning sin and an affront to God's holy nature. Those guilty of it must not be patronized, comforted, or reassured, but confronted and called to repentance. This is no trivial issue; the integrity of God is at stake.

John closed this section by setting out the eternal results of the only two possible responses to God's witness to Jesus Christ: **He who has the Son has the life; he who does not have the Son of God does not have the life.** Here again the exclusivity of the gospel is evident. Only those who believe the Father's witness to the **Son** and acknowledge Jesus as Lord and Savior have eternal **life;** all who refuse to do so do **not have the Son,** and consequently do **not have** eternal **life.**

The glorious promise to those who believe God's testimony is that "as many as received [Jesus], to them He gave the right to become children of God, even to those who believe in His name" (John 1:12). But the sobering warning to those who reject it is, "How will [you] escape if [you] neglect so great a salvation?" (Heb. 2:3).

Christian Certainties (1 John 5:13–21)

18

These things I have written to you who believe in the name of the Son of God, so that you may know that you have eternal life. This is the confidence which we have before Him, that, if we ask anything according to His will, He hears us. And if we know that He hears us in whatever we ask, we know that we have the requests which we have asked from Him. If anyone sees his brother committing a sin not leading to death, he shall ask and God will for him give life to those who commit sin not leading to death. There is a sin leading to death; I do not say that he should make request for this. All unrighteousness is sin, and there is a sin not leading to death. We know that no one who is born of God sins; but He who was born of God keeps him, and the evil one does not touch him. We know that we are of God, and that the whole world lies in the power of the evil one. And we know that the Son of God has come, and has given us understanding so that we may know Him who is true; and we are in Him who is true, in His Son Jesus Christ. This is the true God and eternal life. Little children, guard yourselves from idols. (5:13–21)

Life in this fallen world is filled with uncertainty, with few guarantees and little that can be depended on. "Man, who is born of woman," Job lamented, "is short-lived and full of turmoil" (Job 14:1), being "born for trouble, as sparks fly upward" (5:7). Illness, an accident, violence, or old age catches up with everyone in the end, because all people "are just a vapor that appears for a little while and then vanishes away" (James 4:14; cf. Pss. 39:5; 90:10). In the meantime, life's journey is fraught with doubts, questions, and uncertainties. Jobs vanish as companies downsize and outsource. The volatility of the stock market, the fluctuations of the economy, and increasing taxes create further uncertainty. Relationships come and go, with people's faithfulness often lasting only as long as their felt needs are being met—or until they find someone more attractive. The uncertainty of relationships has made prenuptial agreements commonplace, as people attempt to protect themselves against being exploited by their erstwhile partners. On a larger scale, natural disasters, such as earthquakes, hurricanes, tornadoes, fires, and floods, can sweep away in an instant the accumulated treasures of a lifetime.

Uncertainty over what the future holds drives people to spend a significant percentage of their income on insurance, as they attempt to safeguard against all of the potential negative contingencies. Car insurance provides a measure of security in the event of an accident. Uncertainty about fire, theft, and natural disasters leads people to buy coverage to protect their homes. Health insurance helps guard against financial ruin in case of serious illness; life insurance provides money should the breadwinner in a family die.

But the most profound uncertainty with the most disastrous results exists not in the material realm, but in the spiritual and eternal realm. Because they reject the gospel and are without God, people are also without hope (Eph. 2:12), or protection from divine wrath and eternal hell. Most people put their hope in false religions or personal ideologies to get them into a happy eternal state. And it is popularly believed that all religions lead to heaven and most people are good, thus they are headed there. What is not popular is the reality that only the Bible is the true Word of God, the gospel the only way to heaven, and all who do not believe it go to hell forever.

In a world of uncertainty, relativism, and deception, the Bible proclaims absolute truth. Five words, based on biblical absolutes, frame the paradigm.

The first word is *objectivity*. Truth is objective, not subjective. It exists independently outside of the human mind, having its origin in God, and coming to us by revelation in Scripture (John 17:17; cf. Ps. 119:151, 160; 2 Tim. 2:15).

The second word is *rationality*. The revelation of God is intelligible;

it is not mystical, nor does it contain hidden meanings accessible only to the religious elite. Scripture yields its meaning to the mind that approaches it reasonably.

A third word is *veracity*. The Bible, properly interpreted in a normal, rational fashion, yields divine truth.

The fourth term is *authority*. The divinely revealed truth of Scripture bears God's authority, and hence it is binding in all that it affirms.

A final word is *incompatibility*. Because the Bible contains divine truth, anything that contradicts it is wrong. Biblical Christianity's commitment to absolute truth makes it exclusive in an inclusive world.

The Bible reveals the truth about how the universe began, and how it will end; about why people behave the way they do; about what is right and what is wrong; about heaven and hell, and how people get to those places; about what makes for good human relationships; about God's promises; and, most significant, about the Lord Jesus Christ, including His virgin birth, sinless life, unparalleled teaching, substitutionary death, literal resurrection, bodily ascension, and second coming.

Scripture is filled with absolute certainties, including the reality that sin has consequences (Num. 32:23); that the Bible is true (Ps. 19:7; 111:7; Luke 1:4; 2 Peter 1:19); that righteousness brings a reward (Prov. 11:18); that God alone is God (Deut. 4:39; Isa. 43:10–12; 45:6), can do all things (Job 42:2), will not act wickedly (Job 34:12), judges according to truth (Rev. 16:7; 19:2; cf. Ps. 119:75), is faithful (Deut. 7:9), punishes sin (Rom. 2:2), created everything (Isa. 48:13)—including humans (Ps. 100:3), and is good and merciful (Ps. 23:6); that Jesus Christ bore our griefs and sorrows (Isa. 53:4), is the Messiah, the Holy One of God (John 6:69; cf. Matt. 14:33; Acts 2:36), knows all things (John 16:30; 21:17), was sent by the Father (John 17:8; cf. v. 25; 16:27, 30), has authority to forgive sins (Matt. 9:6), will not reject those who come to Him (John 6:37), knows those who are His (John 10:14; cf. 2 Tim. 2:19), has entered into God's presence on believers' behalf (Heb. 6:19–20), and will return (Rev. 22:20); that God's promise of salvation is guaranteed (Rom. 4:16); that there will be a resurrection (Job 19:25–27); that God causes all things to work together for good for those who love Him (Rom. 8:28); that sinners do not inherit the kingdom of God (Eph. 5:5); that the Day of the Lord will come (1 Thess. 5:2); and that God will help and support His people (Isa. 41:10; cf. 2 Tim. 1:12).

John wrote this epistle to provide his readers with certainty about all that God has revealed concerning salvation. The formal argument of the letter ended in 5:12, and verses 13–21 are its postscript. John's concluding remarks are not a collection of random thoughts, however, but form a powerful climax to all he has written. Throughout the letter, John has recycled tests to identify who is a true Christian. Those tests serve a polemic purpose; they expose the phony believers and the false teachers—the deceiving antichrists. But they also serve a pastoral purpose, giving increasingly stronger confidence and assurance to the genuine believers.

As the epistle builds to a great, if familiar, crescendo, John focuses on five things that genuine Christians can be certain of: eternal life, answered prayer, victory over sin, that they belong to God, and Christ's deity.

ETERNAL LIFE

These things I have written to you who believe in the name of the Son of God, so that you may know that you have eternal life. (5:13)

The phrase **these things** sweeps backward to encompass the entire letter, as is evident from several considerations. First, the shift from the second person in verse 12 ("He who has the Son . . . he who does not have the Son . . .") to the first person (**These things I have written . . .**) suggests that verse 13 does not merely continue the flow of thought from the previous verse. Second, in 1:4 John announced his purpose in writing; in verse 13 he looks back on what he had written. Together, the two verses state John's purpose in writing, since it is assurance of eternal life that produces fullness of joy. Finally, there is a strong parallel between verse 13 and John 20:31 ("these have been written so that you may believe that Jesus is the Christ, the Son of God; and that believing you may have life in His name"). Since that verse unquestionably refers back to the entire gospel of John, the parallel expression in verse 13 most likely refers back to the entire epistle. John wrote his gospel so that people might believe and be saved; he wrote his first epistle so that those who believe would know they are saved.

As has been clear throughout, the blessings of salvation and assurance are only for those **who believe in the name of the Son of God** (cf. the discussion of 3:23 in chapter 13 of this volume). God has guaranteed these blessings to Christians by giving them the Holy Spirit as a pledge (Eph. 1:14). John's uncompromising presentation of the truth in absolute, unqualified terms, the relentless attacks of the false teachers, and the departure of some of the false believers (2:19) had shaken his readers. The apostle assured them that if they passed the doctrinal and practical tests, they could **know** for certain **that** they had **eternal life.**

In its most basic sense, **eternal life** is living forever with God in heaven (Matt. 25:46; Mark 10:30). But as noted in the discussion of 5:11 in the previous chapter of this volume, the term does not refer primarily to duration of life, but to quality of life. Eternal life is to know Jesus Christ (John 17:3), who Himself is eternal life (1 John 5:20), and to share in His life. It is a present possession, not merely a future hope (John 3:36; 5:24; 6:47, 54; 10:28; 1 John 3:15), though it is not fully manifested in this life. But there will come a day in the future when the eternal life believers already possess will no longer be incarcerated in their sinful, fallen flesh. On that glorious day, they will experience their "adoption as sons, the redemption of [the] body" (Rom. 8:23; cf. Phil. 3:21; 1 John 3:2). Then the glory of eternal life—the power of the Trinity that works within them (cf. Eph. 3:16–19)—will shine through them unclouded by their mortal bodies.

ANSWERED PRAYER

This is the confidence which we have before Him, that, if we ask anything according to His will, He hears us. And if we know that He hears us in whatever we ask, we know that we have the requests which we have asked from Him. If anyone sees his brother committing a sin not leading to death, he shall ask and God will for him give life to those who commit sin not leading to death. There is a sin leading to death; I do not say that he should make request for this. All unrighteousness is sin, and there is a sin not leading to death. (5:14–17)

As noted above, the full experience of eternal life awaits Christians in heaven. But though they have not yet entered into their eternal inheritance (cf. 1 Peter 1:4), they have access to all of God's resources through prayer. *Parrēsia* (**confidence**) literally means "freedom of speech" (cf. the discussion of 3:21 in chapter 13 of this volume). It can also be translated "boldness" (Acts 4:31), or "openness" (Acts 28:31). The phrase translated **before Him** has the sense of "in His presence." Through Jesus Christ believers have "boldness and confident access" (Eph. 3:12) to God that enables them to "draw near with confidence to the throne of grace, so that [they] may receive mercy and find grace to help in time of need" (Heb. 4:16).

The sure promise of God is that when believers boldly and freely come to Him with their requests, He will hear and answer. **If we ask anything according to His will,** John wrote, **He hears us.** And if we know that **He hears us in whatever we ask, we know that we have the requests which we have asked from Him.** Hearing in this context refers to more than merely God's being aware of believers' requests; it also means that He grants **the requests which we have asked from Him.** That is nothing less than a blank check to ask God for anything, but it comes with one important qualifier: the requests must be **according to His will.**

To pray according to God's will assumes first of all being saved. God is not obligated to answer the prayers of unbelievers. He may choose to do so when it suits His sovereign purposes, but God does not obligate Himself to any unbeliever. John illustrated this principle when he wrote earlier in this epistle, "Beloved, if our heart does not condemn us, we have confidence before God; and whatever we ask we receive from Him, because we keep His commandments and do the things that are pleasing in His sight" (3:21–22). The Lord Jesus Christ made a similar statement, recorded in John 15:7: "If you abide in Me, and My words abide in you [the definition of a genuine believer], ask whatever you wish, and it will be done for you" (cf. v. 16). Only believers, those who obey God's commandments, can have the certainty that He will answer their prayers.

Praying according to God's will also means confessing sin. The psalmist wrote in Psalm 66:18, "If I regard wickedness in my heart, the Lord will not hear" (cf. 1 Peter 3:7).

Again, the Lord's promise in John 14:13–14 affirms the requirement of praying according to God's will: "Whatever you ask in My name, that will I do, so that the Father may be glorified in the Son. If you ask Me anything in My name, I will do it." To pray in Jesus' name is to pray consistent with who He is, with the goal of bringing Him glory. It is to follow the pattern of His model prayer: "Your kingdom come. Your will be done, on earth as it is in heaven" (Matt. 6:10), and His example of humble submission to the Father's will when He prayed in Gethsemane, "Father, if You are willing, remove this cup from Me; yet not My will, but Yours be done" (Luke 22:42). The goal of prayer is not to gratify our selfish desires (cf. James 4:3), but to align our wills with God's purposes.

Praying according to God's will not only brings glory to the Son, but also joy to believers. "Truly, truly, I say to you," Jesus said, "if you ask the Father for anything in My name, He will give it to you. Until now you have asked for nothing in My name; ask and you will receive, so that your joy may be made full" (John 16:23b–24). When obedient believers delight themselves in the Lord, He will plant the desires in their hearts for what glorifies Him (Ps. 37:4), and those desires will control their prayers. God's answers to those prayers will glorify Him, bring believers' wills into line with His purposes, and fill them with joy.

At first glance, verse 16 appears to introduce an abrupt change of subject. But upon further consideration, the connection of verses 16 and 17 to verses 14 and 15 becomes clear. By giving one important exception, John illustrates in a contrasting manner the extent of God's promise to answer prayer. When a believer sees a **brother** (a real or professing believer) **committing a sin not leading to death,** the apostle writes, **he shall ask and God will for him give life to those who commit sin not leading to death.** On the other hand, **there is a sin leading to death,** and the apostle did not advise Christians to **make request for this** sin.

Evidently John and his readers knew what the **sin leading to death** was, since no explanation is given, but its exact meaning is difficult for us to determine. Two possibilities present themselves.

First, the sin in question may be that of a non-Christian leading to eternal death. In that case it would be a final rejection of Jesus Christ, such as that committed by those who attributed His miracles to the power of Satan (Matt. 12:31–32). Such ultimate apostasy is unforgivable, as Jesus declared:

> Therefore I say to you, any sin and blasphemy shall be forgiven people, but blasphemy against the Spirit shall not be forgiven. Whoever speaks a word against the Son of Man, it shall be forgiven him; but whoever speaks against the Holy Spirit, it shall not be forgiven him, either in this age or in the age to come. (Matt. 12:31–32)

Praying for the restoration of such people to the fellowship from which they have departed (1 John 2:19) is futile, because "it is impossible to renew them again to repentance, since they again crucify to themselves the Son of God and put Him to open shame" (Heb. 6:6). John did not forbid prayer for such people, since it is impossible to know who they are. The apostle merely stated that prayer for them will not be answered; God has already made the final decision about their future. Supporting the view that John is referring to unbelievers is the present tense of the participle _hamartanonta_ ("sinning"; the Greek text literally reads "If anyone sees his brother sinning a sin . . ."); John elsewhere in this epistle uses the present tense to describe the habitual sins that characterize unbelievers (e.g., 3:4, 6, 8; 5:18).

Another possibility is that John is not referring to an unbeliever, but to a believer. According to this view, the **sin leading to death** refers to a Christian's sin that is so serious that God takes the life of the one committing it. He put to death Ananias and Sapphira when they lied to the Holy Spirit in front of the church (Acts 5:1–11). Paul wrote to the Corinthians concerning those who were abusing the Lord's Table, "For this reason many among you are weak and sick, and a number sleep [have died]" (1 Cor. 11:30). The sin is not one particular sin, but any sin that the Lord determines is serious enough to warrant such severe chastisement.

Both of the above views reflect biblical truth, and it is hard to be dogmatic as to which one John had in mind. In either case, John's point is that prayer for those committing a sin leading to death will not result in the outcome that might otherwise be expected.

Although God mercifully does not immediately punish every sin with death, every sin is nonetheless a serious matter to Him. **All unrighteousness is sin,** John reminded his readers, even **sin not leading to death.** Every sin is a violation of His law and an affront to God, and is to be confessed (1:9; Ps. 32:5), forsaken (Prov. 28:13), and mortified (Rom. 8:13; Col. 3:5).

VICTORY OVER SIN

We know that no one who is born of God sins; but He who was born of God keeps him, and the evil one does not touch him. (5:18)

As he winds down this letter, John reiterates a vitally important principle he repeated earlier in this epistle: no one who has been transformed by the new birth goes on living in an unbroken pattern of sin.

The unconverted can do nothing but sin. They are sinners from birth (Ps. 51:5), slaves to sin (John 8:34; Rom. 6:16), defiant, rebellious haters of God (Pss. 5:10; Rom. 1:28–32; 5:10; 8:7), and under the dominion of Satan (Eph. 2:2; cf. Acts 26:18; Col. 1:13). In short, they are "dead in [their] trespasses and sins" (Eph. 2:1).

The **one who is born of God,** however, cannot live in an unbroken pattern of sin, for several reasons. First, sin is incompatible with the law of God (1 John 3:4). The redeemed love God's law (Ps. 119:97, 113, 163, 165) and cannot habitually live in violation of it (cf. 1 John 2:3–4; 3:24; 5:3). Second, sin is incompatible with the work of Christ, who "appeared in order to take away sins" (1 John 3:5; cf. v. 8; Matt. 1:21; John 1:29). Finally, sin is incompatible with the work of the Holy Spirit, who in the new birth plants the principle of divine life in the redeemed (1 Peter 1:23; 1 John 3:9). (For a complete discussion of believers' incompatibility with sin, see chapter 11 of this volume.)

That they do not continually live in sin does not mean that believers can reach a point in this life where they never sin. In fact, John said that those who make such claims are liars (1:8, 10). Further, his description of Jesus as believers' Advocate (2:1) assumes that they will continue to sin and need His intercession. The point here is the same as earlier, that a pattern of righteousness characterizes the redeemed, whereas a pattern of unrighteousness characterizes the unredeemed.

Paul reminded the Romans that since sin's power over them has been broken, it cannot characterize their lives:

> But thanks be to God that though you were slaves of sin, you became obedient from the heart to that form of teaching to which you were committed, and having been freed from sin, you became slaves of righteousness. I am speaking in human terms because of the weakness of your flesh. For just as you presented your members as slaves to impurity and to lawlessness, resulting in further lawlessness, so now present your members as slaves to righteousness, resulting in sanctification. For when you were slaves of sin, you were free in regard to righteousness. Therefore what benefit were you then deriving from the things of which you are now ashamed? For the outcome of those things is death. But now having been freed from sin and enslaved to God, you derive your benefit, resulting in sanctification, and the outcome, eternal life. (Rom. 6:17–22)

The unredeemed are "slaves to sin," but the redeemed are "obedient from the heart" to God's law, and thus "having been freed from sin, [they are] slaves of righteousness." While the inevitable outcome for those who live in sin is spiritual death (Rom. 6:23), those who have "been freed from sin and enslaved to God" gain "eternal life" (v. 22).

A believer can never fall back into a pattern of unbroken sin because **He who was born of God keeps him.** This second reference to one **born of God** is to Jesus Christ, the only begotten Son of God (John 1:14; 3:16, 18; Heb. 1:5; 5:5; 1 John 4:9). As the Good Shepherd, Jesus protects His flock so that **the evil one** (Satan) **does not** so much as **touch** (lay hold of or fasten his grip on) them. They are no longer under his control, having been "rescued ... from the domain of darkness" (Col. 1:13; cf. Acts 26:18; 2 Tim. 2:26; Heb. 2:14–15). Satan can tempt and harass the saints, as he did Job (Job 1–2) and Peter (Luke 22:31), but he can never reclaim them. Jesus will not fail to keep the redeemed (John 10:28; 2 Tim. 1:12; Jude 24–25), who have been given to Him by the Father (John 6:37, 39; 17:2, 6, 9, 24). Christ is the "anchor of the soul" for believers, providing them with "a hope both sure and steadfast and one which enters within the veil, where Jesus has entered as a forerunner for us, having become a high priest forever according to the order of Melchizedek" (Heb. 6:19–20).

The Bible does speak of Christians keeping themselves. They are to keep themselves pure (1 Tim. 5:22), keep the commandments of God (1 John 3:22), keep the faith (2 Tim. 4:7), keep themselves unstained by the world (James 1:27), keep themselves from idols (1 John 5:21), keep God's Word (1 John 2:5), and keep themselves in the love of God (Jude 21).

But John sees here God's work of supernaturally preserving His people, which is as guaranteed as His justifying of them. The promises of God constitute the first guarantee. Paul wrote in Philippians 1:6: "For I am confident of this very thing, that He who began a good work in you will perfect it until the day of Christ Jesus." To the Thessalonians he wrote, "Now may the God of peace Himself sanctify you entirely; and may your spirit and soul and body be preserved complete, without blame at the coming of our Lord Jesus Christ. Faithful is He who calls you, and He also will bring it to pass" (1 Thess. 5:23–24). Nearing the end of his life, with martyrdom looming, Paul still confidently affirmed, "The Lord will rescue me from every evil deed, and will bring me safely to His heavenly kingdom; to Him be the glory forever and ever. Amen" (2 Tim. 4:18).

Second, the power of God guarantees believers' security; what He promised, He can deliver. In Romans 5:10, Paul points out that since God has the power to do the greater work of redemption, He is certainly powerful enough to do the lesser work of preservation: "For if while we were enemies we were reconciled to God through the death of His Son, much more, having been reconciled, we shall be saved by His life."

Third, God's eternal, unchangeable purpose to save the elect (Matt. 25:34; Eph. 1:4; 2 Thess. 2:13; 2 Tim. 1:9; Rev. 13:8; 17:8) guarantees their preservation.

Fourth, the prayer of Christ, "Holy Father, keep them in Your name" (John 17:11b), prompts the Father to preserve the elect.

Fifth, believers' inseparable union with Christ (Rom. 6:3–5; cf. 1 Cor. 6:17) guarantees their preservation.

Sixth, the high price that God paid to redeem the elect—the blood of His Son (Acts 20:28; Heb. 9:12)—guarantees that He will not lose them.

In Romans 8:31–39, Paul eloquently sums up the absolute certainty that God will preserve His own:

> What then shall we say to these things? If God is for us, who is against us? He who did not spare His own Son, but delivered Him over for us all, how will He not also with Him freely give us all things? Who will bring a charge against God's elect? God is the one who justifies; who is the one who condemns? Christ Jesus is He who died, yes, rather who was raised, who is at the right hand of God, who also intercedes for us. Who will separate us from the love of Christ? Will tribulation, or distress, or persecution, or famine, or nakedness, or peril, or sword? Just as it is written, "For Your sake we are being put to death all day long; we were considered as sheep to be slaughtered." But in all these things we overwhelmingly conquer through Him who loved us. For I am convinced that neither death, nor life, nor angels, nor principalities, nor things present, nor things to come, nor powers, nor height, nor depth, nor any

other created thing, will be able to separate us from the love of God, which is in Christ Jesus our Lord.

THAT WE BELONG TO GOD

We know that we are of God, and that the whole world lies in the power of the evil one. (5:19)

Despite the existence of countless political, cultural, and social entities in the world, there are in reality only two realms. It is the comforting privilege of believers, in addition to having eternal life, answered prayer, and victory over sin, to **know** they belong to **God.** Though they exist in this world, they are not part of it (John 15:19; 17:14); they are children of God (John 1:12–13), "aliens and strangers" (1 Peter 2:11; cf. 1:1, 17; 1 Chron. 29:15; Ps. 119:19; Heb. 11:13), whose true citizenship is in heaven (Phil. 3:20).

On the other hand, **the whole world**—its politics, economics, education, entertainment, and, above all, its religion—**lies in the power of the evil one.** The evil world system is hostile to God and believers (John 15:18–19), as John noted earlier in this epistle (see the discussion of 3:13 in chapter 12 of this volume). It takes its cue from its ruler, Satan (John 12:31; 14:30; 16:11; cf. Eph. 2:2; 6:12), the archenemy of God and His people. Because the world is completely under Satan's influence, believers must avoid being contaminated by it (2:15–17; cf. James 1:27).

There is no middle ground, no third option. Everyone is part of God's kingdom, or of Satan's. In the words of Jesus, "He who is not with Me is against Me; and he who does not gather with Me, scatters" (Luke 11:23). Or as James scathingly declares, "You adulteresses, do you not know that friendship with the world is hostility toward God? Therefore whoever wishes to be a friend of the world makes himself an enemy of God" (James 4:4).

THAT CHRIST IS THE TRUE GOD

And we know that the Son of God has come, and has given us understanding so that we may know Him who is true; and we are in Him who is true, in His Son Jesus Christ. This is the true God and eternal life. Little children, guard yourselves from idols. (5:20–21)

These closing verses finally bring the epistle full circle. John began with the coming of the Word of Life (1:1–4); now he closes with the certainty that **the Son of God has come.** The present tense of the verb *hēkō* (**come**) indicates that Jesus has come and is still present. The Christian faith is not theoretical or abstract; it is rooted in the practical truth that God became man in the person of Jesus Christ.

Because no one can know "who the Father is except the Son, and anyone to whom the Son wills to reveal Him" (Luke 10:22), Jesus **has given us understanding so that we may know Him who is true.** But beyond mere knowledge, Christians have a personal union with **Him who is true, in His Son Jesus Christ** (cf. Rom. 8:1; 1 Cor. 1:30; 2 Cor. 5:17; 1 Peter 5:14). The Bible teaches that the only way to know the true and living God is through Jesus Christ. No one can be saved who does not believe in Christ, for there is no salvation apart from Him (cf. 2:1–2; 4:10, 14; 5:1; John 14:6; Acts 4:12).

John's threefold use of the word *alēthinos* (**true**) in this verse stresses the importance of understanding the truth in a world filled with Satan's lies. The last use of the term points to the most significant truth of all—that Jesus Christ **is the true God and eternal life.** The deity of Jesus Christ is an essential element of the Christian faith, and no one who rejects it can be saved. (For a detailed biblical defense of Christ's deity, see *John 1–11,* The MacArthur New Testament Commentary [Chicago: Moody, 2006], chapter 1.)

John's concluding warning, **Little children, guard yourselves from idols,** reflects the crucial significance of worshiping the true God exclusively. The danger of idolatry was especially serious in Ephesus (where John likely wrote this epistle), center of the worship of the goddess Artemis (Diana). A few decades earlier, the ministry of the apostle Paul had sparked a riot by her zealous worshipers (Acts 19:23–41). But the danger was not confined to Ephesus, as Paul's warning to the Corinthians, "You cannot drink the cup of the Lord and the cup of demons; you cannot partake of the table of the Lord and the table of demons" (1 Cor. 10:21), indicates. Though few in our contemporary culture worship physical idols, idolatry is widespread nonetheless. Anything that people elevate above God is an idol of the heart. Every "lofty thing raised up against the knowledge of God" (2 Cor. 10:5) must be smashed, and only Christ exalted.

In a dark world filled with uncertainty, Christians have the glorious certainty based on divine revelation—"the prophetic word made more sure . . . a lamp shining in a dark place" (2 Peter 1:19). While the world stumbles blindly in the darkness (Jer. 13:16), God's Word is for saints "a lamp to [their] feet and a light to [their] path" (Ps. 119:105), because "the commandment is a lamp and the teaching is light" (Prov. 6:23).

Introduction to
2 John

OCCASION AND PURPOSE

The two brief epistles of 2 and 3 John are the shortest New Testament books. Each contains fewer than 300 words in the Greek text and could have fit on a single papyrus sheet (cf. 2 John 12; 3 John 13). They closely approximate the conventional letter form of the contemporary Greco-Roman world.

But despite their brevity, both epistles are significant in that they stress the importance and boundaries of loving in the truth. Second John addresses the same basic historical events as 1 John: false teachers were assaulting the congregations under John's care (v. 7). Having left the fellowship of believers (1 John 2:19), the heretics were traveling from church to church, taking advantage of Christian hospitality as they spread their venomous lies. The lady to whom John addressed this letter may have inadvertently or unwisely shown them hospitality. John cautioned her (as a model for all believers) against participating in false teachers' evil deeds by showing them hospitality.

AUTHOR, DATE AND PLACE OF WRITING

This letter's close affinities with 1 John (e.g., v. 5 and 1 John 2:7; 3:11; v. 6 and 1 John 5:3; v. 7 and 1 John 2:18–26; v. 9 and 1 John 2:23; v. 12 and 1 John 1:4) make it clear that it also was written by John the apostle (see the discussion under The Author of 1 John in the Introduction to 1 John). Second John was most likely composed at Ephesus at about the same time or shortly after 1 John (c. A.D. 90–95).

DESTINATION AND READERS

Many commentators believe the phrase "the chosen lady" (v. 1) refers metaphorically to a local church. The more natural understanding in the context, however, is to take it as a reference to an actual woman and her children, whom John knew personally. The letter's obvious similarity to 3 John, which clearly (v. 1) was written to an individual, favors the view that 2 John also was written to an individual. Further, it would be unnatural to sustain such a figure of speech throughout the whole letter. Such an elaborate metaphor is also not in keeping with the letter's simplicity and the tenderness of its tone. Finally, the change from the singular form of the personal pronoun "you" in v. 5 to the plural form in v. 12 applies more naturally to a woman and her children than to a church and its members.

OUTLINE

I. The Basis of Christian Hospitality (1–3)
II. The Behavior of Christian Hospitality (4–6)
III. The Bounds of Christian Hospitality (7–11)
IV. The Blessings of Christian Hospitality (12–13)

Living in the Truth (2 John 1–4)

19

The elder to the chosen lady and her children, whom I love in truth; and not only I, but also all who know the truth, for the sake of the truth which abides in us and will be with us forever: Grace, mercy and peace will be with us, from God the Father and from Jesus Christ, the Son of the Father, in truth and love. I was very glad to find some of your children walking in truth, just as we have received commandment to do from the Father. (1–4)

When Pilate asked cynically, "What is truth?" (John 18:38) he reflected the view of many today. Postmodernism views the concept of truth with skepticism. Many believe that there is no such thing as absolute truth or, if there is, that it cannot be known. Certainly, they argue, there is no religious truth; religion is merely a personal preference, like one's taste in art, music, or literature.

But truth—absolute, divine truth—*does* exist, and it is the most important reality in the universe. When Martha complained that her sister was not helping her with the serving, Jesus replied, "Martha, Martha, you are worried and bothered about so many things; but only one thing is necessary, for Mary has chosen the good part, which shall not be taken away from her" (Luke 10:41–42). There was no higher priority than for

Mary to be "seated at the Lord's feet, listening to His word" of truth (v. 39). Truth is a precious commodity, more valuable than any earthly riches (cf. Pss. 19:7–10; 119:72, 127); once found, it is to be held on to at all costs. Thus Proverbs 23:23a exhorts, "Buy truth, and do not sell it."

The Bible, the Word of truth (Ps. 119:160; John 17:17; 2 Cor. 6:7; 2 Tim. 2:15; James 1:18), majors on the theme of truth. God is the "God of truth" (Ps. 31:5; Isa. 65:16), who abounds in truth (Ex. 34:6) and always speaks the truth (2 Sam. 7:28; cf. Num. 23:19; Titus 1:2); Christ is the truth (John 14:6; Eph. 4:21), is full of truth (John 1:14), revealed the truth (John 1:17), spoke the truth (John 8:45–46), and testified to the truth (John 18:37); the Holy Spirit is the Spirit of truth (John 14:17; 15:26; 16:13; 1 John 5:6). God's truth is eternal (Ps. 117:2), infinite (Pss. 57:10; 86:15; 108:4), and saving (Ps. 69:13). Salvation comes from faith in the truth (2 Thess. 2:13; cf. 1 Tim. 2:4; 2 Tim. 2:25); believers are sanctified by the truth (John 17:17), love the truth (cf. 2 Thess. 2:10), are set free by the truth (John 8:32), worship in the truth (John 4:23–24), rejoice in the truth (1 Cor. 13:6), speak the truth (Eph. 4:15, 25), meditate on the truth (Phil. 4:8), manifest the truth (2 Cor. 4:2), obey the truth (1 Peter 1:22), are guided by the truth (Pss. 25:5; 43:3) and, most comprehensively, walk in the truth (1 Kings 2:4; 3:6; 2 Kings 20:3; Pss. 26:3; 86:11).

Believers must be committed to the truth, because we exist in the world, which is the realm of Satan (1 John 5:19), the "father of lies" (John 8:44). He strives to keep sinners from understanding and believing the truth; he is "the god of this world [who] has blinded the minds of the unbelieving so that they might not see the light of the gospel of the glory of Christ, who is the image of God" (2 Cor. 4:4). As a result, "Everyone deceives his neighbor and does not speak the truth, they have taught their tongue to speak lies" (Jer. 9:5). Unbelievers are "men of depraved mind and deprived of the truth" (1 Tim. 6:5), who "oppose the truth" (2 Tim. 3:8) and "turn away their ears from the truth" (2 Tim. 4:4) because "they exchanged the truth of God for a lie" (Rom. 1:25).

In a world of lies, the church is called to be the "pillar and support of the truth" (1 Tim. 3:15). Paul's metaphor would have been readily understood by Timothy and his congregation at Ephesus. Located in that city was the temple of Diana (Artemis; Acts 19:23–28), one of the Seven Wonders of the Ancient World. The temple's immense roof was supported by 127 pillars, which rested on a massive foundation. Just as that temple was a monument to the lies of Satan, so the church is to be a monument to the truth of God. The church's mission is to immovably, unshakably live, uphold, guard, and proclaim the truth of God's Word. It is to proclaim the "whole purpose of God" (Acts 20:27), not merely that part of divine truth that is inoffensive to the surrounding culture. In the words of Martin Luther, a stalwart champion of necessary controversy,

> If I profess with the loudest voice and clearest exposition every portion of the truth of God except precisely that little point which the world and the devil are at that moment attacking, I am not *confessing* Christ, however boldly I may be *professing* Christ. Where the battle rages, there the loyalty of the soldier is proved, and to be steady on all the battle-field besides, is mere flight and disgrace if he flinches at that point. (*D. Martin Luthers Werke, Kritische Gesamtausgabe. Briefwechsel*, 18 vols. [Weimar: Verlag Hermann Bohlaus Nachfolger, 1930–1985], 3:81, emphases added)

Any so-called church that fails to exercise its stewardship of His truth faces God's judgment—just as the Jews did for failing to uphold and live the Old Testament truth entrusted to them (cf. Rom. 2:23–24). But throughout its history, the true church has clung tenaciously to the truth, despite the storms of persecution, the sting of rejection, and the assaults of enemies both from inside and outside its ranks (cf. Acts 20:29–30). And countless thousands have suffered martyrdom rather than compromise or abandon the truth.

Strategically, the final epistles of the New Testament emphasize the priority of the truth (2 and 3 John), and the need to contend for it in the face of apostate liars (Jude).

John wrote his two brief letters—more postcards than letters—to stress the importance of truth. *Alētheia* ("truth") appears five times in this opening section of 2 John and six times in the more brief 3 John. Though each is a personal letter to an individual, John was writing the inspired revelation of God that was to God's people throughout time. Recognizing that all the readers of his letter faced and always would face a world of lies and deceit, he wrote to call them to live in God's truth, to love within the bounds of truth, and to be loyal to and look out for the truth. In the opening verses John reveals four features of living in the truth: the truth unites, indwells, blesses, and controls believers.

THE TRUTH UNITES BELIEVERS

The elder to the chosen lady and her children, whom I love in truth; and not only I, but also all who know the truth, (1)

By the time he wrote this epistle, John was a very old man, the last surviving apostle. Even so, his reference to himself as **the elder** (*presbuteros* with the definite article) stresses not so much his age as his position of spiritual oversight for the church. In the New Testament the term, borrowing from familiar Old Testament usage (cf. Lev. 4:15; Num. 11:25; Deut. 25:7–8, etc.), generally refers to the office of elder (the exception is in 1 Tim. 5:1, where it refers simply to an older man); the related term *pres-butēs* (translated "old man" in Luke 1:18 and "aged" in Philem. 9) describes an older man without reference to a leadership role. John's description of himself reinforces the truth that he wrote this epistle; someone impersonating him would likely have chosen the title "apostle," while a writer not trying to impersonate him would not likely have called himself *the* elder (cf. Alfred Plummer, *The Epistles of St. John,* The Cambridge Bible for Schools and Colleges [Cambridge: Cambridge Univ., 1911], 175). John did not need to refer to himself as an apostle because his readers knew and accepted him as such, though in the experience of the church, he served them as their pastor.

In the New Testament, churches were always taught and ruled by a plurality of elders (Acts 11:30; 14:23; 15:2, 4, 6, 22, 23; 16:4; 20:17; 21:18; 1 Tim. 5:17; Titus 1:5; James 5:14; 1 Peter 5:1, 5). But though there were other elders serving with John in Ephesus (cf. Acts 20:17; see the Introduction to 1 John in this volume for evidence that John wrote his epistles from that city), he was the patriarchal elder, whose authority and oversight extended well beyond Ephesus. Like Peter (1 Peter 5:1), John was both an elder and an apostle; as the last of the apostles, he was *the* elder, the most distinguished of all elders; the only living elder who was chosen to be an apostle by the Lord Jesus Christ and was a member of the innermost circle of the twelve apostles; the one self-confessed as the "disciple whom Jesus loved" (John 20:2; cf. 13:23; 19:26; 21:7, 20). In contrast to the false teachers, John was the torchbearer of apostolic tradition.

As noted in the Introduction to 2 John, the **chosen lady** to whom John addressed this letter was an actual woman, not a church. **Lady** translates the feminine form of the noun *kurios* ("lord," "sir"). The husband is the "lord" of the household as its divinely ordained head (cf. 1 Cor. 11:3; Eph. 5:23), but the **lady** has her sphere of authority and responsibility as well (cf. Titus 2:3–5 and 1 Tim. 5:14, where "keep house" translates a Greek verb that literally means "to rule or manage a household"). That her husband is not mentioned may indicate that she was a widow. In any case, she was responsible for providing hospitality in the home, as is clear from 1 Timothy 5:9–10. Since John addressed her **children** too, they may still have been living at home with her. Families typically shared a common house, even after the children were married.

Chosen translates a form of the Greek word *eklektos* ("elect," "chosen," "choice"). The term describes those selected by God for eternal glory, whether Christ (Luke 23:35; 1 Peter 2:4, 6), the holy angels (1 Tim. 5:21), or the redeemed (Matt. 22:14; 24:22, 24, 31; Mark 13:20, 22, 27; Luke 18:7; Rom. 8:33; Col. 3:12; 2 Tim. 2:10; Titus 1:1; 1 Peter 1:1; 2:9; 2 John 13; Rev. 17:14). The only other time outside of this epistle that it is used of an individual is in Romans 16:13, where Paul described Rufus as a "choice [from *eklektos*] man in the Lord."

John's description of this woman (and her sister; v. 13) as **chosen** reflects the biblical truth that God sovereignly chooses believers for salvation (in addition to the vv. cited above, see Mark 13:20; Acts 13:48; Rom. 8:28–30; Eph. 1:4–5, 11; 2 Thess. 2:13; 2 Tim. 1:9; James 2:5). Unlike those who hold a weak view of divine sovereignty, the New Testament writers did not hesitate to refer to believers as "the elect." In fact, the Lord Jesus Christ Himself did so in Matthew 24:22: "Unless those days had been cut short, no life would have been saved; but for the sake of the elect those days will be cut short." The term is no less appropriate than the more popular terms "child of God," "saved," "born again," "believer," or "Christian."

John's statement **whom I love in truth** reveals his personal connection to this family (the relative pronoun *hous* [**whom**] is plural and encompasses both the lady and her children). *Egō* (**I**) is emphatic, stressing the apostle's personal, ongoing (the verb is in the present tense) **love** for them. The **love** in view here is that willful, spiritual devotion and service conveyed by the familiar verb *agapaō*. The phrase **in truth** explains and qualifies the sphere of John's love for them. It does not refer to his sincerity; he was not merely claiming to "truly" love them, though he obviously did. Rather, **truth** refers here to the embodiment of truth in the gospel. It is parallel to the frequent New Testament expression "the faith" (Acts 6:7; 13:8; 14:22; 16:5; 1 Cor. 16:13; 2 Cor. 13:5; Gal. 1:23; Eph. 4:13; Phil. 1:27; Col. 1:23; 1 Tim. 1:2; 3:9; 4:1; 5:8; 6:10, 21; 2 Tim. 3:8; Titus 1:13; Jude 3). John's expression is similar to Paul's exhortation to Titus, "Greet those who love us in the faith" (Titus 3:15*b*); that is, in the objective truth of the gospel. It was the truth that bound **not only** John, **but also all who** knew **the truth** to this lady and her children. It is their common belief in the gospel truth that unites all believers.

John's statement encapsulates the main theme of this brief epistle, that truth must always govern the exercise of love. Christians' deep, mutual affection flows out of their shared commitment to the truth. In his first epistle John wrote, "Whoever believes that Jesus is the Christ is born of God, and whoever loves the Father loves the child born of Him" (1 John 5:1). We can have no real communion with those who reject the truth of the gospel, since we share no common spiritual life with them. Such people are outside the fellowship of believers, because it is only those who "have in obedience to the truth purified [their] souls" who can have "a sincere love of the brethren" (1 Peter 1:22).

Because salvation requires belief in the truth, it is critically important for the church to proclaim the right message. A simple, accurate presentation of the gospel is sufficient, through the transforming power of the Holy Spirit, to bring about salvation. On the other hand, the most carefully crafted, smoothly polished presentation of anything less than the gospel will not save.

John's linking of love and truth shows that they are anything but incompatible, as some are always eager to suggest. Believers are to speak in love, but they are also to speak the truth (Eph. 4:15). To minimize the truth in the name of love is to abandon biblical love, which is based on the truth. God's purposes will never be accomplished by compromising His truth; love for souls is never manifested by minimizing the truth.

THE TRUTH INDWELLS BELIEVERS

for the sake of the truth which abides in us and will be with us forever (2)

In keeping with his passionate commitment to the truth, John wrote this epistle **for the sake of the truth.** His concern was that the Christian lady to whom he addressed it might compromise truth in the name of hospitality. Christian love, fellowship, and hospitality are vitally important, since they manifest the transforming power of the gospel (cf. Rom. 12:13; 1 Tim. 3:2; Titus 1:8; 1 Peter 4:9). Believers share a spiritual love that flows from their common eternal life in Christ. But they cannot genuinely manifest that love apart from an unswerving commitment to the truth of God's Word. That truth permeates all aspects of the church's individual and corporate life, underlying all of its preaching, evangelism, and fellowship.

In language reminiscent of Jesus' promise concerning the Holy Spirit (John 14:17), John wrote that the **truth . . . abides in us and will be with us forever.** The parallel is appropriate, since the Holy Spirit is the "Spirit of truth" (John 14:17; 15:26; 16:13; 1 John 5:6). Though in a lifetime we cannot comprehend the vast depth of all biblical truth, all true Christians know the truth of the Scripture that saves. They know that they are sinners, facing God's just judgment, and that forgiveness comes only by divine grace, apart from works, through faith in the Lord Jesus Christ and His atoning sacrifice and resurrection. If they did not comprehend those facts, they would not be Christians since, as noted above, understanding the truth is necessary for salvation.

In his first epistle, John taught that all believers are able to discern the truth from error:

> You have an anointing from the Holy One, and you all know. I have not written to you because you do not know the truth, but because you do know it. . . . As for you, the anointing which you received from Him

abides in you, and you have no need for anyone to teach you; but as His anointing teaches you about all things, and is true and is not a lie, and just as it has taught you, you abide in Him. (1 John 2:20–21, 27)

Menō (**abides**) is one of John's favorite terms, appearing more than sixty times in his writings. It is used in a theological sense to refer to the truth that resides in believers (1 John 2:14, 24–27; cf. John 5:38 where Jesus upbraids the unbelieving Jews for not having the Word abiding in them), to true believers abiding in the Word (John 8:31) and thus not being in spiritual darkness (John 12:46), to the Spirit abiding in believers (John 14:17; cf. 1 John 4:12, 15, 16) and, most significant, to believers abiding in Christ (John 6:56; 14:10; 15:4–7, 9–10; 1 John 2:6, 10, 28; 3:6, 24; 4:13). The truth of the Word, which abides in believers **forever**, gives them "the mind of Christ" (1 Cor. 2:16).

THE TRUTH BLESSES BELIEVERS

Grace, mercy and peace will be with us, from God the Father and from Jesus Christ, the Son of the Father, in truth and love. (3)

Although they appear together only here and in Paul's letters to Timothy (1 Tim. 1:2; 2 Tim. 1:2), **grace, mercy,** and **peace** are familiar New Testament terms. They are often used in the salutations of the epistles. **Grace** combines with **peace** in Romans 1:7, 1 Corinthians 1:3, 2 Corinthians 1:2, Galatians 1:3, Ephesians 1:2, Philippians 1:2, Colossians 1:2, 1 Thessalonians 1:1, 2 Thessalonians 1:2, Titus 1:4, Philemon 3, 1 Peter 1:2, 2 Peter 1:2, and Revelation 1:4; **mercy** with **peace** in Jude 2. The three terms summarize the progression of the plan of salvation: God's **grace** caused Him to grant **mercy,** which results in **peace. Grace** views sinners as guilty and undeserving (Rom. 5:20; Eph. 1:7); **mercy** views them as needy and helpless (Matt. 5:3; Rom. 11:30–32; Eph. 2:4–5; Titus 3:5; 1 Peter 1:3); **peace** is the result of God's outpouring of both (Acts 10:36; Rom. 5:1; Eph. 2:14; Col. 1:20). These divine blessings, like everything in the Christian life, come only **from God the Father and from Jesus Christ, the Son of the Father.** From God, "the Father of lights, with whom there is no variation or shifting shadow" comes down "every good thing given and every perfect gift" (James 1:17). And through the Son, all "the promises of God . . . are yes" (2 Cor. 1:20). They are present when divine **truth** dominates the mind and heart, resulting in genuine **love.** The twofold repetition of *para* (**from**) stresses Jesus' equality with the Father. John emphasized Christ's identity as God's Son because the false teachers were denying that truth (cf. the discussion of the false teachers and their heretical teaching in the Introduction to 1 John).

THE TRUTH CONTROLS BELIEVERS

I was very glad to find some of your children walking in truth, just as we have received commandment to do from the Father. (4)

In light of his commitment to the truth, it comes as no surprise that John **was very glad to find some of** this Christian lady's **children walking in truth.** Surely the apostle was exuberant at the news of their obedience to divine revelation, which he may have heard from her sister or her sister's children (cf. v. 13). That he mentions only **some** of her children does not necessarily mean that the others were not saved; John was referring only to those of whom he had personal knowledge.

The truth of God's Word is to be lived as well as believed (cf. Matt. 7:21; 12:50; Luke 6:46–49; 11:28; John 13:17; Rom. 2:13; James 1:22; 1 John 2:3). The phrase **walking in truth** refers to moving through life controlled by the truth; it is the equivalent to walking in the light (1 John 1:7). **Walking** is a frequent New Testament metaphor for the Christian life. Believers "walk in newness of life" (Rom. 6:4), "walk by faith, not by sight" (2 Cor. 5:7), "walk by the Spirit" (Gal. 5:16, 25), "walk in good works" (Eph. 2:10), "walk in a manner worthy of the calling with which [they] have been called" (Eph. 4:1), "walk in love" (Eph. 5:2), "walk as children of Light" (Eph. 5:8), "walk in wisdom" (Eph. 5:15), "walk in a manner worthy of the Lord, to please Him in all respects" (Col. 1:10), "walk in a manner worthy of the God who calls [them] into His own kingdom and glory" (1 Thess. 2:12), "walk in the same manner as [Jesus] walked" (1 John 2:6), and "walk according to His commandments" (2 John 6).

John's reference to the **commandment** believers have received **from the Father** to walk in the truth is not a reference to one particular command, but reflects the general and obvious mandate of Scripture to obey. Scripture is even called "the commandment of the Lord" (Ps. 19:8; cf. the similar use of "commandment" in 1 Tim. 6:14). Obedience to God's truth is not optional. "God has not revealed His truth in such a way as to leave us free at our pleasure to believe or disbelieve it, to obey or disobey it. Revelation carries with it responsibility, and the clearer the revelation, the greater the responsibility to believe and obey it" (John R. W. Stott, *The Epistles of John*, The Tyndale New Testament Commentaries [Grand Rapids: Eerdmans, 1964], 206).

This brief letter opens with a ringing call for Christians to live consistently with the truth they believe. The only true basis for unity in the church is the truth of God's Word that indwells, blesses, and controls the lives of individual believers. And it is only those Christians and churches who are firmly planted on the solid foundation of the truth who will be able to withstand the storms of persecution, temptation, and false doctrine that constantly assail them.

The Limits of Love
(2 John 5–13)

20

Now I ask you, lady, not as though I were writing to you a new commandment, but the one which we have had from the beginning, that we love one another. And this is love, that we walk according to His commandments. This is the commandment, just as you have heard from the beginning, that you should walk in it. For many deceivers have gone out into the world, those who do not acknowledge Jesus Christ as coming in the flesh. This is the deceiver and the antichrist. Watch yourselves, that you do not lose what we have accomplished, but that you may receive a full reward. Anyone who goes too far and does not abide in the teaching of Christ, does not have God; the one who abides in the teaching, he has both the Father and the Son. If anyone comes to you and does not bring this teaching, do not receive him into your house, and do not give him a greeting; for the one who gives him a greeting participates in his evil deeds. Though I have many things to write to you, I do not want to do so with paper and ink; but I hope to come to you and speak face to face, so that your joy may be made full. The children of your chosen sister greet you. (5–13)

Verse 9 jumps out of this section: **Anyone who goes too far and does not abide in the teaching of Christ, does not have God; the one who abides in the teaching, he has both the Father and the Son.** There again (as throughout 1 John) is the test of a true Christian and a true preacher—pure doctrine concerning Christ.

The true church of Jesus Christ has always understood that fact. Through the centuries, even in the church's darkest hours, there have always been those who were faithful to evangelize the lost with the pure gospel of Jesus Christ. People searched the Scriptures, without all the Bible study tools available today, to understand the gospel in preparation for spreading the message of salvation. Many unsung heroes of the faith labored for decades translating the Word so people could read it in their own languages. Missionaries traveled in arduous and threatening circumstances to reach difficult places with the truth of Christ. There they endured long periods of separation from family, friends, and country, suffered the loss of coworkers and loved ones, and battled disease, danger, and satanic opposition for the gospel's sake (cf. Eph. 6:12). Tens of thousands of faithful evangelists have been martyred for their unwavering commitment to obey the Lord's command to proclaim the truth that saves.

There are some, however, who advocate a radical and alarming shift from this commission, suggesting that preaching the gospel to the lost may actually be unnecessary, along with the immense sacrifices that have been made to do so. Going beyond the Bible's teaching about the general revelation of God in nature (see the discussion of Rom. 1:18–32 below), some argue that natural theology ("the attempt to attain an understanding of God and his relationship with the universe by means of rational reflection, without appealing to special revelation such as the self-revelation of God in Christ and in Scripture" [Colin Brown, "Natural Theology," in Sinclair B. Ferguson, David F. Wright, and J. I. Packer, eds., *New Dictionary of Theology* (Downers Grove, Ill.: InterVarsity, 1988), 452]) alone is sufficient to save—apart from any knowledge of the true God, or of Jesus Christ or the gospel. Some imagine that God saves people apart from the gospel by treating them as He did those who lived before the time of the New Testament (a view labeled trans-dispensationalism). But as the writer of Hebrews emphasizes, "God, after He spoke long ago to the fathers in the prophets in many portions and in many ways, in these last days has spoken to us in His Son, whom He appointed heir of all things, through whom also He made the world" (Heb. 1:1–2). Having given His final revelation in His Son, God will not turn back the clock to another era. John 1:12 fixes the necessity of faith in Christ: "But as many as received Him, to them He gave the right to become children of God, even to those who believe in His name."

Others, advocates of the so-called wider mercy view, propose something even more radical. They, too, believe that lost sinners can be saved apart from the gospel. But they go one step further and argue that those in non-Christian religions may actually be aided in coming to God by those false religions. Clark Pinnock writes,

> When we approach the man of a faith other than our own, it will be in a spirit of expectancy to find how God has been speaking to him and what new understanding of the grace and love of God we may ourselves discover in this encounter. Our first task in approaching another people, another culture, another religion is to take off the shoes, for the place we are approaching is holy. . . . We may forget that God was here before our arrival. (Cited in Erwin Lutzer, *Christ Among Other gods* [Chicago: Moody, 1994], 185.)

Then, shockingly, he adds,

> God . . . has more going on by way of redemption than what happened in first-century Palestine. (ibid., p. 185)

Pinnock's universalism rejects the teaching of the apostles, who unhesitatingly declared, "There is salvation in no one else [than Jesus Christ]; for there is no other name under heaven that has been given among men by which we must be saved" (Acts 4:12; cf. 1 Cor. 3:11; 1 Tim. 2:5). It also rejects the teaching of the Lord Jesus Christ, who stated unequivocally, "I am the way, and the truth, and the life; no one comes to the Father but through Me" (John 14:6).

In Romans 10:9–10 Paul explains the essential for salvation: "If you confess with your mouth Jesus as Lord, and believe in your heart that God raised Him from the dead, you will be saved; for with the heart a person believes, resulting in righteousness, and with the mouth he confesses, resulting in salvation." Then in verses 13–15 the apostle—in sharp contrast to the "wider mercy" view—stresses the absolute necessity of the church carrying out the Great Commission:

> "Whoever will call on the name of the Lord will be saved." How then will they call on Him in whom they have not believed? How will they believe in Him whom they have not heard? And how will they hear without a preacher? How will they preach unless they are sent? Just as it is written, "How beautiful are the feet of those who bring good news of good things!"

Paul's progression is crystal clear: only those who call on the name of the Lord can be saved (cf. Acts 16:31). But no one can call on the Lord without first believing in Him. And no one can believe in Him until they hear the gospel. Therefore the church must send out preachers to proclaim the gospel message to lost sinners because, as Paul summarized in Romans 10:17, "[Saving] faith comes from hearing, and hearing by the word [about] Christ." In 2 Corinthians 5:18–21 it is clear that the message and ministry of reconciliation is to preach Christ, since we are "ambassadors for Christ" through whom God makes His appeal for reconciliation (v. 20).

In keeping with the biblical mandate, the early church, at great cost, took the gospel to the farthest reaches of the Roman world and beyond, clearly understanding that people cannot be saved apart from believing in Christ. If they could, the suffering the gospel preachers endured (cf. 2 Cor. 11:22–33) was surely pointless. If the lost could be saved through natural theology or their pagan religions, the Christian missionaries could have stayed safely at home. Even exposing pagans to the gospel may have damned them, since they might not believe it. It would be better, on those terms, if they never heard it.

Paul's encounter with the pagan Athenians on Mars Hill is instructive of how the early church approached those of other faiths. The apostle began by commending them for their religious zeal (Acts 17:22–23), much as he did the unbelieving Jews (Rom. 10:2). Then, as was his custom when evangelizing Gentiles (cf. Acts 14:15–17), Paul appealed to God's general revelation in nature. He noted that he had "found an altar with this inscription, 'to an unknown god'" (Acts 17:23). Despite the pantheon of gods they worshiped, the Athenians had a nagging concern that there might be one that they still did not know. To avoid giving offense, they erected a sort of catchall altar to appease any god they might have inadvertently overlooked.

The apostle's reaction is illuminating. He did not approach those pagans expecting to discover how God had been speaking to them. Nor did he seek a new understanding of God's grace and love in his encounter with them. Instead, he confronted them with the fact that they were worshiping in ignorance (Acts 17:23), and explained to them who God really is (vv. 24–29). And far from assuming that they could know Him and be saved from hell through their false religion, Paul closed his message by calling them to repent and turn to Jesus Christ, the only way to God, saying, "Therefore having overlooked the times of ignorance, God is now declaring to men that all people everywhere should repent, because He has fixed a day in which He will judge the world in righteousness through a Man whom He has appointed, having furnished proof to all men by raising Him from the dead" (vv. 30–31).

Paul's encounter with the Athenians illustrates the impossibility of anyone being saved through general revelation alone. General revelation demonstrates that an all-powerful Creator exists. But it does not reveal the way of salvation, "since in the wisdom of God the world through its wisdom did not come to know God" (1 Cor. 1:21*a*). Human reason, even aided by general revelation, cannot produce a saving knowledge of God. Therefore, as Paul went on to write, "God was well-pleased through the foolishness of the message preached to save those who believe" (1 Cor. 1:21*b*). Only those who believe the message of "Christ crucified, to Jews a stumbling block and to Gentiles foolishness, but to those who are the called, both Jews and Greeks, Christ the power of God and the wisdom of God" (vv. 23–24; cf. 2:1–5) will be saved (cf. 2 Thess. 1:8, where Paul defines those who do not know God as those who "do not obey the gospel of our Lord Jesus").

No human has the power in himself to come to God, even by the gospel. Scripture is clear that humanity is dead and cannot in the flesh please God (Rom. 8:7–8). No person can by his own strength, works, or faith please God at all, especially not so as to earn salvation even under the hearing of the gospel, let alone apart from it. God alone saves sovereignly and always through the gospel. Only He can give life and light producing repentance and faith—always directed toward Jesus Christ.

To say that all men are totally depraved is not to say each is as bad as the other, or as evil as possible. That cannot be true because even "evil men" in general "proceed from bad to worse" (2 Tim. 3:13). But all men are alienated, "excluded from the life of God because of the ignorance that is in them" (Eph. 4:18), unable to do anything to please God—especially to do the highest good: to repent and believe. If an unregenerate sinner, on his own, by a free act of his will, could believe in God or Christ, then he would do the greatest work of all. But Scripture says that he cannot please God. The Bible would lie if he could, and it would have to be said that sinners are not dead, powerless, alienated, darkened, and hopeless. But unregenerate sinners do not have the ability to believe savingly. If they did have the power to do what pleases God, they should be glorified for it—maybe even worshiped. But no one can be saved except by divine, sovereign, regenerating grace—and God grants that apart from any righteous act, but only in connection with the hearing and believing of the gospel of the Lord Jesus Christ.

If the salvation of one who heard the gospel was conditioned on his ability to believe, then there would be no need for efficacious grace. And God would be taking too much credit for His part in salvation by saying it is all through His grace. But this is a foolish, if not blasphemous, notion. No sinner can do anything that pleases God, and only God can sovereignly grant saving faith by grace alone, and He does so only through Christ. Paul writes on this matter:

> Blessed be the God and Father of our Lord Jesus Christ, who has blessed us with every spiritual blessing in the heavenly places in Christ, just as He chose us in Him before the foundation of the world, that we would be holy and blameless before Him. In love He predestined us to adoption as sons through Jesus Christ to Himself, according to the kind intention of His will, to the praise of the glory of His grace, which He freely bestowed on us in the Beloved. In Him we have redemption through His blood, the forgiveness of our trespasses, according to the riches of His grace. (Eph. 1:3–7)

If salvation is by man's will, then what is the point of God's electing a people? But all the redeemed are elect in Christ, the Beloved, and saved through the divine gift of trust in Him and His work (Eph. 2:8–9; cf. Rom. 1:16).

God does not save by sovereign grace through general revelation; rather, unaided by God, the sinner is rendered by that revelation under judgment and without excuse. All men have ample evidence for God's existence, "because that which is known about God is evident within them; for God made it evident to them. For since the creation of the world His invisible attributes, His eternal power and divine nature, have been clearly seen, being understood through what has been made, so that they are without excuse" (Rom. 1:19–20). That knowledge, however, does not lead them to God. On the contrary, it only leaves them without excuse when He judges them, because "the wrath of God is revealed from heaven against all ungodliness and unrighteousness of men who suppress the truth in unrighteousness" (v. 18). General revelation is not sufficient for salvation, but is enough for damnation. Human reason alone will never lead sinners to a saving knowledge of God because they suppress the knowledge of Him that is available in general revelation (cf. Rom. 3:9–18). Apart from God's special revelation in His Son and in the Scriptures, people remain ungodly, defiant, depraved sinners, hopelessly lost in the darkness of idolatrous false religion (Rom. 1:22–32). And far from accepting them, God in reality has utterly abandoned them (vv. 24–32).

The apostle John knew that there is no substitute for teaching that the "truth is in Jesus" (Eph. 4:21) and stressed the importance of it in this brief epistle. John had called his readers to live in the truth of Christ that unites, indwells, blesses, and controls them (see the exposition of vv. 1–4 in the previous chapter of this volume). He was about to exhort them to remain loyal to, guard, and learn the truth. But before he did so, the apostle paused to add an important caveat: truth and love are inseparably linked. Love is an integral part of obedience to the truth, being repeatedly commanded in Scripture (cf. the discussion below); therefore, those who do not love do not practice the truth. And those who uphold the truth do so in love (Eph. 4:15).

Loving in the Truth

Now I ask you, lady, not as though I were writing to you a new commandment, but the one which we have had from the beginning, that we love one another. And this is love, that we walk according to His commandments. This is the commandment, just as you have heard from the beginning, that you should walk in it. (5–6)

The Greek phrase *kai nun* ("And now") that begins verse 5 provides a logical link to verse 4. John did not hesitate to **ask** this Christian **lady** to love; his request was perfectly consistent with living in the gospel truth. The parenthetical statement, **not as though I were writing to you a new commandment, but the one which we have had from the beginning, that we love one another,** echoes 1 John 2:7–11 (see the exposition of that passage in chapter 6 of this volume). John was not writing **a new commandment** never before revealed, **but** was reiterating **the one which** she **had** heard **from the beginning** of her Christian life. All believers are called into a fellowship marked by **love** for **one another.** Divine revelation is clear that love is the defining mark of a true believer, and the lack of it characterizes unbelievers. In 1 John 2:9–11 John declared,

> The one who says he is in the Light and yet hates his brother is in the darkness until now. The one who loves his brother abides in the Light and there is no cause for stumbling in him. But the one who hates his brother is in the darkness and walks in the darkness, and does not know where he is going because the darkness has blinded his eyes. (cf. 4:20–21)

In one sense, what John wrote was not **a new commandment. New** translates *kainos*, which refers not to something new in time, but in essential character. The command to love is not unique to the New Testament. The Old Testament Law provided a summary of how to love. Deuteronomy 6:5 commands, "You shall love the Lord your God with all your heart and with all your soul and with all your might," while Leviticus 19:18 adds, "You shall love your neighbor as yourself." When asked to name the greatest commandment in the Law, Jesus replied by citing those same two commands: "'You shall love the Lord your God with all your heart, and with all your soul, and with all your mind.' This is the great and foremost commandment. The second is like it, 'You shall love your neighbor as yourself.' On these two commandments depend the whole Law and the Prophets" (Matt. 22:37–40). The Ten Commandments, the summation of the Law, are divided into two sections. The first four commandments describe how to love God; the last six describe how to love people. Thus Paul could write that "love is the fulfillment of the law" (Rom. 13:10).

But though the **commandment** John spoke of was from one perspective an old one, viewed from another it was new. In 1 John 2:8 John wrote, "On the other hand, I am writing a new commandment to you, which is true in Him and in you, because the darkness is passing away and the true Light is already shining." There are three senses in which the commandment is new. First, love is "true in Him"; that is, it has now been perfectly modeled in a human life by the Lord Jesus Christ. In his gospel John wrote concerning Christ's love, "Having loved His own who were in the world, He loved them to the end (lit., "perfectly," "completely," or "to the fullest measure")" (John 13:1). Jesus offered Himself as an example of how to love when He said, "A new commandment I give to you, that you love one another, even as I have loved you, that you also love one another. By this all men will know that you are My disciples, if you have love for one another" (John 13:34–35; cf. 15:13; Phil. 2:5–9). Paul exhorted believers to "walk in love, just as Christ also loved you and gave Himself up for us" (Eph. 5:2).

Christians also have a new understanding of love through the indwelling of the Holy Spirit. As John pointed out in his first epistle, it is only possible for us to love "because He first loved us" (1 John 4:19; cf. Eph. 3:16–19). Paul wrote in Romans 5:5 that "the love of God has been poured out within our hearts through the Holy Spirit who was given to us." That supernatural love is one aspect of the fruit of the Spirit (Gal. 5:22); thus Paul could write that believers "are taught by God to love one another" (1 Thess. 4:9).

Finally, the commandment to love is new in that it belongs to the new age inaugurated by the coming of Christ. We now live in the spiritual kingdom (Luke 17:20–21), which is growing (Luke 13:18–20) into the glorious millennial kingdom to be established when Christ returns, and after that the eternal kingdom. During this present spiritual kingdom "the darkness is passing away and the true Light is already shining" (1 John 2:8). The "true Light" is Jesus Christ (cf. John 8:12; 9:5; 12:35), through whom God has "rescue[d] us from this present evil age" (Gal. 1:4) and "from the domain of darkness, and transferred us to the kingdom of His beloved Son" (Col. 1:13). We are blessed "with every spiritual blessing in the heavenly places in Christ" (Eph. 1:3), including divine, supernatural love, which is a way of life for those in the kingdom of Jesus Christ.

The defining characteristic of **love** is **that we walk according to His commandments.** Love and obedience are inseparably linked, as Jesus made clear in John 14:15 when He declared, "If you love Me, you will keep My commandments" (cf. vv. 23–24; 15:10). Believers manifest their love for God by their obedience to Him. In his first epistle, John wrote, "For this is the love of God, that we keep His commandments" (1 John 5:3). The Old Testament also views obedience to God as the ultimate expression of love for Him. In Deuteronomy 11:1 Moses commanded Israel, "You shall therefore love the Lord your God, and always keep His charge, His statutes, His ordinances, and His commandments." Moses' successor, Joshua, gave Israel a similar charge: "Only be very careful to observe the commandment and the law which Moses the servant of the Lord commanded you, to love the Lord your God and walk in all His ways and keep His commandments and hold fast to Him and serve Him with all your heart and with all your soul" (Josh. 22:5). Love and obedience are also linked in such Old Testament passages as Exodus 20:6; Deuteronomy 5:10; 7:9; 30:16; Nehemiah 1:5; and Daniel 9:4.

Repeating himself to stress the importance of this truth, John wrote, **This is the commandment, just as you have heard from the beginning, that you should walk in it.** Those who truly love will **walk** in obedience to biblical truth and vice versa.

BEING LOYAL TO THE TRUTH

For many deceivers have gone out into the world, those who do not acknowledge Jesus Christ as coming in the flesh. This is the deceiver and the antichrist. Watch yourselves, that you do not lose what we have accomplished, but that you may receive a full reward. (7–8)

Biblical love does not imply a naïve, uncritical, undiscerning acceptance of anyone who claims to represent Jesus Christ. Thus, having stressed the importance of love, John immediately set limits on it. Believers cannot, in the name of love, embrace any of the **many deceivers** who **have gone out into the world.** Followers of the true Christ cannot love antichrists; those who are committed to biblical truth cannot have fellowship with those who pervert it (cf. 2 Cor. 6:14–15). **Deceivers** translates the plural form of *planos,* which literally means "a wanderer" (the English word "planet" derives from it). In this case, it refers to those who wander from the truth of Scripture; who corrupt it; who lead others astray from it; who are impostors (Paul called such people "false brethren" in 2 Cor. 11:26 and Gal. 2:4; cf. Jude's description of them as "wandering stars" headed for the "black darkness" of eternal judgment [v. 13]).

These wolves in sheep's clothing (Matt. 7:15) become especially dangerous when they infiltrate the church; hence the New Testament is full of warnings about them. In the Olivet Discourse Jesus predicted that in the end times "false Christs and false prophets will arise and will show great signs and wonders, so as to mislead, if possible, even the elect" (Matt. 24:24). Paul called them "savage wolves" (Acts 20:29); "false apostles, deceitful workers, disguising themselves as apostles of Christ" (2 Cor. 11:13); servants of Satan who, like their wicked master (v. 14), "disguise themselves as servants of righteousness, whose end will be according to their deeds" (v. 15). The apostle told Timothy that "the Spirit explicitly says that in later times some will fall away from the faith, paying attention to deceitful spirits and doctrines of demons" (1 Tim. 4:1). In his first letter John pleaded with his readers,

> Beloved, do not believe every spirit, but test the spirits to see whether they are from God, because many false prophets have gone out into the world. By this you know the Spirit of God: every spirit that confesses that Jesus Christ has come in the flesh is from God; and every spirit that does not confess Jesus is not from God; this is the spirit of the antichrist, of which you have heard that it is coming, and now it is already in the world. (1 John 4:1–3)

Jude vividly and extensively denounced these deceivers as

> certain persons [who] have crept in unnoticed, those who were long beforehand marked out for this condemnation, ungodly persons who turn the grace of our God into licentiousness and deny our only Master and Lord, Jesus Christ. . . . Woe to them! For they have gone the way of Cain, and for pay they have rushed headlong into the error of Balaam, and perished in the rebellion of Korah. These are the men who are hidden reefs in your love feasts when they feast with you without fear, caring for themselves; clouds without water, carried along by winds; autumn trees without fruit, doubly dead, uprooted; wild waves of the sea, casting up their own shame like foam; wandering stars, for whom the black darkness has been reserved forever. It was also about these men that Enoch, in the seventh generation from Adam, prophesied, saying, "Behold, the Lord came with many thousands of His holy ones, to execute judgment upon all, and to convict all the ungodly of all their ungodly deeds which they have done in an ungodly way, and of all the harsh things which ungodly sinners have spoken against Him." (Jude 4, 11–15; cf. Peter's similar denunciation of them in 2 Peter 2:1–21)

Everywhere the true gospel goes, Satan's emissaries are sure to follow. They preach a false, satanic gospel and thereby pervert the true gospel message and pollute the church. Paul warned the Galatians against them in the strongest possible terms:

I am amazed that you are so quickly deserting Him who called you by the grace of Christ, for a different gospel; which is really not another; only there are some who are disturbing you and want to distort the gospel of Christ. But even if we, or an angel from heaven, should preach to you a gospel contrary to what we have preached to you, he is to be accursed! As we have said before, so I say again now, if any man is preaching to you a gospel contrary to what you received, he is to be accursed! (Gal. 1:6–9)

John defined the particular false teachers in his sights as **those who do not acknowledge Jesus Christ as coming in the flesh.** There are many ways to undermine the gospel, such as by denying the deity of Jesus Christ, or that salvation is by grace alone through faith alone. But these heretics denied the true humanity of **Jesus Christ,** refusing to **acknowledge** that He was God who had become fully human. They were forerunners of the dangerous second-century heresy known as Gnosticism, which posed one of the gravest threats to the early church. (For further information on the heresy against which John wrote, see the Introduction to 1 John in this volume.)

John countered the false teachers' diverse attacks on the person of Jesus Christ by stressing the truth about Him in his epistles. In 1 John 1:3 he identified Jesus Christ as God the Son (cf. 3:23; 2 John 3); in 2:1 he presented Him as the believers' Advocate with the Father, whose death propitiated God's wrath against their sin (v. 2; cf. 1:7; 4:9–10); in 2:22–23 he declared that those who deny that Jesus is the Christ do not know God; in 3:8 he pointed out that Jesus has destroyed the works of Satan; in 4:14 he affirmed that the Father sent the Son into the world as Savior, and reiterated in verse 15 that only those who confess Jesus as the Son of God know the Father (cf. 2 John 9); and in 5:9–13 John wrote that only those who believe the divine revelation about Jesus Christ have eternal life.

To deny the biblical truth that in Jesus Christ, the promised Messiah, God became fully human is to propagate demon doctrine. Anyone who does so is a **deceiver and** an **antichrist** (cf. 1 John 2:18, 22; 4:3). To teach, as these heretics did, that Jesus' humanity was merely an illusion is to strike a blow at the heart of the gospel. If Jesus were not the God-man, fully human as well as fully divine, He could not have died as the substitute for men.

Knowing the serious threat the false teachers posed, John warned his readers, **Watch yourselves.** The church must be vigilant, discerning, even suspicious, because what is at stake is so vital. Having labored in the lives of this lady and her children, John wanted to see the full fruit of that effort; he did not want them to **lose what** they together had **accomplished.** Paul expressed a similar concern for the Corinthians:

> I wish that you would bear with me in a little foolishness; but indeed you are bearing with me. For I am jealous for you with a godly jealousy; for I betrothed you to one husband, so that to Christ I might present you as a pure virgin. But I am afraid that, as the serpent deceived Eve by his craftiness, your minds will be led astray from the simplicity and purity of devotion to Christ. For if one comes and preaches another Jesus whom we have not preached, or you receive a different spirit which you have not received, or a different gospel which you have not accepted, you bear this beautifully. (2 Cor. 11:1–4)

Like every faithful pastor, John and Paul were concerned that those under their care not lose ground spiritually. It was that concern that prompted Paul to sharply rebuke the Galatians for dabbling in false doctrine:

> You foolish Galatians, who has bewitched you, before whose eyes Jesus Christ was publicly portrayed as crucified? This is the only thing I want to find out from you: did you receive the Spirit by the works of the Law, or by hearing with faith? Are you so foolish? Having begun by the Spirit, are you now being perfected by the flesh? (Gal. 3:1–3)

The church today has a legacy that has been handed down to it, a heritage that must be preserved at all costs. Men of God throughout history have preached, taught, and defended the true gospel, often at great cost of time, effort, and persecution—even to the point of death. As his life drew to a close, Paul repeatedly exhorted Timothy to protect the truth that had been handed down to him: "O Timothy, guard what has been entrusted to you" (1 Tim. 6:20); "Retain the standard of sound words which you have heard from me, in the faith and love which are in Christ Jesus. Guard, through the Holy Spirit who dwells in us, the treasure which has been entrusted to you" (2 Tim. 1:13–14); "You, however, continue in the things you have learned and become convinced of, knowing from whom you have learned them" (2 Tim. 3:14; cf. 2 Thess. 2:15).

But those who, influenced by false teachers, slip backwards risk far more than undoing the labor of faithful shepherds. The tragic consequences of their spiritual regression will include failing to **receive a full reward.** The Bible teaches that believers will be rewarded in heaven for their service in this life (e.g., Matt. 5:12; 10:41–42; Luke 6:35; 1 Cor. 3:10–15; 4:3–5; 2 Cor. 5:10; Col. 3:24; Rev. 22:12). While salvation cannot be lost (cf. John 6:37–40; Rom. 5:1; 8:1, 28–39; Heb. 7:25; 1 Peter 1:4), unfaithful believers may forfeit some of the reward that faithfulness to the truth would have gained them. John did not want to see that happen to those whom he loved and labored among. Paul had the same concern in mind when he warned the Colossians, "Let no one keep defrauding you of your prize by delighting in self-abasement and the worship of the angels, taking his stand on visions he has seen, inflated without cause by his fleshly mind" (Col. 2:18).

Believers must be discerning and decisively reject deceiving false teachers, no matter how loudly they clamor for love and tolerance. Loyalty to the truth, written and incarnate, demands it, and the consequences of not doing so—both now and in eternity—are sufficient reason to be faithful.

Guarding the Truth

Anyone who goes too far and does not abide in the teaching of Christ, does not have God; the one who abides in the teaching, he has both the Father and the Son. If anyone comes to you and does not bring this teaching, do not receive him into your house, and do not give him a greeting; for the one who gives him a greeting participates in his evil deeds. (9–11)

Those who are loyal to Scripture will naturally seek to protect and guard it. No matter what he may claim, **anyone who goes too far and does not abide in the teaching of Christ does not have God.** *Proagō* (**goes too far**) means in this context "to go beyond established bounds of teaching or instruction, with the implication of failure to obey properly " ("proagō," *Louw-Nida Greek-English Lexicon of the New Testament Based on Semantic Domains,* 2nd Edition, Edited by J. P. Louw and E. A. Nida. Copyright © 1988 by the United Bible Societies, New York, NY 10023. Electronic edition, BibleWorks 7). The "established bounds of teaching or instruction" are revealed in Scripture. In 1 Corinthians 4:6 Paul wrote, "Now these things, brethren, I have figuratively applied to myself and Apollos for your sakes, so that in us you may learn *not to exceed what is written,* so that no one of you will become arrogant in behalf of one against the other" (emphasis added). Any teaching not consistent with Scripture is to be rejected (cf. Rev. 22:18–19).

Abide again translates the present participle of the verb *menō,* which means "to remain," "continue," or "persist in." The **teaching of Christ** can refer either to His teaching, or to the biblical teaching about Him, since both are in total agreement. False teachers are not content to remain within the confines of Scripture, but invariably add erroneous interpretations, revelations, visions, words as if from the Lord, or esoteric distortions of the biblical text, while claiming to have advanced knowledge, new truth, or hidden wisdom available only to them and their followers.

But such claims are specious. John plainly states that anyone who alters, adds to, denies, or misrepresents what the Bible says about Jesus Christ **does not have God** (cf. Matt. 11:27; John 5:23; 15:23; 1 John 2:23; Rev. 22:18–19). Conversely, **the one who abides in the teaching, he has both the Father and the Son.** This is salvation language; having God and Christ must mean their indwelling presence. As Jesus declared in John 14:23, "If anyone loves Me, he will keep My word; and My Father will love him, and We will come to him and make Our abode with him." There is no way to know God apart from faith in the Christ of Scripture (John 14:6; Acts 4:12; 1 Tim. 2:5).

In verse 10 John sets out one practical application of how to defend the truth: **If anyone comes to you and does not bring this teaching, do not receive him into your house.** Hospitality for traveling teachers was common in the culture (cf. Luke 9:1–6; 10:1–12). The prohibition here is not to turn away the ignorant; it does not mean that believers may not invite unbelievers—even those who belong to a cult or false religion—into their midst. That would make giving the truth to them difficult, if not impossible. The point is that believers are not to welcome and provide care for traveling false teachers, who seek to stay in their homes, thereby giving the appearance of affirming what they teach and lending them credibility.

John's use of the conjunction *ei* (**if**) with an indicative verb indicates a condition that is likely true. Apparently, the lady to whom he wrote had for whatever reason, in the name of Christian fellowship, already welcomed false teachers into her home. It was just such compassionate, well-meaning people that the false teachers sought out (cf. 2 Tim. 3:6); since churches were supposed to be protected by elders who were skilled teachers of the Word (1 Tim. 3:2; Titus 1:9), they should have been less susceptible to the lies propagated by the deceivers. Having established themselves in homes, the false teachers hoped eventually to worm their way into the churches. It is much the same today, as false teaching insidiously invades Christian homes through television, radio, the Internet, and literature.

So threatening are these emissaries of Satan that John went on to forbid even giving them **a greeting; for the one who gives him a greeting participates in his evil deeds.** Irenaeus relates that the church father Polycarp, when asked by the notorious heretic Marcion, "Do you know me?" replied, "I do know you—the firstborn of Satan" (*Against Heresies,* 3.3.4). John himself once encountered Cerinthus (another notorious heretic) in a public bathhouse in Ephesus. Instead of greeting him, however, John turned and fled, exclaiming to those with him, "Let us fly, lest even the bath-house fall down, because Cerinthus, the enemy of the truth, is within" (Irenaeus, *Against Heresies,* 3.3.4).

Chairein (**greeting**) means "Rejoice." It was a common Christian greeting, conveying the joy believers had in one another's presence. But it is an affirmation of solidarity that is totally inappropriate for false teachers, who have no part in the truth or genuine Christian fellowship. Such emissaries of Satan must be exposed and shunned, not affirmed and welcomed.

False teachers like to decry such treatment as harsh, intolerant, and unloving. But love forbids allowing dangerous spiritual deception to find a foothold among Christians. John's pastoral admonition is perfectly consistent with Jesus' denunciation of false teachers as "ravenous wolves" (Matt. 7:15; cf. Acts 20:29); thieves and robbers (John 10:1) whose only purpose is "to steal and kill and destroy" (v. 10). The church cannot aid or abet with impunity such spiritual outlaws by doing anything that would acknowledge them as Christians. The one who does so —even by doing something as seemingly innocuous as greeting them— **participates in** their **evil deeds** by helping them further their deception.

LEARNING THE TRUTH

Though I have many things to write to you, I do not want to do so with paper and ink; but I hope to come to you and speak face to face, so that your joy may be made full. The children of your chosen sister greet you. (12–13)

The conclusion of this marvelous little epistle reveals one last responsibility believers have toward the truth. If they are to live in it, love consistent with it, be loyal to it, and guard it, they must constantly be learning it. Despite all that she had learned from John and her other pastors and teachers, there were still **many things** about which he needed **to write to** her. The apostle still had much to teach her, but he did **not want to do so with paper** (papyrus) **and ink** (lit., "black"; a reference to ink made from water, charcoal, and gum resin). It was his **hope to come to** her **and speak face to face.** The Greek text literally reads "mouth to mouth," an idiomatic expression comparable to the English expression "eyeball to eyeball." In Numbers 12:8 God declared that He spoke "mouth to mouth" with Moses. The phrase reveals John's pastoral heart; he longed to have a personal conversation with this influential Christian lady to further her instruction in the truth.

The result of her learning the truth would be **that** her **joy** would **be made full** (cf. 1 John 1:4). The greater the knowledge of the truth, the greater the believer's joy. Jeremiah said, "Your words were found and I ate them, and Your words became for me a joy and the delight of my heart"

(Jer. 15:16). Jesus also connected knowing and obeying the truth with experiencing joy (John 15:11; 17:13).

John's concluding statement, **The children of your chosen sister greet you,** was a personal greeting he passed along from this lady's nieces and nephews. As noted in the discussion of verse 1 in the previous chapter of this volume, John did not hesitate to refer to believers as **chosen. Greet** translates a form of the verb *aspazomai,* which is frequently used at the conclusion of New Testament epistles (Rom. 16:22, 23; 1 Cor. 16:19–20; 2 Cor. 13:12–13; Phil. 4:21–22; Col. 4:10, 12, 14, 15; 1 Thess. 5:26; 2 Tim. 4:19, 21; Titus 3:15; Philem. 23; Heb. 13:24; 1 Peter 5:13–14; 3 John 14). From his location in Ephesus, John signed off after calling this dear lady, and by implication all Christians, to the truth.

In an age of relativism and skepticism, the church must remain firmly anchored to the solid foundation of divine truth. There is no place for insipid, shallow, theologically contentless preaching, for worship based on emotion devoid of truth, or for tolerating false teaching. There is no virtue in ignorance; no substitute for learning, loving, and guarding the truth. Only by so doing will the church be able to fulfill its divine calling to be the "pillar and support of the truth" (1 Tim. 3:15), shining the light of God's truth in the world of darkness.

Introduction to 3 John

OCCASION AND PURPOSE

Third John is the most personal of the three Johannine epistles. Like 2 John, it addresses the issue of believers' duty to show love and hospitality within the bounds of faithfulness to the truth. Second John revealed the negative side: false teachers are not to be granted hospitality in the name of showing love. Third John expresses the positive counterpart to that principle: all who embrace the truth are to be loved and cared for.

Gaius, to whom this letter was written, was known to John personally. A powerful and influential man (Diotrephes) in Gaius's church refused to show hospitality to itinerant teachers of whom John approved (vv. 5–8). Not only that, Diotrephes also excommunicated those who defied him and showed hospitality to the teachers (v. 10). He even went so far as to slander the apostle John and defy his apostolic authority (v. 10). John wrote to encourage Gaius to remain loyal to the truth by continuing to show hospitality to strangers, as he had done in the past (vv. 5–6). John also promised to deal personally with Diotrephes (v. 10) when he arrived (v. 14).

Further information concerning Gaius and Diotrephes may be found in the exposition of this epistle.

AUTHOR, DATE AND PLACE OF WRITING

Since 3 John's style, structure, and vocabulary closely parallel 2 John (e.g., v. 1 and 2 John 1; v. 4 and 2 John 4; v. 13 and 2 John 12; v. 14 and 2 John 12), it too was penned by the apostle John. Third John was most likely written from Ephesus at about the same time as 1 and 2 John (c. A.D. 90–95).

OUTLINE

I. The Commendation Regarding Christian Hospitality (1–8)
II. The Condemnation Regarding Violating Christian Hospitality (9–11)
III. The Conclusion Regarding Christian Hospitality (12–14)

Sacrificial Love for Those Faithful to the Truth (3 John 1–8)

21

The elder to the beloved Gaius, whom I love in truth. Beloved, I pray that in all respects you may prosper and be in good health, just as your soul prospers. For I was very glad when brethren came and testified to your truth, that is, how you are walking in truth. I have no greater joy than this, to hear of my children walking in the truth. Beloved, you are acting faithfully in whatever you accomplish for the brethren, and especially when they are strangers; and they have testified to your love before the church. You will do well to send them on their way in a manner worthy of God. For they went out for the sake of the Name, accepting nothing from the Gentiles. Therefore we ought to support such men, so that we may be fellow workers with the truth. (1–8)

Truth is the theme of this letter, especially in the opening section where the word appears five times. It is a call to give hospitality, but especially to those who were faithful teachers of the gospel truth (cf. 2 John 10–11).

When the apostle Paul detailed his suffering for the cause of Christ (2 Cor. 11:22–33), some of that suffering involved travel far different from the comfort and safety of modern travel. But the apostle's experience reflected the common reality of life in the ancient world:"I have been on frequent journeys," he wrote,"in dangers from rivers, dangers from robbers, dangers from my countrymen, dangers from the Gentiles, dangers in the city, dangers in the wilderness, dangers on the sea" (v. 26) . . . "three times I was shipwrecked, a night and a day I have spent in the deep" (v. 25). As that list indicates, travel was arduous, unpleasant, and even dangerous. The few inns that existed (cf. Luke 2:7; 10:34) were often little more than vermin-infested brothels and their keepers dishonest and of ill repute. As a result, travelers seeking safety were largely dependent on people opening their homes to them.

Hospitality therefore was both a necessity and a duty. Even in pagan cultures necessity rendered it one of the highest virtues. In fact, some of the gods invented by the Canaanites were designed to act as protectors of strangers and travelers. The Greeks also viewed travelers as being under the protection of the deities and hence to be shown hospitality, as William Barclay notes:

> In the ancient world hospitality was a sacred duty. Strangers were under the protection of Zeus Xenios, Zeus the god of strangers (*Xenos* is the Greek word for a *stranger*). . . . The ancient world had a system of *guest-friendships* whereby families in different parts of the country undertook to give each other's members hospitality when the occasion arose. This connection between families lasted throughout the generations and when it was claimed the claimant brought with him a *sumbolon*, or *token*, which identified him to his hosts. Some cities kept an official called the *Proxenos* in the larger cities to whom their citizens, when travelling, might appeal for shelter and for help. (*The Letters of John and Jude* [rev. ed.; Philadelphia: Westminster, 1976], 149)

The Bible certainly stresses the importance of hospitality. What the false god Zeus Xenios supposedly did, the true God actually did. Psalm 146:9*a* says,"The Lord protects the strangers" (cf. Deut. 10:18). God charged Israel, "You shall not oppress a stranger, since you yourselves know the feelings of a stranger, for you also were strangers in the land of Egypt" (Ex. 23:9; cf. 22:21; Lev. 19:33–34; 25:35; Deut. 10:19). Among those whom God indicted in Malachi 3:5 were those who turned away aliens.

The Old Testament relates many examples of hospitality. Melchizedek provided Abraham with bread and wine after he returned from rescuing Lot (Gen. 14:18). Abraham provided food for the Lord and two angels (Gen. 18:1–8), and soon afterward Lot took the two angels into his house (Gen. 19:1–3). Laban offered hospitality to Abraham's servant (Gen. 24:31–33), Jethro to Moses (Ex. 2:20), Samson's parents to the angel of the Lord (Judg. 13:15), an old man in Gibeah to a Levite (Judg. 19:15, 20–21), and the Shunammite woman to Elisha (2 Kings 4:8).

Defending his integrity against the false allegations of his friends, Job declared, "The alien has not lodged outside, for I have opened my doors to the traveler" (Job 31:32).

Hospitality is equally stressed in the New Testament. The general Jewish cultural view of hospitality underlies Jesus' charge to the seventy in Luke 10:4–7:

> "Carry no money belt, no bag, no shoes; and greet no one on the way. Whatever house you enter, first say, 'Peace be to this house.' If a man of peace is there, your peace will rest on him; but if not, it will return to you. Stay in that house, eating and drinking what they give you; for the laborer is worthy of his wages. Do not keep moving from house to house."

Zaccheus extended hospitality to Jesus (Luke 19:5–7), as did the Samaritan village of Sychar (John 4:40), Simon the Pharisee (Luke 7:36), another unnamed Pharisee (Luke 14:1), Mary, Martha, and Lazarus (Luke 10:38), Simon the leper (Matt. 26:6), and the two disciples on the road to Emmaus (Luke 24:29–30).

The apostles also enjoyed the hospitality of both Jews and Gentiles. Peter stayed in the homes of Simon the tanner (Acts 9:43; 10:5–6) and Cornelius (Acts 10:24–33, 48). Paul and his companions received hospitality from Lydia (Acts 16:14–15), the jailer at Philippi (Acts 16:34), Jason (Acts 17:5–7), Priscilla and Aquila (Acts 18:1–3), Titius Justus (Acts 18:7), Philip the evangelist (Acts 21:8), Mnason (Acts 21:16), and Publius (Acts 28:7).

Hospitality was not merely a cultural obligation, but even more a Christian duty. It is one very necessary and practical expression of the love that should mark the fellowship of believers (cf. John 13:34–35). In Romans 12:13 Paul wrote that believers are to be "practicing hospitality," while Peter exhorted, "Be hospitable to one another without complaint" (1 Peter 4:9). The writer of Hebrews commanded his readers, "Do not neglect to show hospitality to strangers, for by this some have entertained angels without knowing it" (Heb. 13:2). In 1 Timothy 5:10 Paul listed hospitality as one of the virtues of a godly Christian woman. Elders in particular are required to be hospitable as one of the exemplary qualifications for that office (1 Tim. 3:2; Titus 1:8).

Hospitality was also a significant responsibility because the home was central to the life of the early church (cf. Acts 2:46; 5:42; 12:12; 16:40; 18:7; 20:20; Rom. 16:5; 1 Cor. 16:19; Col. 4:15; Philem. 2). The believers met in homes for worship (the earliest known church building dates from early in the third century), prayer, fellowship, teaching, preaching, and discipleship. Thus it was common for Christians to open their doors to travelers visiting the church, especially the faithful teachers of the truth (3 John 6–8).

While the theme of showing love by hospitality is clearly commanded in both 2 and 3 John, the foundational reality below that duty is love for and obedience to the truth. John exalts the truth in his second letter in that he sets the exclusive limit that only those who embrace the truth are to be shown hospitality. In his third letter he affirms the inclusive approach that all who are in the truth are to be loved and cared for. That emphasis is made evident in John's greeting, **the elder to the beloved Gaius.**

Unlike modern correspondence, it was customary for the ancient writer to name himself at the opening of the letter. As noted in the discussion of 2 John 1 in chapter 19 of this volume, **elder** does not only designate John's age (he was a very old man when he wrote this letter), but more significant, it points to his position of spiritual oversight. As the last surviving apostle of Jesus Christ, John was not just *an* elder, but *the* elder, the most revered and respected figure in the church.

Details concerning **Gaius** are not known. There are several other men with that name in the New Testament (Acts 19:29; 20:4; Rom. 16:23; 1 Cor. 1:14). But since Gaius was one of the most common names in Roman society, it is impossible to identify this individual with any of them. He evidently was a prominent member of a local church, probably somewhere in Asia Minor, whom the apostle John knew personally.

Although his life remains hidden, Gaius's sterling character is disclosed in a grand tribute by the noble apostle. The rich term *agapētos* (**beloved**) can include not only the thought that this Gaius was loved by the Christian community (cf. its use in Acts 15:25; Eph. 6:21; Col. 1:7; 2 Peter 3:15), but also by the Lord (cf. Rom. 1:7; Eph. 5:1). John addressed the lady to whom he wrote his second epistle as "chosen" (2 John 1); here he addresses Gaius as **beloved.** All who love the Lord Jesus Christ are both chosen by God and loved by Him. In Colossians 3:12 Paul referred to Christians as "those who have been chosen of God, holy and beloved." The Bible repeatedly speaks of God's love for His elect (Zeph. 3:17; John 13:1, 34; 14:21, 23; 15:9, 12–13; 16:27; 17:23, 26; Rom. 5:5, 8; 8:35–39; 2 Cor. 13:14; Gal. 2:20; Eph. 1:4–5; 2:4; 5:2, 25; 2 Thess. 2:16; Heb. 12:6; 1 John 3:1; 4:9–11, 16, 19; Rev. 1:5; 3:9, 19).

John, too, loved this man (cf. vv. 2, 5, 11) and confessed so by saying that Gaius is a man **whom I love in truth** (cf. 2 John 1). **Truth,** as always, is the common sphere in which genuine biblical love is shared by believers; again, love and truth are inseparably linked (cf. vv. 3, 4, 8, 12). There is a sense in which Christians are to love all people (cf. Gal. 6:10), just as God loves the world (Matt. 5:44–45; cf. John 3:16; Mark 10:21). But the love John spoke of here is the unique love that believers have for those who are in Christ and faithful to the truth (John 13:34–35; 15:12,17; Rom. 12:10; 13:8; 1 Thess. 3:12; 4:9; 2 Thess. 1:3; 1 Peter 1:22; 4:8; 1 John 3:11,23; 4:7,11,12; 2 John 5).

This letter revolves around three individuals and their relationship to truth and love: Gaius, who walked in the truth and loved sacrificially (vv. 1–8); Diotrophes, who rejected the truth and hindered sacrificial love (vv. 9–11); and Demetrius, who was to receive sacrificial love for his faithfulness to the truth (v. 12). John opens by expressing to Gaius his concern, commendation, and counsel.

JOHN'S CONCERN FOR GAIUS

Beloved, I pray that in all respects you may prosper and be in good health, just as your soul prospers. (2)

The phrase **I pray that in all respects you may prosper and be in good health** was a standard greeting in ancient letters, so it does not imply that Gaius was ill. **Prosper** translates a form of the verb *euodoō*. The term, used only here, Romans 1:10, and 1 Corinthians 16:2, means "to succeed," "to have things go well," or "to enjoy favorable circumstances." The first use of **prosper** in verse 2 refers to Gaius's physical **health,** as the contrast with the last part of the verse makes clear. The apostle's wish was that Gaius's physical health would be as good as that of his spiritual.

John's concern for Gaius is a pastoral desire that he be free from the turmoil, pain, and debilitation of illness so as to be unrestricted in his service to the Lord and His church. This attitude mirrors God's concern for the physical health of His people. The Old Testament dietary laws, and the regulations concerning hygiene (e.g., Deut. 23:13), even circumcision, were designed to protect the health of the people of Israel for their usefulness as well as their preservation. In the New Testament, Paul advised Timothy, "No longer drink water exclusively, but use a little wine for the sake of your stomach and your frequent ailments" (1 Tim. 5:23). Wine in biblical times was usually mixed with water, which the alcohol in the wine helped disinfect. Drinking that relatively purified water would help guard Timothy from further illness. Paul's concern for Timothy's physical health was characteristic of any apostle's affection for a child in the faith (cf. Titus 1:4). The same was certainly true of John's love for Gaius.

But Gaius's healthy **soul** brought far more delight to John. He knew he had a vibrant spiritual life. To borrow from some other apostles, Gaius was among those who are "sound in the faith" (Titus 1:13); constantly "grow[ing] in the grace and knowledge of our Lord and Savior Jesus Christ" (2 Peter 3:18); "walk[ing] in a manner worthy of the Lord, to please Him in all respects, bearing fruit in every good work and increasing in the knowledge of God" (Col. 1:10). John knew this to be true by the testimony of those who had personal knowledge of Gaius, as he states in the next verse.

JOHN'S COMMENDATION OF GAIUS

For I was very glad when brethren came and testified to your truth, that is, how you are walking in truth. I have no greater joy than this, to hear of my children walking in the truth. Beloved, you are acting faithfully in whatever you accomplish for the brethren, and especially when they are strangers; and they have testified to your love before the church. (3–6a)

John was **very glad when** some **brethren,** probably traveling preachers to whom Gaius had shown hospitality, **came and testified to** him of the **truth** that was operative and evident in Gaius's life. The repeatedly used image of **walking** refers metaphorically in the New Testament to daily conduct (e.g., Mark 7:5; Luke 1:6; John 8:12; 11:9–10; 12:35; Acts 21:21, 24; Rom. 6:4; 8:4; 14:15; 1 Cor. 3:3; 7:17; 2 Cor. 4:2; 5:7; 10:2–3; Gal. 5:16, 25; 6:16; Eph. 2:2, 10; 4:1, 17; 5:2, 8, 15; Phil. 3:17–18; Col. 1:10; 2:6; 3:7; 1 Thess. 2:12; 4:1; 1 John 1:6–7; 2:6, 11; 2 John 4, 6).

Showing hospitality was a manifestation of love—all the more remarkable when contrasted with Diotrophes' ugly rejection (v. 10). John, however, did not commend Gaius for his love but, more fundamentally, for his commitment to the truth. As is always the case with believers, Gaius's genuine love flowed from his obedience to the truth. John commended him because he not only knew the truth, but lived in it.

Such commendations are not unusual in the New Testament. Phoebe was commended for being a faithful servant and helper in her church (Rom. 16:1). Priscilla and Aquila, the husband and wife team who were so dear to Paul, were commended for the great sacrifices they made on his behalf (Rom. 16:3). Stephanas and his household, along with Fortunatus and Achaicus, were commended for their service to the saints (1 Cor. 16:15–18). Epaphroditus was commended for ministering to Paul—even at the risk of his own life (Phil. 2:25–30). Epaphras was twice commended for his fruitful service to Christ, especially his laboring in prayer for the saints (Col. 1:7; 4:12). Despite his earlier lapse (Acts 13:13; cf. 15:37–39), Paul commended John Mark for his useful service to him (2 Tim. 4:11). Peter commended Silvanus as a "faithful brother" (1 Peter 5:12). But there is no higher commendation for a Christian than the one given to Gaius by John—that he not only knew the truth revealed by God, but also lived in conformity to it (cf. Luke 6:46–49; 11:28; John 13:17; James 1:22–23).

John's general comment, **I have no greater joy than this, to hear of my children walking in the truth** (cf. 2 John 4), expresses the ultimate goal of every true minister. That goal is not just to teach the truth, or even to know that his people understand it, but to know that his people believe, love, and obey the truth (cf. 1 Cor. 4:14–16; 1 Thess. 2:11, 19–20; 3:1–10). The writer of Hebrews exhorted his readers, "Obey your leaders and submit to them, for they keep watch over your souls as those who will give an account. Let them do this with joy and not with grief, for this would be unprofitable for you" (Heb. 13:17). The great grief of ministry is people who are indifferent or rebellious toward the Word of God.

With Gaius there was no dichotomy between creed and conduct, between profession and practice. The emphatic position of **my** in the Greek text may mean that Gaius had been converted under John's ministry.

The apostle spells out Gaius's obedience to the truth as **acting faithfully in whatever** he labored to **accomplish for the brethren.** Gaius no doubt gave the gospel preachers shelter, food, and perhaps money, meeting their needs even though they were **strangers** to him. Genuine saving faith, such as Gaius possessed, always produces good works (Eph. 2:8–10; 1 Tim. 2:10; 5:10; 6:18; James 2:14–26). The missionaries were so impressed with Gaius's humble service to them that after returning to Ephesus **they . . . testified to** his **love before the church.** Consistent with Gaius's devotion to the truth, he was a model of one who "contributed to the needs of the saints [by] practicing hospitality" (Rom. 12:13).

JOHN'S COUNSEL TO GAIUS

You will do well to send them on their way in a manner worthy of God. For they went out for the sake of the Name, accepting nothing from the Gentiles. Therefore we ought to support such men, so that we may be fellow workers with the truth. (6*b*–8)

John encouraged this godly man to continue his generous love when other preachers of the truth arrived in the future. The apostle advised Gaius, **You will do well to send them on their way in a manner worthy of God. You will do well** is an idiomatic Greek expression equivalent to the English word "please." John entreated him to **send** any

missionaries that came to him **on their way** refreshed and fully sup-
plied for the next stage of their journey. John's exhortation is reminiscent
of Paul's command to Titus, "Diligently help Zenas the lawyer and Apollos on their way so that nothing is lacking for them" (Titus 3:13).

The standard is high; Gaius was to treat them **in a manner worthy of God.** He was to give to them generously as God would give. Three
reasons are suggested for supporting all faithful servants of Christ.

First, they **went out for the sake of the Name.** God's **Name** represents all that He is. Their work is the work of God Himself for His own
glory (1 Cor. 10:31; Col. 3:17), the motive that underlies the church's evangelistic efforts (cf. Matt. 6:9; Luke 24:47; Acts 5:41; 9:15–16; 15:26; 21:13;
Rom. 1:5). It is an affront to God when people do not believe in the name
of His Son, who is worthy to be loved, praised, honored, and confessed as
Lord. When believers proclaim the good news of the gospel of Jesus
Christ, people are saved, and as a result, "the grace which is spreading to
more and more people . . . cause[s] the giving of thanks to abound to the
glory of God" (2 Cor. 4:15).

Second, preachers of the truth could expect **nothing from the
Gentiles.** It goes without saying that unbelievers are not going to support those who preach the true gospel. If Christians do not support them,
no one will. And, as Paul explained to Timothy, those who faithfully proclaim the Word of God are worthy of financial compensation (1 Tim.
5:17–20).

Of course, while it is right for them to be paid for their labor, true
ambassadors of the gospel are never in the ministry for the sake of
money. In fact, it is precisely the issue of money that separates true
preachers from false ones. Scripture is clear that the latter are invariably
in it for the money, and have no honest commitment to the truth. They
are hucksters, spiritual con men guilty of "peddling the word of God"
(2 Cor. 2:17), "teaching things they should not teach for the sake of sordid
gain" (Titus 1:11). "Woe to them!" Jude exclaimed, "For they have gone the
way of Cain, and for pay they have rushed headlong into the error of Balaam, and perished in the rebellion of Korah" (Jude 11). The Didache, an
early Christian writing, offered the following wise advice about how to
distinguish a false prophet:

> Welcome every apostle [teacher; evangelist] on arriving, as if he were
> the Lord. But he must not stay beyond one day. In case of necessity,
> however, the next day too. If he stays three days, he is a false prophet.
> On departing, an apostle must not accept anything save sufficient food
> to carry him till his next lodging. If he asks for money, he is a false
> prophet. (11:4–6; cited in Cyril C. Richardson, ed., *Early Christian
> Fathers* [New York: Macmillan, 1978], 176)

To avoid any suspicion that he might be a charlatan, Paul worked with his own hands to support himself (Acts 20:34; 1 Cor. 4:12; 9:18; 1 Thess. 2:9; 2 Thess. 3:7–9; cf. 1 Peter 5:1–2).

Finally, we **ought to support such men, so that we may be fellow workers with the truth.** In 2 John 10–11, John cautioned against participating in false teachers' evil deeds by supporting them, even verbally. But by supporting those who present the **truth,** Christians partner with them. Jesus said in Matthew 10:41, "He who receives a prophet in the name of a prophet shall receive a prophet's reward; and he who receives a righteous man in the name of a righteous man shall receive a righteous man's reward." Thus, He promised eternal reward, as if the one caring for a prophet was himself a prophet. In His limitless grace God not only rewards a true prophet, preacher, or missionary for his faithfulness, but also rewards anyone else who receives him. Receiving a prophet refers to embracing his ministry—affirming his call and supporting his work. Receiving a righteous man is that same principle, extended to every believer who is accepted for Christ's sake. In an incomprehensible sharing of blessing, God showers His rewards on every person who receives His people because they are His people.

Whenever we become the source of blessing for others, we are blessed; and whenever other believers become a source of blessing to us, they are blessed. In God's magnificent economy of grace, the least believer can share the blessings of the greatest, and no one's good work will go unrewarded.

The Man Who Loved the Preeminence
(3 John 9–14)

22

I wrote something to the church; but Diotrephes, who loves to be first among them, does not accept what we say. For this reason, if I come, I will call attention to his deeds which he does, unjustly accusing us with wicked words; and not satisfied with this, he himself does not receive the brethren, either, and he forbids those who desire to do so and puts them out of the church. Beloved, do not imitate what is evil, but what is good. The one who does good is of God; the one who does evil has not seen God. Demetrius has received a good testimony from everyone, and from the truth itself; and we add our testimony, and you know that our testimony is true. I had many things to write to you, but I am not willing to write them to you with pen and ink; but I hope to see you shortly, and we will speak face to face. Peace be to you. The friends greet you. Greet the friends by name. (9–14)

One of the defining characteristics of every sinful human heart is pride (Prov. 21:4). Pride causes people to forget God (Deut. 8:14; Hos. 13:6), be unfaithful to Him (2 Chron. 26:16), be ungrateful to Him (2 Chron. 32:24–25), and become an abomination to Him (Prov. 16:5). It was through

251

pride that sin entered the universe, when Satan sought to exalt himself above God (Isa. 14:12–14; cf. 1 Tim. 3:6).

As was the case with the Devil, pride drives people to seek to exalt themselves. There have always been proud, egotistical, self-promoting people, who try to usurp authority, seize a place of preeminence, and elevate themselves over others, even God. They tend to gravitate to and even manipulate themselves into positions of power, influence, and prominence. Scripture records many such people; they form a sort of "Hall of Shame," in contrast to the heroes of the faith listed in Hebrews 11.

The story of human pride began in the Garden of Eden. As it had been in Satan's fall, pride was a major component in the act of disobedience that catapulted the human race into sin. Eve ate the forbidden fruit in part because she believed Satan's lie that it would make her wise like God (Gen. 3:5–6). Moreover, by choosing to eat the fruit, without consulting Adam, she elevated herself above her husband, usurping his role in the created order (1 Tim. 2:13; cf. 1 Cor. 11:3–10). Clearly, then, pride was at work from the very moment sin entered the world.

The next chapter of Genesis introduces Lamech, a descendant of the first murderer, Cain. Like his ancestor, Lamech was also a murderer (as well as the first recorded polygamist). As Cain's murder had been motivated by proud envy, Lamech's killings were a result of pride. In the first recorded poetry in human history, Lamech boasted arrogantly to his wives,

> "Adah and Zillah,
> Listen to my voice,
> You wives of Lamech,
> Give heed to my speech,
> For I have killed a man for wounding me;
> And a boy for striking me;
> If Cain is avenged sevenfold,
> Then Lamech seventy-sevenfold." (Gen. 4:23–24)

Perhaps Enoch had Lamech in mind when he prophesied, "Behold, the Lord came with many thousands of His holy ones, to execute judgment upon all, and to convict all the ungodly of all their ungodly deeds which they have done in an ungodly way, and of all the harsh things which ungodly sinners have spoken against Him" (Jude 14–15).

Genesis 10 and 11 relate the story of Nimrod, another proud figure. Genesis 10:8 describes him as "a mighty one on the earth." His name probably is related to a Hebrew word meaning "to rebel," while the word translated "mighty one" refers to someone who magnifies himself, acts proudly, or is tyrannical. The description of Nimrod as a renowned hunter (v. 9) may indicate his skill in hunting animals—or in hunting people to enslave them. It was under his leadership that the Tower of Babel, a monument to human pride and rebellion against God, was built (Gen. 11:1–9). Nimrod also was the founder of what later became the Babylonian and Assyrian empires (cf. Gen. 10:10–12). Derek Kidner writes concerning Nimrod's character, "Nimrod looks out of antiquity as the first of 'the great men that are in the earth', remembered for two things the world admires, personal prowess and political power" (*Genesis,* The Tyndale Old Testament Commentaries [Downers Grove, Ill.: Inter-Varsity, 1979], 107).

During Israel's wilderness wandering, "Nadab and Abihu, the sons of Aaron, took their respective firepans, and after putting fire in them, placed incense on it and offered strange fire before the Lord, which He had not commanded them. And fire came out from the presence of the Lord and consumed them, and they died before the Lord" (Lev. 10:1–2). These two priests, sons of Aaron, in their first priestly act violated in some unspecified way the divine prescription for offering incense. Their behavior, possibly while they were drunk (cf. Lev. 10:8–10), betrayed their rebellious carelessness, irreverence, and preference for their own will over God's very specific commands. The two decided to do things their own way, and paid the ultimate price for such proud independence. Also during the wilderness wandering, Moses' own brother and sister, Aaron and Miriam, sought to elevate themselves to his level (Num. 12:1–3). The Lord severely judged both of them for their arrogance and presumption (vv. 4–15).

During the lawless days of the judges, Abimelech, the son of Gideon, wanted to be king. So passionate was his lust for power that he murdered seventy of his brothers in an attempt to eliminate any possible rivals (Judg. 9:1–6). But Abimelech's reign came to an untimely and embarrassing end. During his siege of the city of Thebez, "a certain woman threw an upper millstone on Abimelech's head, crushing his skull" (v. 53). In the throes of death, he made a desperate, prideful attempt to avoid the shame of being killed by a woman. He "called quickly to the young man, his armor bearer, and said to him, 'Draw your sword and kill me, so that it will not be said of me, "A woman slew him."' So the young man pierced him through, and he died" (v. 54). Despite his attempt to cover it up, Abimelech's shameful death was recorded for all time in Scripture.

Absalom's quest for power and prominence led him to stage a coup against his own father, King David. But his day in the sun was short-lived, and he met an ignominious end. While he was fleeing from David's men through a dense forest, Absalom's mule went under an oak tree. His flowing hair became entangled in the tree's thick branches, leaving him dangling helplessly in midair. He was soon executed by David's general, Joab (2 Sam. 18:9–15).

Another of David's sons, Adonijah, also sought to usurp the throne of his father. In the waning days of David's life, "Adonijah the son of Haggith exalted himself, saying, 'I will be king.' So he prepared for himself chariots and horsemen with fifty men to run before him [like his brother Absalom had done; 2 Sam. 15:1]" (1 Kings 1:5). His attempt to claim the throne failed, however, thwarted by the quick action of Nathan the prophet (vv. 11–48). Granted mercy by King Solomon (vv. 50–53), Adonijah repaid that kindness by scheming to overthrow him (1 Kings 2:13–21). Solomon saw through his plot, however, and had him executed (vv. 22–25).

Not content with being king, Uzziah attempted to usurp the function of the priests. According to 2 Chronicles 26:16, "When he became strong, his heart was so proud that he acted corruptly, and he was unfaithful to the Lord his God, for he entered the temple of the Lord to burn incense on the altar of incense." Uzziah was courageously opposed by Azariah and eighty priests, who warned him that he was overstepping his bounds (vv. 17–18). Enraged, the proud and self-confident Uzziah threatened the priests, and was immediately stricken by God with leprosy (v. 19). For the rest of his life Uzziah, the outcast, lived in a separate house and his son Jotham assumed his royal duties (v. 21).

The book of Esther relates the story of Haman, the great foe of the Jewish people. Obsessed with his self-importance after being elevated to a high position in the Persian Empire, Haman was enraged at Mordecai's refusal to do homage to him (Est. 3:5). He therefore instigated a pogrom to exterminate Mordecai's people, the Jews (v. 6). In the end, however, it was Haman who perished, hanged on the very gallows on which he had planned to hang Mordecai (Est. 7:10).

Nebuchadnezzar was the king of the mighty Babylonian Empire. One day as he walked on the roof of his royal palace in Babylon, "the king reflected and said, 'Is this not Babylon the great, which I myself have built as a royal residence by the might of my power and for the glory of my majesty?'" (Dan. 4:30). But his pride was swiftly and humiliatingly crushed:

> While the word was in the king's mouth, a voice came from heaven, saying, "King Nebuchadnezzar, to you it is declared: sovereignty has been removed from you, and you will be driven away from mankind, and your dwelling place will be with the beasts of the field. You will be given grass to eat like cattle, and seven periods of time will pass over you until you recognize that the Most High is ruler over the realm of mankind and bestows it on whomever He wishes." Immediately the

word concerning Nebuchadnezzar was fulfilled; and he was driven away from mankind and began eating grass like cattle, and his body was drenched with the dew of heaven until his hair had grown like eagles' feathers and his nails like birds' claws. (vv. 31–33)

In the New Testament, pompous King Herod Agrippa I decided to hold a celebration. As he gave a speech his enraptured subjects, unable to contain themselves, "kept crying out, 'The voice of a god and not of a man!'" (Acts 12:22). Because Herod neglected to give glory to God, an angel of the Lord struck him and he died (v. 23), thus bringing an abrupt and unexpected end to the festivities.

The four Gospels describe an entire group of boastful men who sought the preeminence, namely the scribes and Pharisees. Jesus said of them,

> They do all their deeds to be noticed by men; for they broaden their phylacteries and lengthen the tassels of their garments. They love the place of honor at banquets and the chief seats in the synagogues, and respectful greetings in the market places, and being called Rabbi by men. (Matt. 23:5–7)

They were those who justified themselves in the sight of men (Luke 16:15), "for appearance's sake offer[ed] long prayers" (Luke 20:47), "receive[d] glory from one another" (John 5:44), and "loved the approval of men rather than the approval of God" (John 12:43).

Prideful ambition had an ugly presence even among Jesus' own disciples. In Matthew 20:20–21 "The mother of the sons of Zebedee came to Jesus with her sons, bowing down and making a request of Him. And He said to her, 'What do you wish?' She said to Him, 'Command that in Your kingdom these two sons of mine may sit one on Your right and one on Your left.'" James and John used their mother's presumed influence with Jesus to ask for preeminent places in the kingdom. But instead of granting their request, Jesus used the occasion to instruct His disciples concerning the importance of humility:

> But Jesus called them to Himself and said, "You know that the rulers of the Gentiles lord it over them, and their great men exercise authority over them. It is not this way among you, but whoever wishes to become great among you shall be your servant, and whoever wishes to be first among you shall be your slave; just as the Son of Man did not come to be served, but to serve, and to give His life a ransom for many." (vv. 25–28)

In this third epistle the apostle John introduces Diotrephes, another in the long line of men who sought the preeminence. Verse 9 marks an abrupt shift in the tone of the letter. The first eight verses praise Gaius for showing sacrificial love to missionaries who came to his church. But beginning in verse 9, the tone is just the opposite, as John sharply rebukes a man called Diotrephes for refusing to show hospitality to the servants of the gospel, and for refusing to permit others to do so. The apostle exposed Diotrephes' personal ambition and perverted actions, and offered yet another man, Demetrius, as a commendable contrast to him.

DIOTREPHES' PERSONAL AMBITION

I wrote something to the church; but Diotrephes, who loves to be first among them, does not accept what we say. (9)

The contrast between righteous Gaius and unrighteous **Diotrephes** is striking; the two men were poles apart. Gaius was graciously hospitable, Diotrephes ungraciously inhospitable. Gaius loved the truth and loved everyone humbly (vv. 3–6); Diotrephes refused the truth and loved himself, and threatened everyone from his position of self-appointed authority in the church. One submitted to the words of truth; the other spouted words of contempt. The difference between the two men was not primarily doctrinal but behavioral; John did not rebuke Diotrephes for heresy, but for haughtiness.

The letter John **wrote** to Gaius's **church** is now lost, perhaps because Diotrephes intercepted and destroyed it. It could not have been 2 John, since that letter was not written to a church but to an individual. Nor could it have been 1 John, which does not address the issue of showing hospitality to missionaries.

John's parenthetical description of **Diotrephes** as one **who loves to be first among them** goes to the heart of the issue. **Loves to be first** translates a participial form of the Greek verb *philoprōteuō*, a compound word from *philos* ("love") and *prōtos* ("first"). It describes a person who is selfish, self-centered, and self-seeking. The present tense of the participle indicates that this was the constant pattern of Diotrephes' life. *Prōteuō* appears in the New Testament only in Colossians 1:18, where it refers to the preeminence of the Lord Jesus Christ. By rejecting those who were representing Christ, Diotrephes was in effect usurping His role as head of the church. The name **Diotrephes** (lit., "nourished by Zeus" or "foster child of Zeus") was as uncommon as Gaius was common. Some believe that it was used exclusively in noble families. If Diotrephes was from a noble family, his arrogant behavior may have been cultivated in that elevated environment.

That Diotrephes did **not accept what** John said indicates just how far he had gone in his arrogance. Shockingly, his desire for power and self-glory had driven him to reject the authority of Christ mediated through the apostle John. Diotrephes was guilty of spiritual pride of the rankest kind. His attitude was that of a self-promoting demagogue, who refused to serve anyone but wanted all to serve him. That attitude utterly defies the New Testament's teaching on servant leadership (cf. Matt. 20:25–28; 1 Cor. 3:5; 2 Cor. 4:5; Phil. 2:5–11; 1 Peter 5:3).

DIOTREPHES' PERVERTED ACTIONS

For this reason, if I come, I will call attention to his deeds which he does, unjustly accusing us with wicked words; and not satisfied with this, he himself does not receive the brethren, either, and he forbids those who desire to do so and puts them out of the church. (10)

For this reason (Diotrephes' prideful defiance of John's apostolic authority) the apostle declared, **If I come, I will call attention to his deeds which he does.** John would not overlook this challenge to his apostolic authority and to Christ's rule in the church. He would expose Diotrephes before the congregation, make his conduct a matter of church discipline (1 Tim. 5:19–20), and, if need be, use his apostolic authority to deal with him. Paul issued a similar challenge to the rebels at Corinth when he wrote, "I will come to you soon, if the Lord wills, and I shall find out, not the words of those who are arrogant but their power" (1 Cor. 4:19), and again in his second letter to Corinth, when he stated,

> This is the third time I am coming to you. Every fact is to be confirmed by the testimony of two or three witnesses. I have previously said when present the second time, and though now absent I say in advance to those who have sinned in the past and to all the rest as well, that if I come again I will not spare anyone. (2 Cor. 13:1–2)

John indicted Diotrephes on four counts. In each case, the present tense of the verb indicates that these were continual, habitual behaviors on Diotrephes' part.

First, he was guilty of **unjustly accusing** John **with wicked words.** Character assassination is an all too common ploy of those who seek to elevate themselves. They gain people's trust not positively by manifesting a godly character but negatively by destroying people's trust in other leaders. The verb translated **unjustly accusing** appears only here in the New Testament, but a related word is translated "gossips" in 1 Timothy 5:13. Scripture repeatedly condemns gossip (Prov. 20:19; Rom. 1:29; 2 Cor. 12:20; 1 Tim. 3:11; 5:13; 2 Tim. 3:3; Titus 2:3), and slander (Lev. 19:16; Ps. 15:3; 101:5; 140:11; Prov. 10:18; 16:28; Matt. 15:19; Rom. 1:30; 2 Cor. 12:20; Eph. 4:31; Col. 3:8; 1 Peter 2:1). The adjective translated **wicked** is used five times in 1 John to describe the Devil (2:13, 14; 3:12; 5:18, 19) and once of Cain's evil deeds (3:12). In 2 John 11, it describes the evil deeds of the false teachers. Diotrephes' malicious accusations were evil, false, and slanderous. He saw John as a threat to his power and prestige in the church and savagely attacked him. This is similar to the way the false teachers in Corinth had assaulted Paul (2 Cor. 7:2–3; 10:10; 11:5–7; 12:15; 13:3).

Second, **not satisfied with** merely assaulting John, Diotrephes defiantly did **not receive the brethren,** the traveling preachers who proclaimed the apostolic message of the gospel. Seeing the preachers as a threat to his own power in the church, Diotrephes refused to extend hospitality to them. Since Scripture commands such hospitality (Rom. 12:13; Heb. 13:2; 1 Peter 4:9), Diotrephes was also guilty of rejecting the Word of God. As one commentator explains,

> Not only are Diotrephes' words vicious; his deeds are equally reprehensible. He willfully breaks the rules of Christian hospitality by refusing to receive missionaries sent out to proclaim the gospel. By denying them shelter and food, he hinders the progress of the Word of God. In brief, Diotrephes is thwarting God's plans and purposes and consequently he faces divine wrath. (Simon J. Kistemaker, *III John*, New Testament Commentary [Grand Rapids: Baker, 1986], 9–10)

Not only did Diotrephes personally refuse to extend hospitality to the brethren; he also forbade **those who desire**[d] **to do so.** He further abused his power by obstructing or preventing others in the church from showing hospitality to the itinerant preachers.

Those who defied Diotrephes and showed hospitality were put **out of the church.** So threatening was Diotrephes that he had the clout to excommunicate anyone he perceived as an apparent threat. Perhaps that had actually happened to Gaius, which could explain why John had to tell him about what was going on in the church. If he was still in the church, Gaius was facing hostility and opposition from Diotrephes, prompting John to encourage him not to give in, but to continue to show hospitality in the future (cf. the discussion of 3 John 5–8 in the previous chapter of this volume).

Like most conflicts in the church, this one stemmed from pride. It was pride that caused Diotrephes to slander John, snub the missionaries, and eliminate those who defied him. His arrogance led to ambition, which resulted in false, slanderous accusations, defiance toward apostolic authority, and the crushing of any opposition to his power. Sadly, there have always been people like Diotrephes in churches. Even more tragically, many churches, either because they are fearful of them, or in the name of tolerance, refuse to deal with their own Diotrephes types. The apostle John, however, had no hesitation in confronting such a sinner for the good of the church and the honor of Christ.

DEMETRIUS' COMMENDABLE CONTRAST

Beloved, do not imitate what is evil, but what is good. The one who does good is of God; the one who does evil has not seen God. Demetrius has received a good testimony from everyone, and from the truth itself; and we add our testimony, and you know that our testimony is true. I had many things to write to you, but I am not willing to write them to you with pen and ink; but I hope to see you shortly, and we will speak face to face. Peace be to you. The friends greet you. Greet the friends by name. (11–15)

At first glance verse 11 appears to interrupt John's flow of thought. But it is a necessary introduction to the section commending Demetrius. John urged Gaius **not** to **imitate** Diotrephes' **evil** behavior by refusing to welcome Demetrius. Instead, the apostle urged Gaius to pattern his life after **what is good,** like Demetrius did. John's reminder that **the one who does good is of God; the one who does evil has not seen God** is a practical application of the moral test of genuine faith that he gave in his first epistle (see the exposition of 1 John 2:3–6 and 5:2–3 in chapters 5 and 16 of this volume). The Bible is clear that good works do not save; "a man is not justified by the works of the Law but through faith in Christ Jesus . . . since by the works of the Law no flesh will be justified" (Gal. 2:16; cf. Rom. 3:20). Obedience is, however, the external, visible proof of salvation (John 14:15, 21). Diotrephes' refusal to obey God's commands demonstrates that he was not saved.

In contrast to his strong indictment of Diotrephes, John warmly commended **Demetrius.** Like Gaius, the name Demetrius ("belonging to Demeter," the Greek goddess of grain and the harvest) was common. A silversmith in Ephesus by that name sparked a riot over Paul's teaching, because the gospel was financially damaging to him and his fellow idol makers (Acts 19:23–41). Demas (Col. 4:14; 2 Tim. 4:10; Philem. 24) was a shortened form of Demetrius.

Nothing is known apart from this verse of the Demetrius whom John commended. He may have delivered this letter from John to Gaius. That he was a man of noble Christian character is evident from three sources. First, he had **received a good testimony from everyone.** His reputation was well known among the Christian community in that region. Second, Demetrius was committed to living **the truth** (v. 3). Finally, John added his own **testimony**—which Gaius knew to be **true** —to commend Demetrius' character. The example of Demetrius shows that a man's worth can be measured by his reputation in the community, his faithfulness to the truth of Scripture, and the opinion godly Christian leaders have of him. Demetrius received high marks on all counts.

The conclusion of this epistle closely parallels that of 2 John. John wrote, **I had many things to write to you, but I am not willing to write them to you with pen and ink; but I hope to see you shortly, and we will speak face to face.** In both epistles John had much more to say to those to whom he wrote, but he preferred to do so not **with pen and ink,** but **face to face.**

The apostle's farewell wish, **peace be to you,** was an appropriate one for that strife-torn congregation. Gaius and John evidently had mutual **friends** who asked John to **greet** Gaius for them. John also asked Gaius to **greet** some other mutual **friends** who were with him. The phrase **by name** adds a personal, intimate touch. Though well into his nineties, John still cherished those to whom he had ministered throughout his life.

Without question, the concept of the truth stands out in this brief letter. First, believers must know the truth and obey it (v. 3). Second, they are to be hospitable to other faithful believers, who preach the truth (vv. 6–8). Finally, they are to pattern their lives after godly examples who live in the truth (v. 11; cf. Heb. 13:7). Where the truth prevails, the Lord is glorified in His church.

Bibliography

Brooke, A. E. *A Critical and Exegetical Commentary on the Johannine Epistles.* The International Critical Commentary. Edinburgh: T. & T. Clark, 1912.

Bruce, F. F. *The Epistles of John.* Grand Rapids: Eerdmans, 1970.

Burdick, Donald W. *The Letters of John the Apostle.* Chicago: Moody, 1985.

Carson, D. A., Douglas J. Moo, and Leon Morris. *An Introduction to the New Testament.* Grand Rapids: Zondervan, 1992.

Gundry, Robert H. *A Survey of the New Testament.* Grand Rapids: Zondervan, 1970.

Guthrie, Donald. *New Testament Introduction.* Revised Edition. Downers Grove, Ill.: InterVarsity, 1990.

Hiebert, D. Edmond. *An Introduction to the Non-Pauline Epistles.* Chicago: Moody, 1962.

_____. *The Epistles of John.* Greenville, S.C.: Bob Jones University Press, 1991.

Kistemaker, Simon J. *New Testament Commentary: Exposition of the Epistle of James and the Epistles of John.* Grand Rapids: Baker, 1986.

Law, Robert. *The Tests of Life.* Edinburgh: T. & T. Clark, 1914.

Lloyd-Jones, Martyn. *Life in Christ: Studies in 1 John.* Wheaton, Ill.: Crossway, 2002.

MacArthur, John. *The MacArthur Bible Commentary.* Nashville: Thomas Nelson, 2005.

_____. *John 1–11.* The MacArthur New Testament Commentary. Chicago: Moody, 2006.

Marshall, I. Howard. *The Epistles of John.* The New International Commentary on the New Testament. Grand Rapids: Eerdmans, 1978.

Moulton, J. H. *A Grammar of New Testament Greek.* Vol. IV: *Style,* by Nigel Turner. Edinburgh: T. & T. Clark, 1976.

Plummer, Alfred. *The Epistles of St. John.* The Cambridge Bible for Schools and Colleges. Cambridge: Cambridge University Press, 1911.

Smith, David. "The Epistles of John." In W. Robertson Nicoll, ed., *The Expositor's Greek Testament Vol. V.* Reprint. Peabody, Mass.: Hendrickson, 2002.

Stott, John R. W. *The Epistles of John.* The Tyndale New Testament Commentaries. Grand Rapids: Eerdmans, 1964.

Westcott, Brooke Foss. *The Epistles of St. John.* Reprint. Grand Rapids: Eerdmans, 1966.

Indexes

Index of Greek Words and Phrases

Index of Scripture

Index of Subjects

Salome, 6
Salutations, 219
Salvation
    Arminian position on, 140, 141
    assurance of, 52–60, 140, 141, 142
    for believers only, 202, 210
    believers' perfect love and, 171
    conscience, cleansed, as a gift of,
      143
    elect or "chosen" and, 217
    faith and, 120–22, 227
    general revelation and, 227, 228
    God's Covenants and, 39
    God's perfect love in, 164–65
    God's saving plan and purpose, 107,
      158
    gospel needed for, 227
    grace and, 227
    knowing Jesus Christ in, 55, 56, 187,
      198, 210
    natural theology and, 224
    new birth and, 127–28, 133
    no-lordship or Free Grace view, 140,
      141
    propitiation and, 46–50, 124
    redemption by Jesus Christ, 55–56,
      187–89, 198, 210
    Reformed view, 140
    righteousness as proof of, 140, 144,
      171, 207
    sanctification and, 164, 125–26
    Scripture truth, understanding, and,
      218, 227
    tests of
      confession, 37–41
      forgiveness of sins, 33–36
      overview of, 42, 122
      sin, certainty of, 25–31
    universalism and, 225
    "wider mercy" view and, 225
Samson's parents, 242
Sanctification, 29, 36–37, 117–18,
    124–25
Sapphira, 2–5
Sardis, 2, 185
Satan. *See* Hell
    Adam and Eve and deceit of, 252
    antichrists, energizer of, 94, 96

children of
    children of God and, 128
    eternal life of, 135, 136
    hatred of God's children, 131,
      133–35
    indifference of toward God's
      children, 131, 135–37
    murdering God's children, 131,
      132–33
    sinners, unsaved, as, 126
counterfeit conversions, tactic of,
    140
darkness and death, 62, 126, 132
deception and falsehood tactics of,
    89–90, 214
defeat of certain, 175
description of as the devil, 126
emissaries of, 232, 236, 237
God's enmity to at the fall, 188–80
hope a defense against attacks of,
    108
inability of to reclaim the saints, 207
opposition of to God's plan, 94, 126
serving God's sovereign purpose, 99
strategy for attacking the truth, 153,
    155, 210, 214
temptations of, threefold, 90
Trojan horse stratagem of, 155
works of, 126, 140, 210
Saving faith. *See* Faith
Scribes and Pharisees, 255
Scripture. *See* Bible, the
Seven churches of Revelation, 2,
    184–86
Shunammite woman, 242
Simon the leper, 243
Simon the Pharisee, 243
Simon the tanner, 243
Sin. *See* Forgiveness
    avenues used to incite
      boastful pride of life, 87–90, 92
      lust of the eyes, 88–90, 92
      lust of the flesh, 87–90, 92
    believer's personal responsibility
      for, 121, 122
    certainty of, 25–28
    characteristics of, 85–86

The MacArthur New Testament Commentary series includes:

Matthew 1–7
Matthew 8–15
Matthew 16–23
Matthew 24–28
Mark 1–8
Mark 9–16
Luke 1–5
Luke 6–10
Luke 11–17
Luke 18–24
John 1–11
John 12–21
Acts 1–12
Acts 13–28
Romans 1–8
Romans 9–16
First Corinthians
Second Corinthians
Galatians
Ephesians
Philippians
Colossians & Philemon
First & Second Thessalonians
First Timothy
Second Timothy
Titus
Hebrews
James
First Peter
Second Peter & Jude
First–Third John
Revelation 1–11
Revelation 12–22

www.MoodyPublishers.com | 1-800-678-6928